THE Eminence IN Shadow

3

Art **Anri Sakano**

Original Story **Daisuke Aizawa**

Character Design **Touzai**

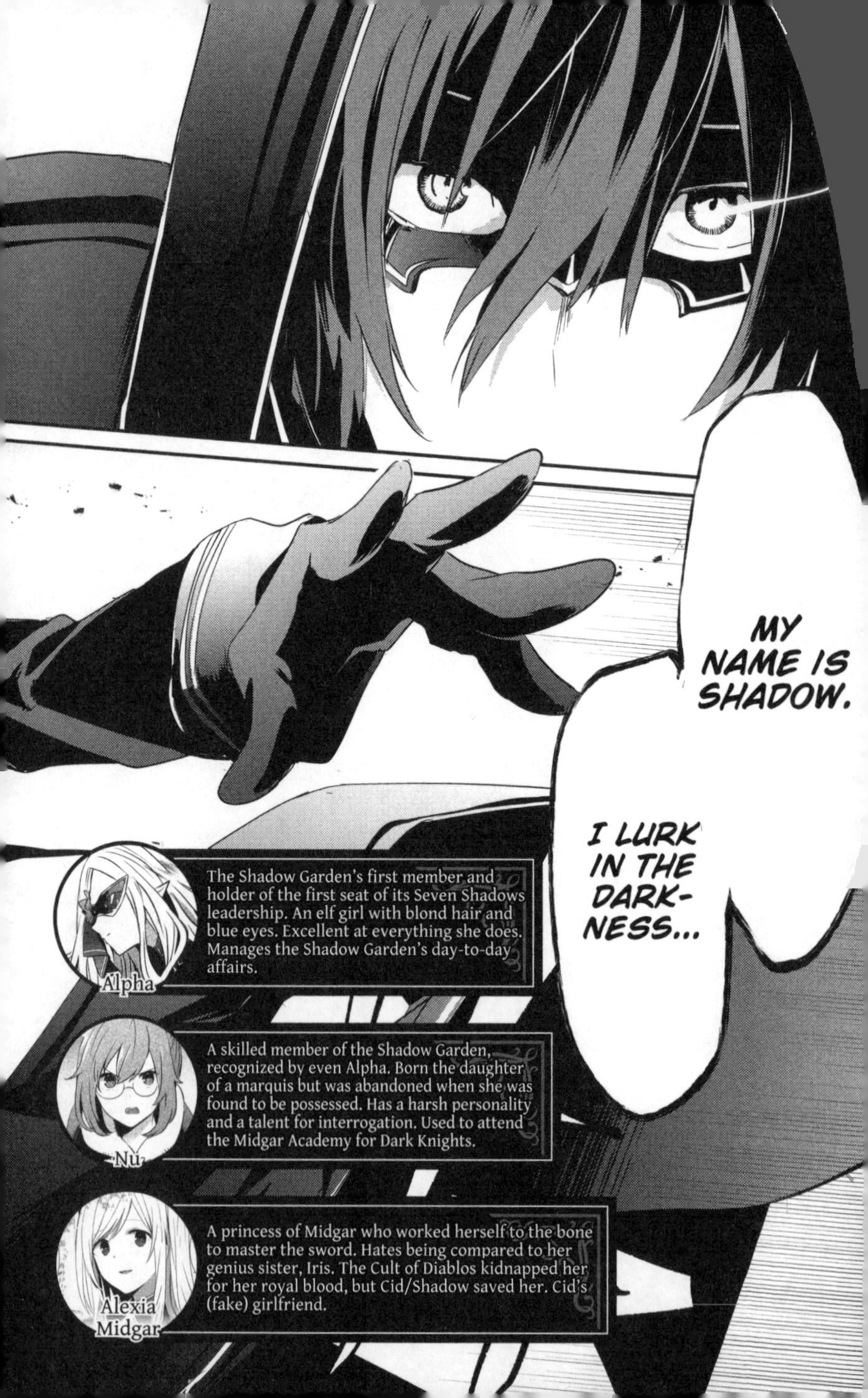
MY NAME IS SHADOW.
I LURK IN THE DARK-NESS...
The Shadow Garden's first member and holder of the first seat of its Seven Shadows leadership. An elf girl with blond hair and blue eyes. Excellent at everything she does. Manages the Shadow Garden's day-to-day affairs.
Alpha
A skilled member of the Shadow Garden, recognized by even Alpha. Born the daughter of a marquis but was abandoned when she was found to be possessed. Has a harsh personality and a talent for interrogation. Used to attend the Midgar Academy for Dark Knights.
Nu
A princess of Midgar who worked herself to the bone to master the sword. Hates being compared to her genius sister, Iris. The Cult of Diablos kidnapped her for her royal blood, but Cid/Shadow saved her. Cid's (fake) girlfriend.
Alexia Midgar

The Story So Far

Cid doesn't want to be the protagonist or the final boss—he wants to be an "eminence in shadow" manipulating things from behind the scenes. As he reincarnates into another world and enrolls in the Midgar Academy for Dark Knights, he enjoys himself by stealthily (?) acting out a made-up scenario in which he, as the puppet mastermind Shadow, starts a secret society called the Shadow Garden whose mission is to wipe out an evil cult... But what he doesn't realize is...the wicked Cult of Diablos actually exists...!

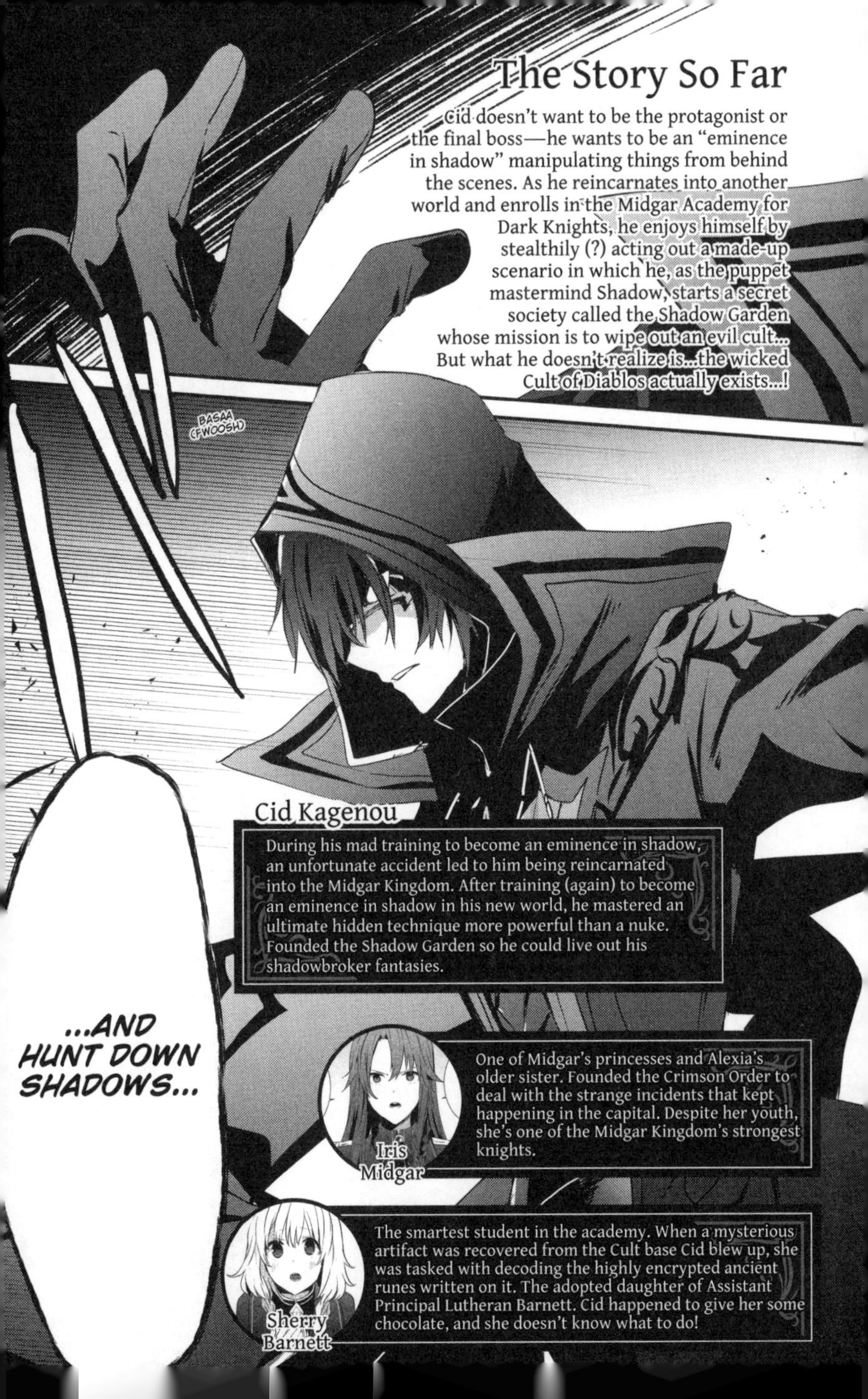
BASAA (FWOOSH)
...AND HUNT DOWN SHADOWS...

Cid Kagenou

During his mad training to become an eminence in shadow, an unfortunate accident led to him being reincarnated into the Midgar Kingdom. After training (again) to become an eminence in shadow in his new world, he mastered an ultimate hidden technique more powerful than a nuke. Founded the Shadow Garden so he could live out his shadowbroker fantasies.

Iris Midgar

One of Midgar's princesses and Alexia's older sister. Founded the Crimson Order to deal with the strange incidents that kept happening in the capital. Despite her youth, she's one of the Midgar Kingdom's strongest knights.

Sherry Barnett

The smartest student in the academy. When a mysterious artifact was recovered from the Cult base Cid blew up, she was tasked with decoding the highly encrypted ancient runes written on it. The adopted daughter of Assistant Principal Lutheran Barnett. Cid happened to give her some chocolate, and she doesn't know what to do!

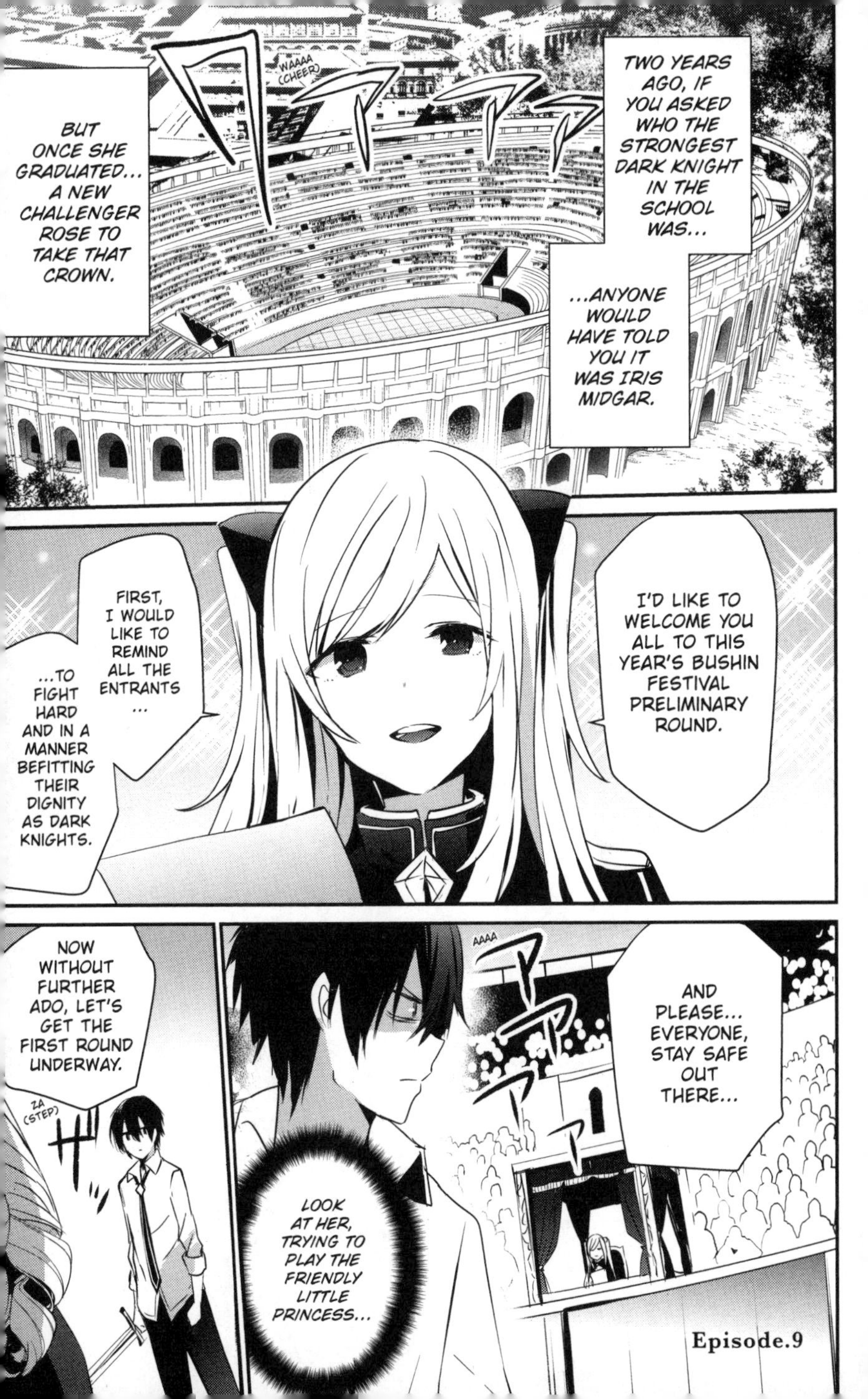
TWO YEARS AGO, IF YOU ASKED WHO THE STRONGEST DARK KNIGHT IN THE SCHOOL WAS...
WAAAA (CHEER)
...ANYONE WOULD HAVE TOLD YOU IT WAS IRIS MIDGAR.
BUT ONCE SHE GRADUATED... A NEW CHALLENGER ROSE TO TAKE THAT CROWN.
I'D LIKE TO WELCOME YOU ALL TO THIS YEAR'S BUSHIN FESTIVAL PRELIMINARY ROUND.
FIRST, I WOULD LIKE TO REMIND ALL THE ENTRANTS...
...TO FIGHT HARD AND IN A MANNER BEFITTING THEIR DIGNITY AS DARK KNIGHTS.
AND PLEASE... EVERYONE, STAY SAFE OUT THERE...
AAAA
LOOK AT HER, TRYING TO PLAY THE FRIENDLY LITTLE PRINCESS...
NOW WITHOUT FURTHER ADO, LET'S GET THE FIRST ROUND UNDERWAY.
ZA (STEP)
Episode.9

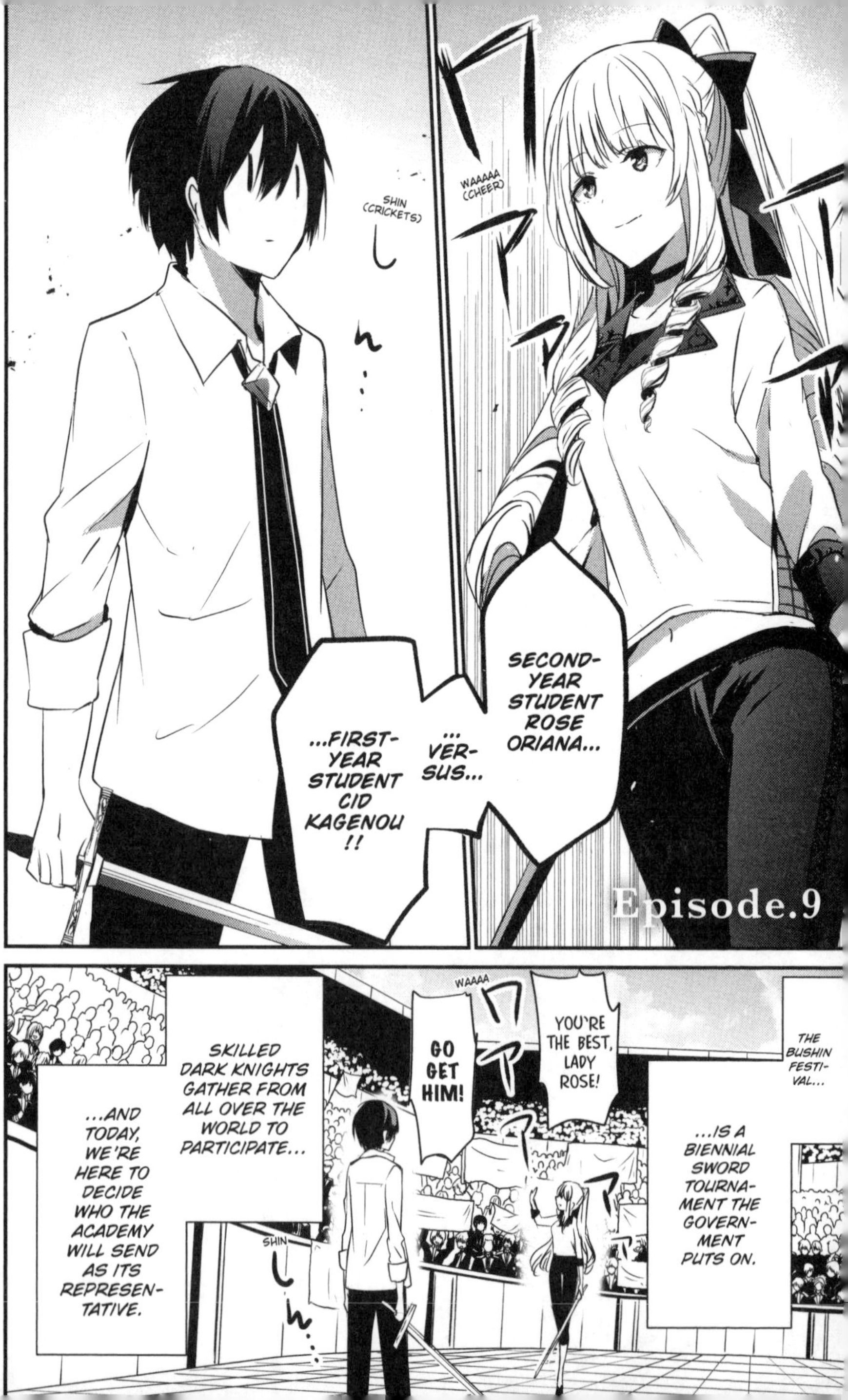

WAAAAA (CHEER)
SECOND-YEAR STUDENT ROSE ORIANA...
...VERSUS...
...FIRST-YEAR STUDENT CID KAGENOU!!
SHIN (CRICKETS)
Episode.9
THE BUSHIN FESTIVAL...
...IS A BIENNIAL SWORD TOURNAMENT THE GOVERNMENT PUTS ON.
YOU'RE THE BEST, LADY ROSE!
WAAAA
GO GET HIM!
SKILLED DARK KNIGHTS GATHER FROM ALL OVER THE WORLD TO PARTICIPATE...
...AND TODAY, WE'RE HERE TO DECIDE WHO THE ACADEMY WILL SEND AS ITS REPRESENTATIVE.
SHIN

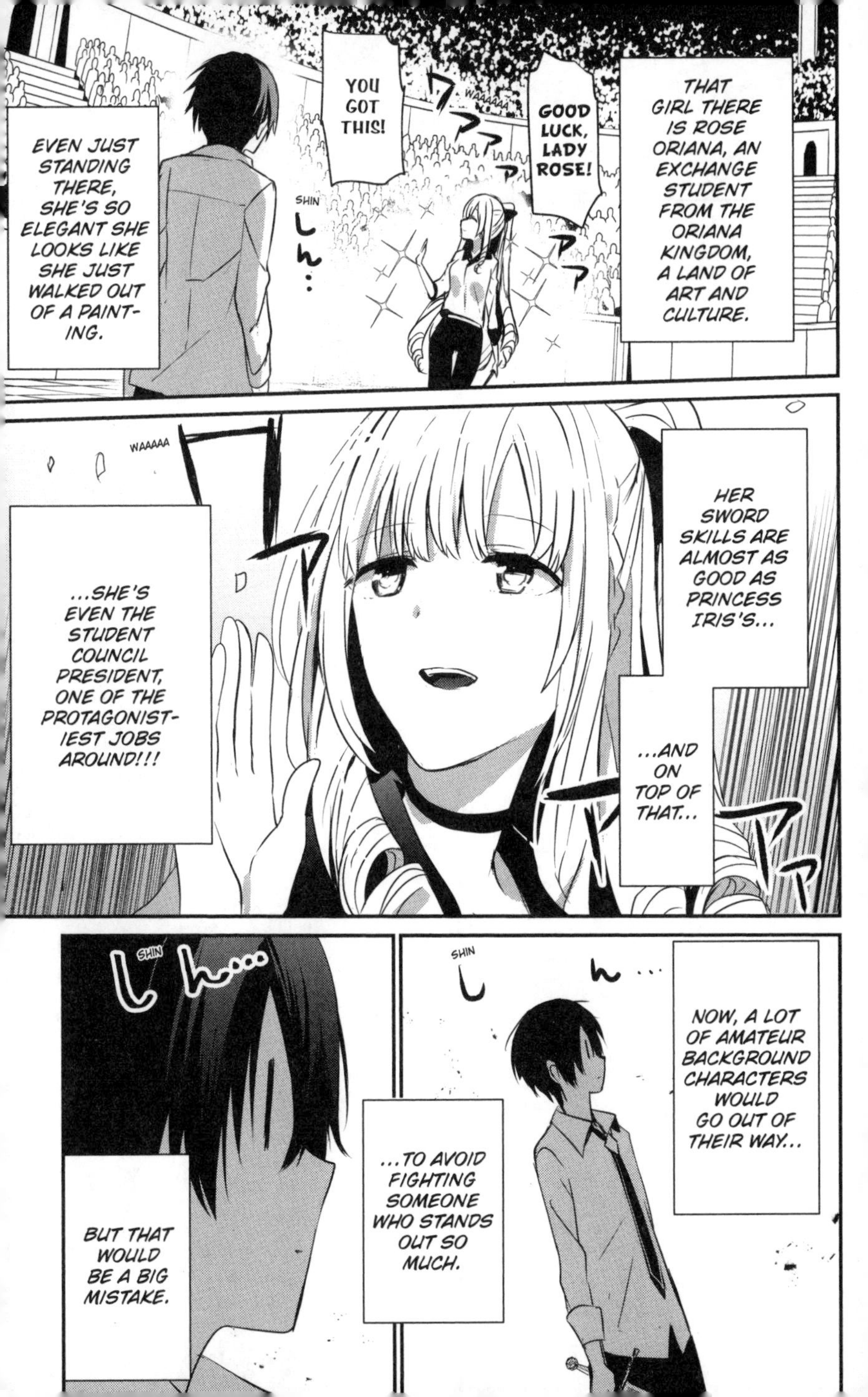
THAT GIRL THERE IS ROSE ORIANA, AN EXCHANGE STUDENT FROM THE ORIANA KINGDOM, A LAND OF ART AND CULTURE.
GOOD LUCK, LADY ROSE!
WAAAAAA
YOU GOT THIS!
SHIN
EVEN JUST STANDING THERE, SHE'S SO ELEGANT SHE LOOKS LIKE SHE JUST WALKED OUT OF A PAINT-ING.
HER SWORD SKILLS ARE ALMOST AS GOOD AS PRINCESS IRIS'S...
...AND ON TOP OF THAT...
WAAAAA
...SHE'S EVEN THE STUDENT COUNCIL PRESIDENT, ONE OF THE PROTAGONIST-IEST JOBS AROUND!!!
SHIN
NOW, A LOT OF AMATEUR BACKGROUND CHARACTERS WOULD GO OUT OF THEIR WAY...
...TO AVOID FIGHTING SOMEONE WHO STANDS OUT SO MUCH.
SHIN
BUT THAT WOULD BE A BIG MISTAKE.

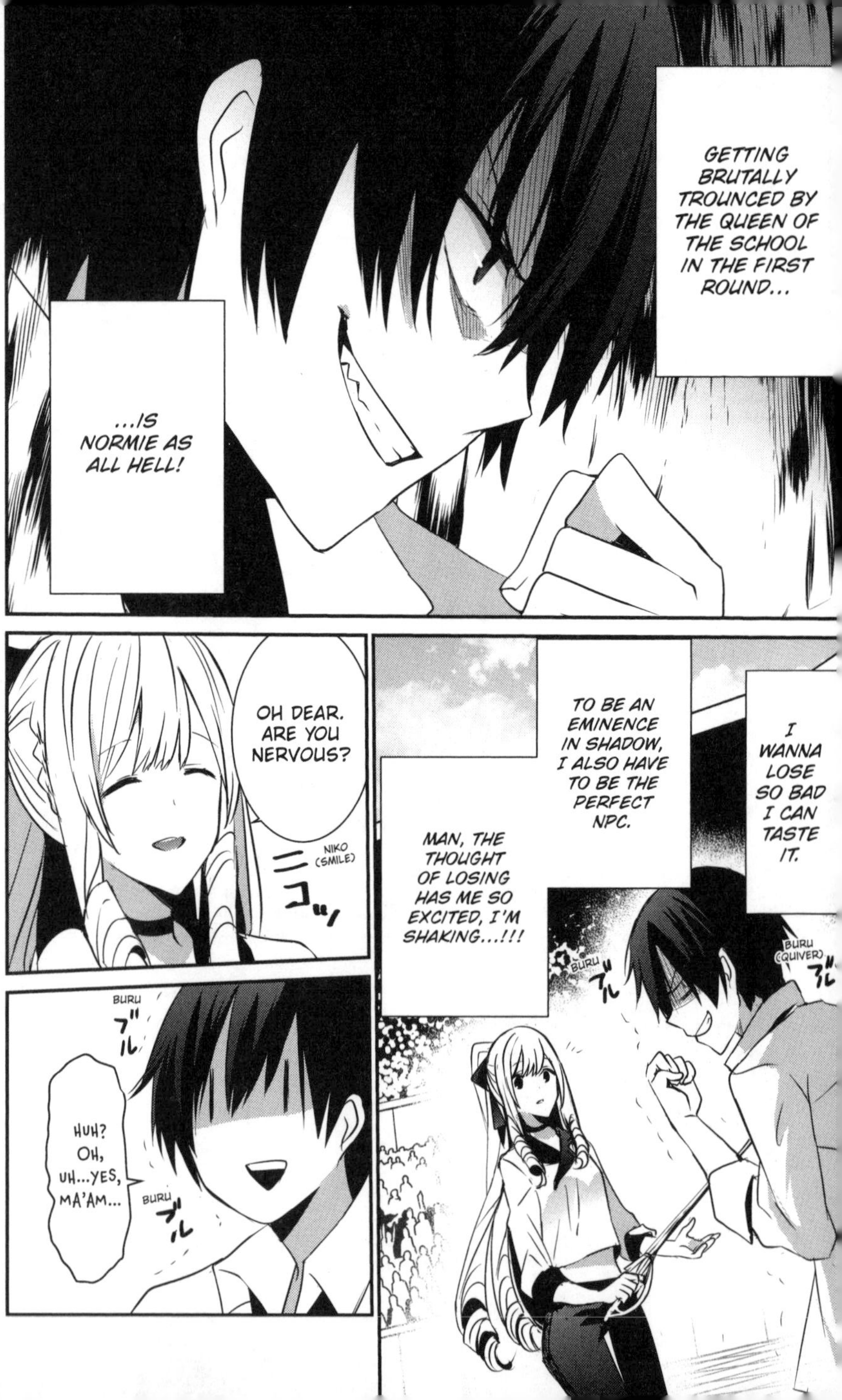
GETTING BRUTALLY TROUNCED BY THE QUEEN OF THE SCHOOL IN THE FIRST ROUND...
...IS NORMIE AS ALL HELL!
I WANNA LOSE SO BAD I CAN TASTE IT.
TO BE AN EMINENCE IN SHADOW, I ALSO HAVE TO BE THE PERFECT NPC.
MAN, THE THOUGHT OF LOSING HAS ME SO EXCITED, I'M SHAKING...!!!
BURU (QUIVER)
BURU
OH DEAR. ARE YOU NERVOUS?
NIKO (SMILE)
BURU
HUH? OH, UH...YES, MA'AM...
BURU

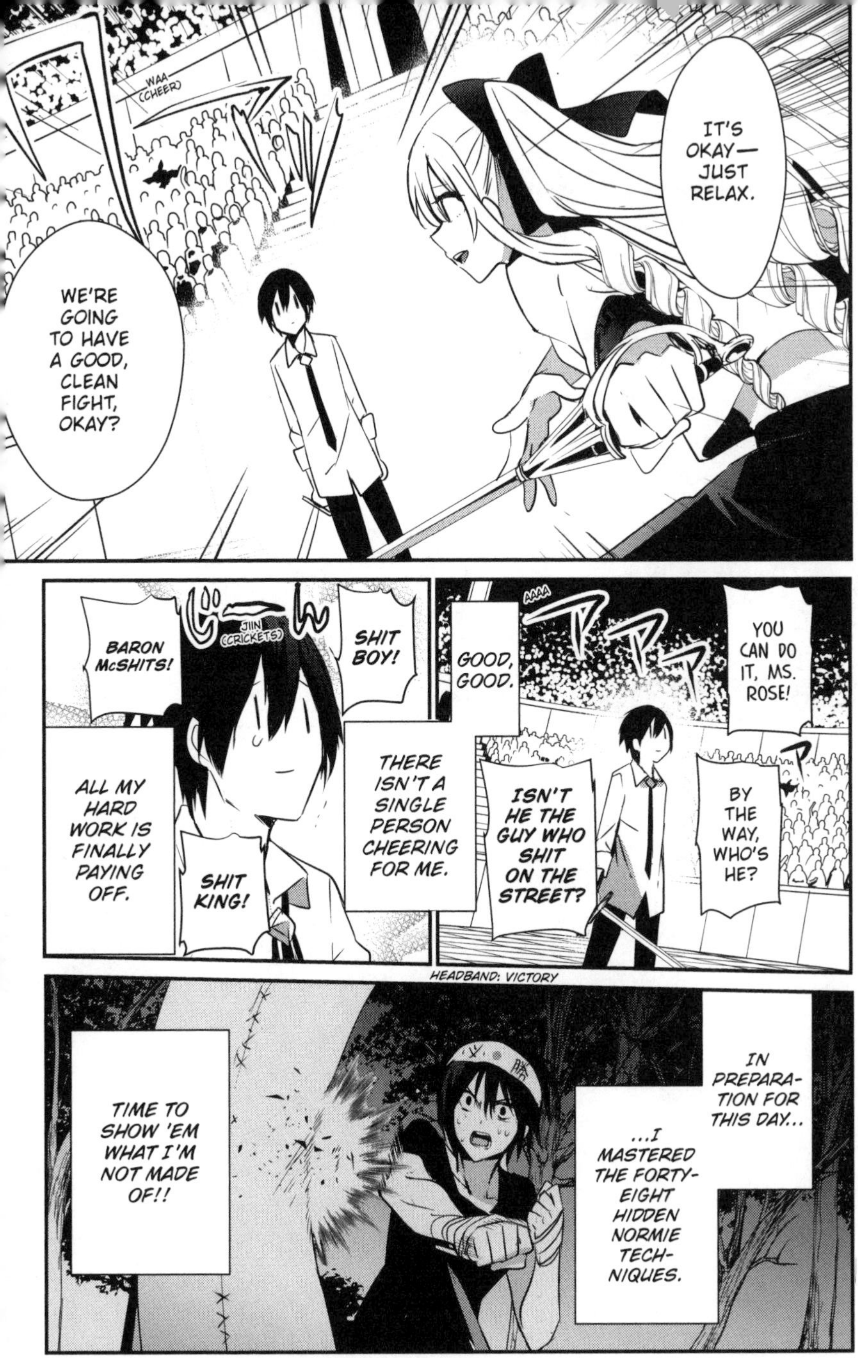
IT'S OKAY—JUST RELAX.
WAA (CHEER)
WE'RE GOING TO HAVE A GOOD, CLEAN FIGHT, OKAY?
AAAA
YOU CAN DO IT, MS. ROSE!
GOOD, GOOD.
BY THE WAY, WHO'S HE?
ISN'T HE THE GUY WHO SHIT ON THE STREET?
SHIT BOY!
JIIN (CRICKETS)
BARON McSHITS!
THERE ISN'T A SINGLE PERSON CHEERING FOR ME.
SHIT KING!
ALL MY HARD WORK IS FINALLY PAYING OFF.
HEADBAND: VICTORY
IN PREPARATION FOR THIS DAY...
...I MASTERED THE FORTY-EIGHT HIDDEN NORMIE TECHNIQUES.
TIME TO SHOW 'EM WHAT I'M NOT MADE OF!!

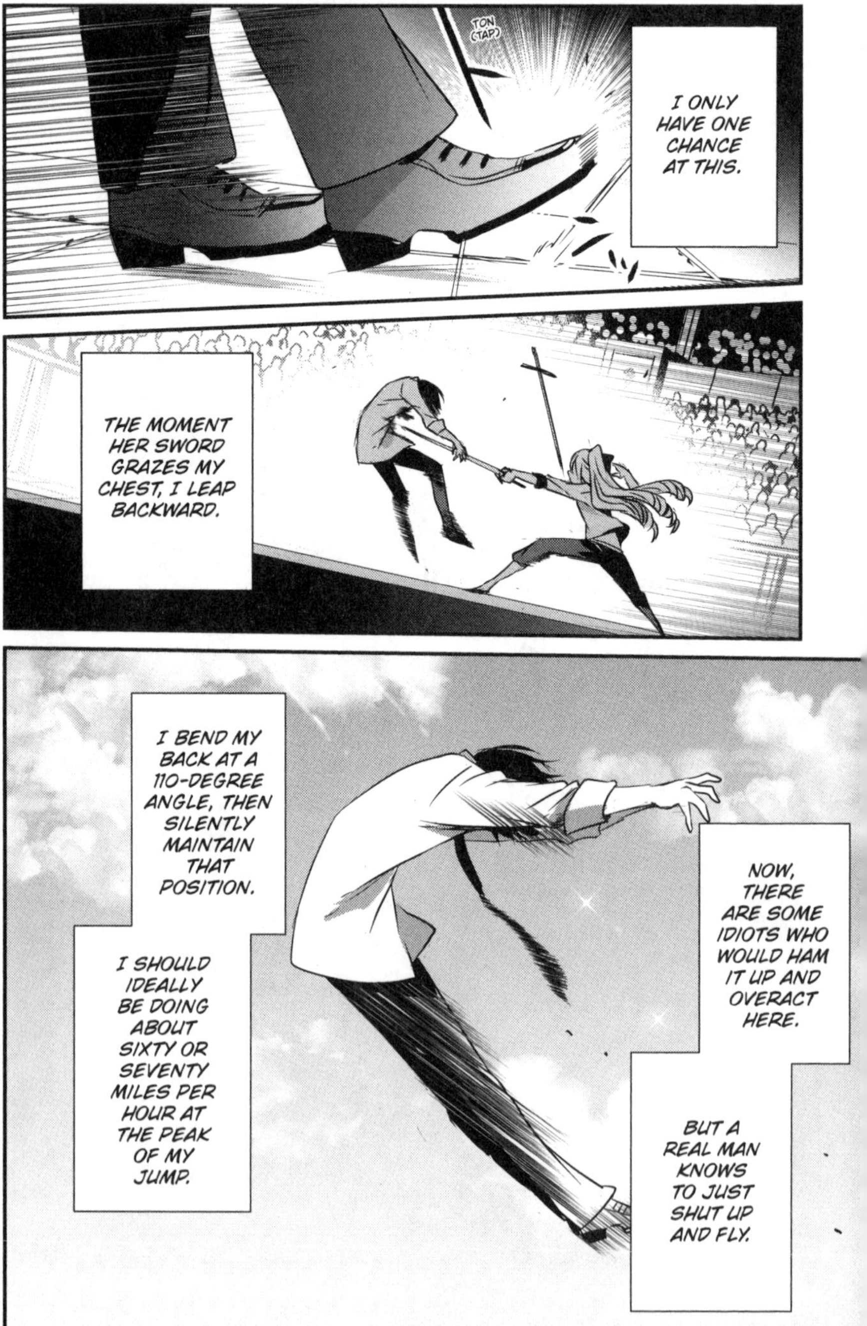
I ONLY HAVE ONE CHANCE AT THIS.
TON (TAP)
THE MOMENT HER SWORD GRAZES MY CHEST, I LEAP BACKWARD.
I BEND MY BACK AT A 110-DEGREE ANGLE, THEN SILENTLY MAINTAIN THAT POSITION.
I SHOULD IDEALLY BE DOING ABOUT SIXTY OR SEVENTY MILES PER HOUR AT THE PEAK OF MY JUMP.
NOW, THERE ARE SOME IDIOTS WHO WOULD HAM IT UP AND OVERACT HERE.
BUT A REAL MAN KNOWS TO JUST SHUT UP AND FLY.

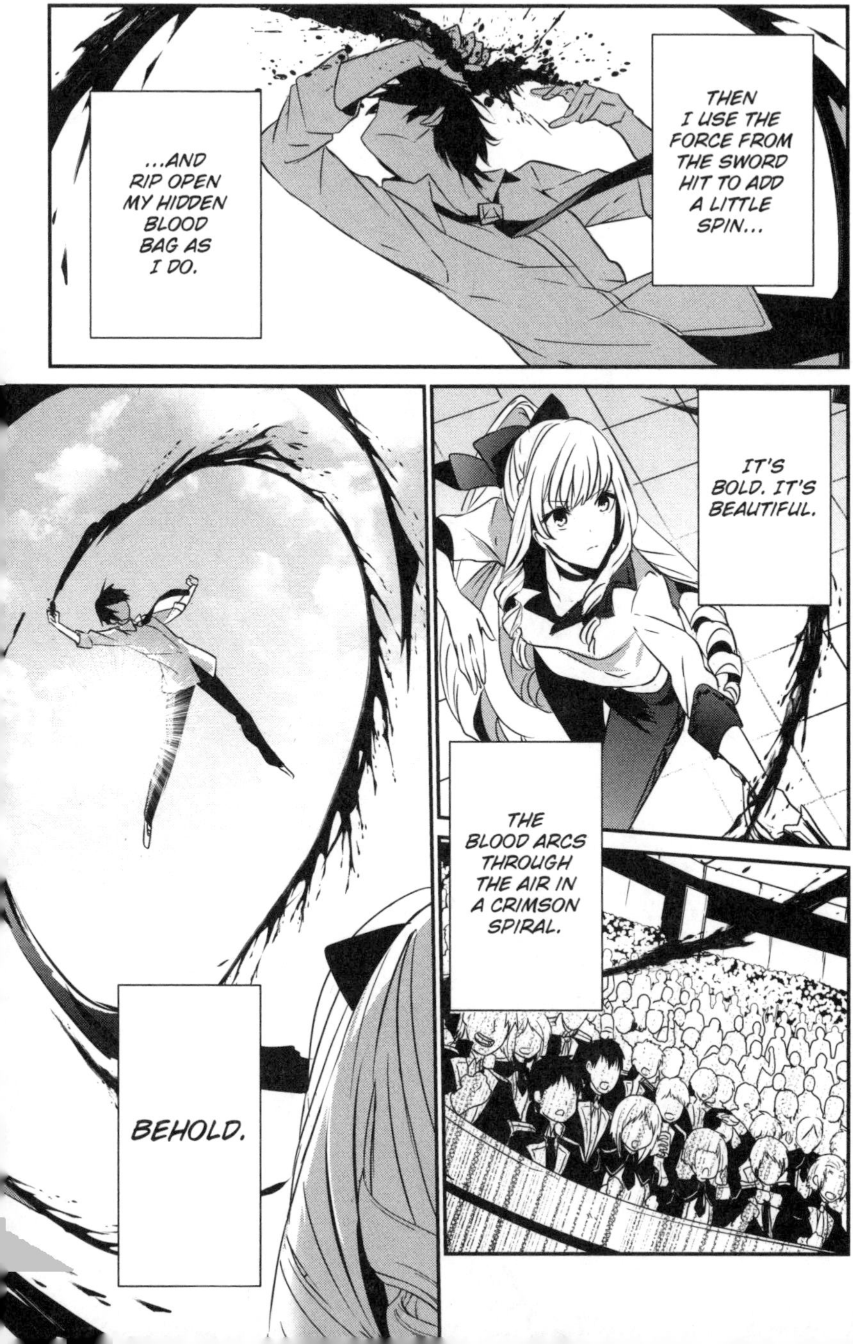
THEN I USE THE FORCE FROM THE SWORD HIT TO ADD A LITTLE SPIN...
...AND RIP OPEN MY HIDDEN BLOOD BAG AS I DO.
IT'S BOLD. IT'S BEAUTIFUL.
THE BLOOD ARCS THROUGH THE AIR IN A CRIMSON SPIRAL.
BEHOLD.

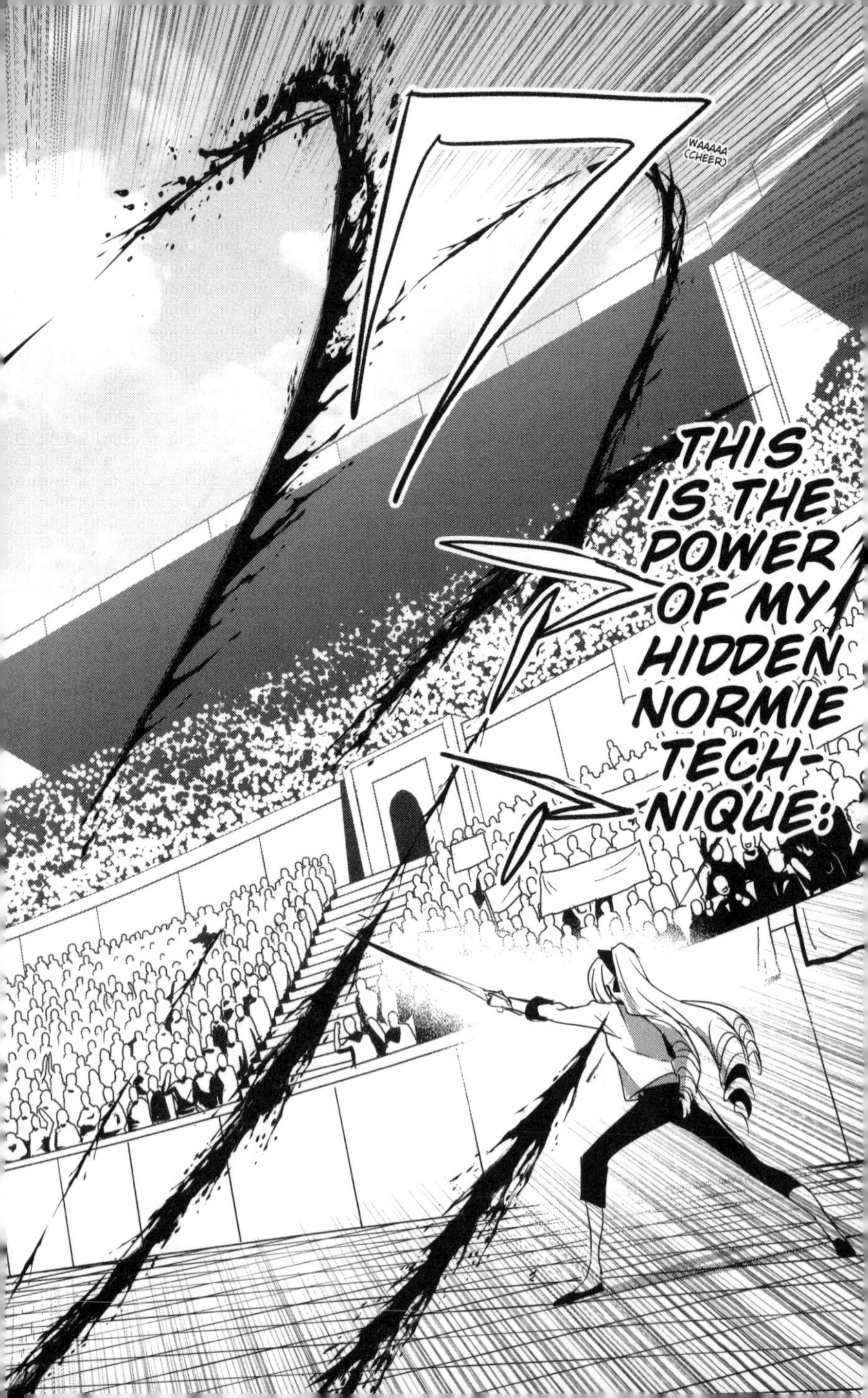
WAAAAA (CHEER)
THIS IS THE POWER OF MY HIDDEN NORMIE TECH-NIQUE:

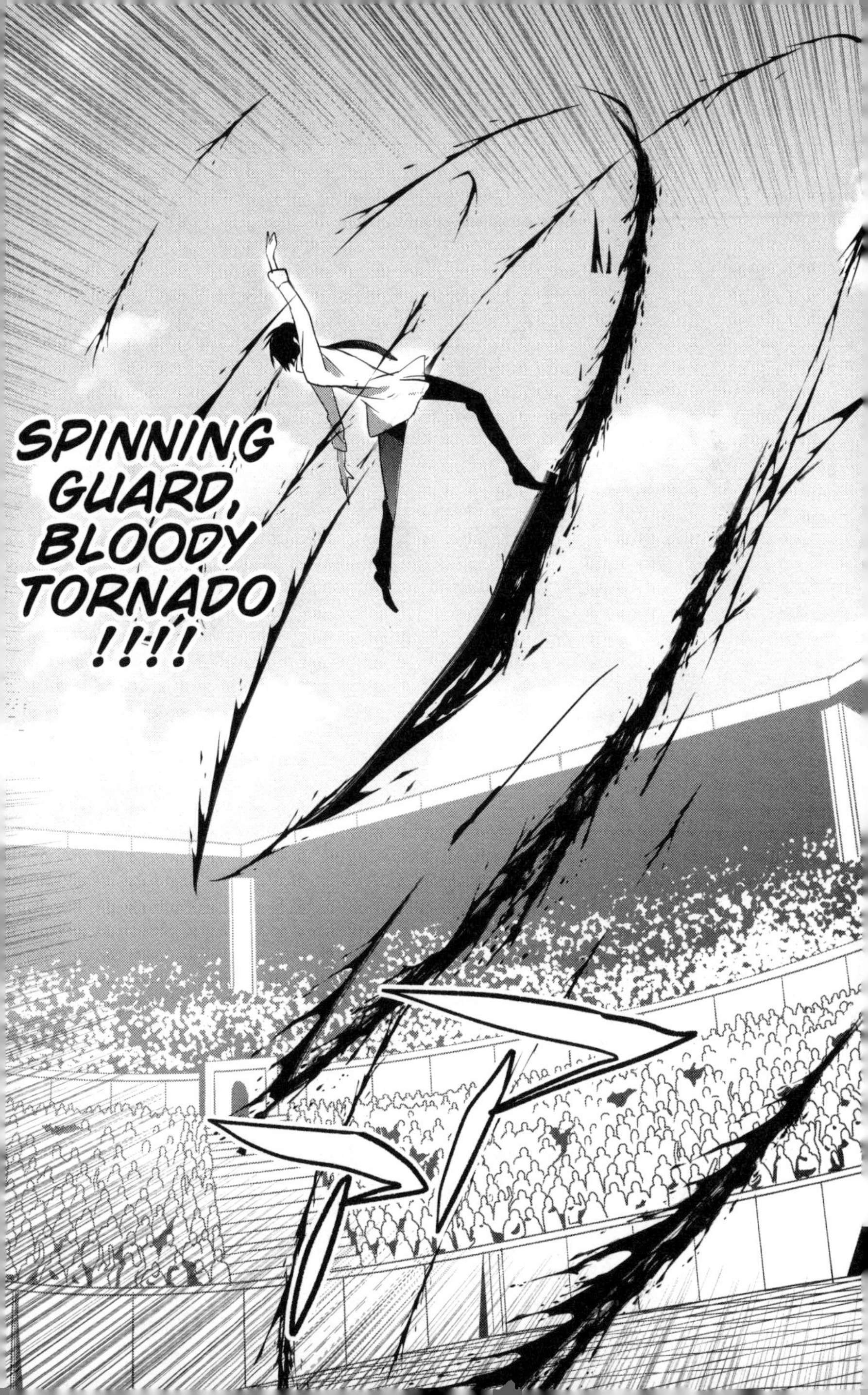
SPINNING GUARD, BLOODY TORNADO !!!!

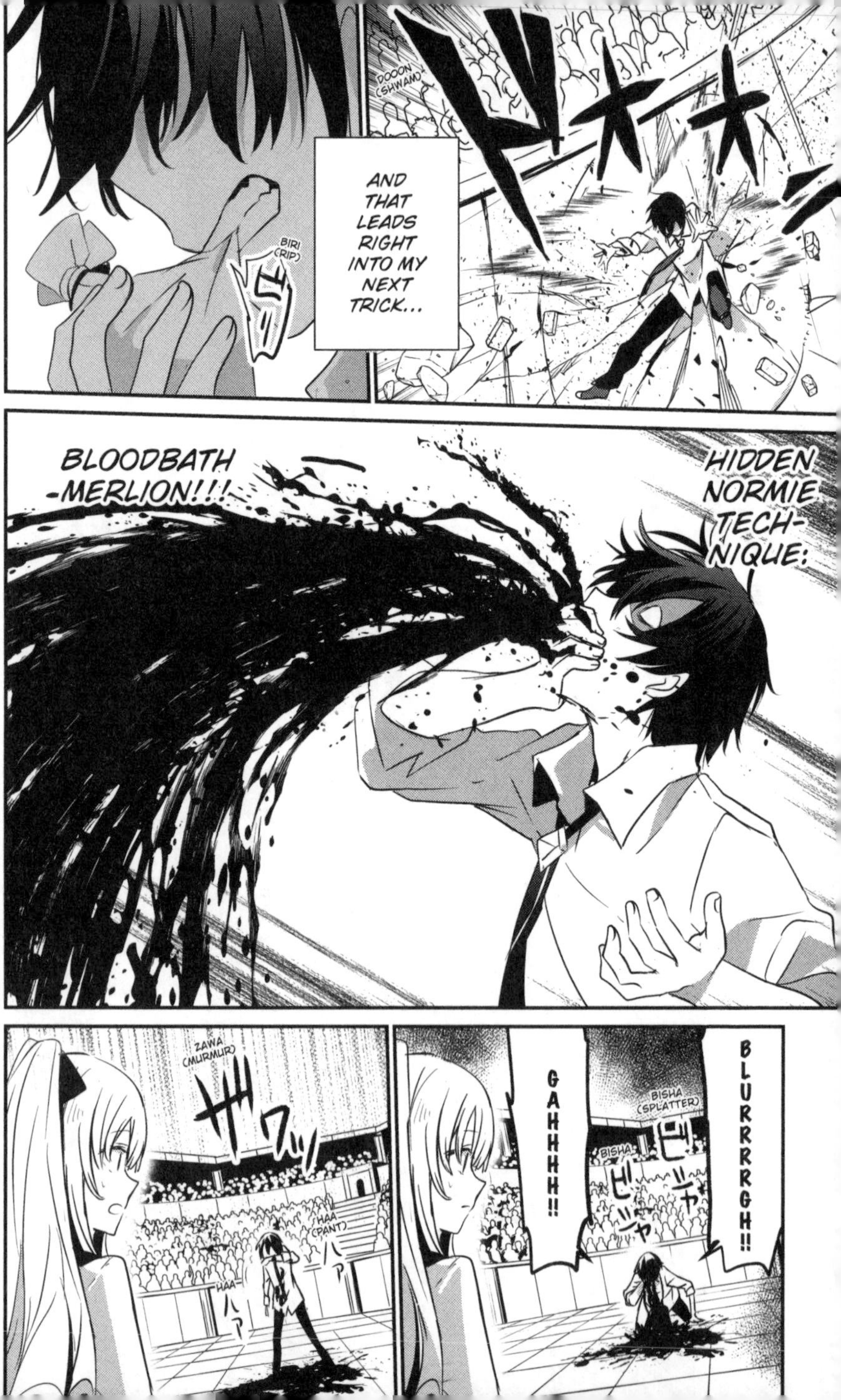
DOOON (SHWAM)
AND THAT LEADS RIGHT INTO MY NEXT TRICK...
BIRI (RIP)
HIDDEN NORMIE TECH-NIQUE:
BLOODBATH-MERLION!!!
BLURRRRGH!!
GAHHHHH!!
BISHA (SPLATTER)
BISHA
ZAWA (MURMUR)
HAA (PANT)
HAA

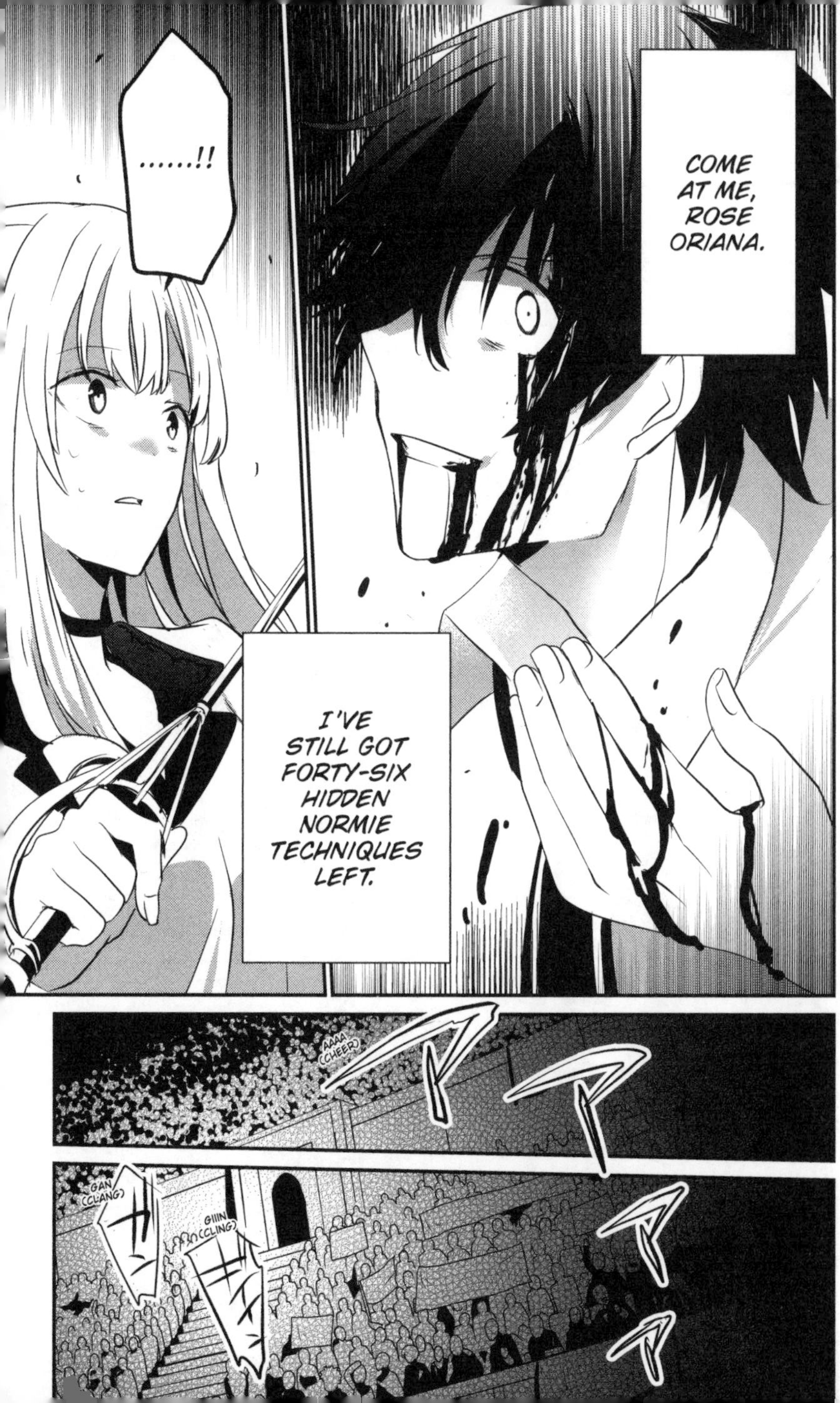
COME AT ME, ROSE ORIANA.
I'VE STILL GOT FORTY-SIX HIDDEN NORMIE TECHNIQUES LEFT.
......!!
AAAA (CHEER)
GAN (CLANG)
GIIIN (CLING)

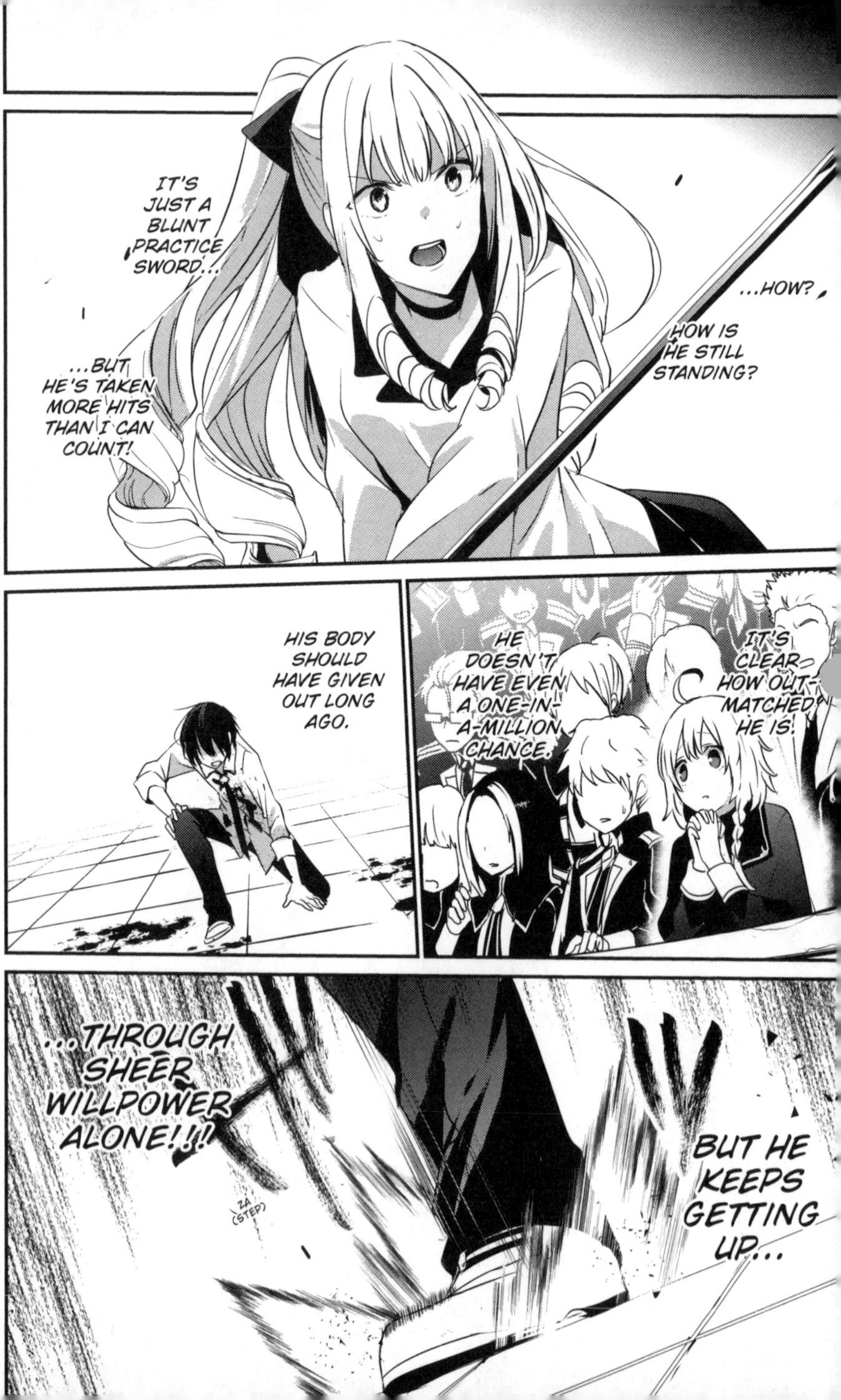
...HOW?
HOW IS HE STILL STANDING?
IT'S JUST A BLUNT PRACTICE SWORD...
...BUT HE'S TAKEN MORE HITS THAN I CAN COUNT!
IT'S CLEAR HOW OUTMATCHED HE IS!
HE DOESN'T HAVE EVEN A ONE-IN-A-MILLION CHANCE.
HIS BODY SHOULD HAVE GIVEN OUT LONG AGO.
BUT HE KEEPS GETTING UP...
ZA (STEP)
...THROUGH SHEER WILLPOWER ALONE!!!

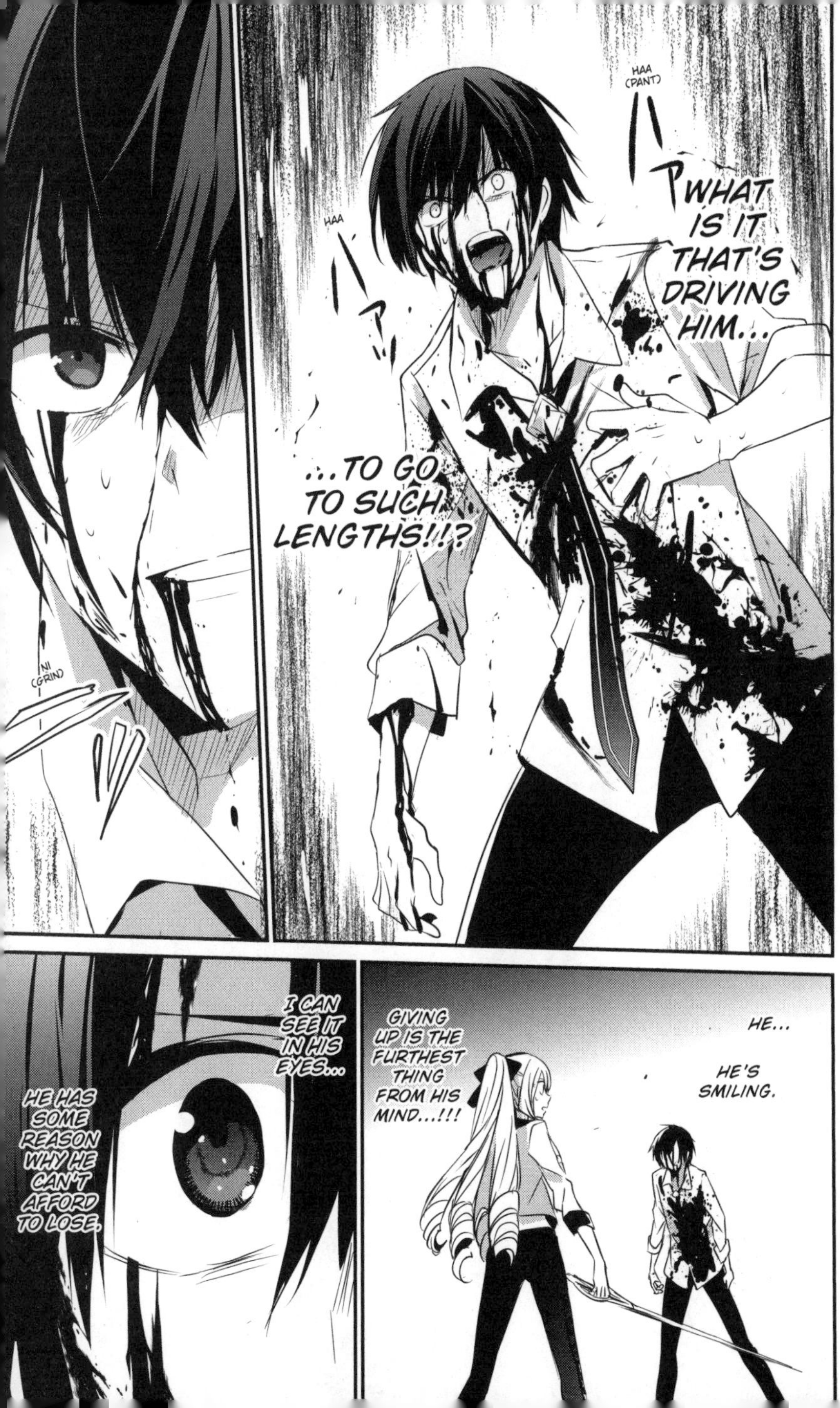
HAA (PANT)
WHAT IS IT THAT'S DRIVING HIM...
HAA
...TO GO TO SUCH LENGTHS!!?
NI (GRIND)
HE...
HE'S SMILING.
GIVING UP IS THE FURTHEST THING FROM HIS MIND...!!!
I CAN SEE IT IN HIS EYES...
HE HAS SOME REASON WHY HE CAN'T AFFORD TO LOSE.

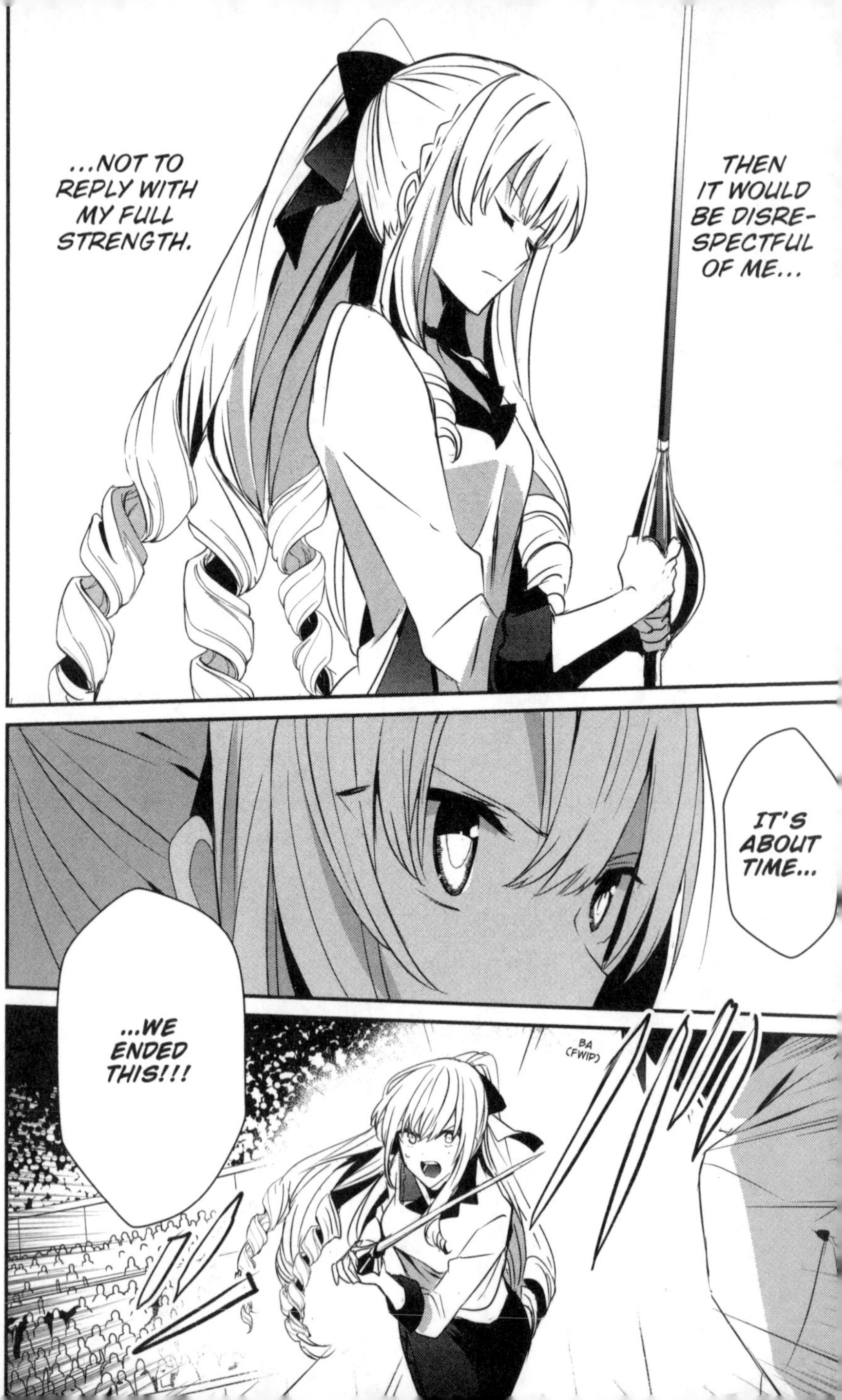
THEN IT WOULD BE DISRE-SPECTFUL OF ME...
...NOT TO REPLY WITH MY FULL STRENGTH.
IT'S ABOUT TIME...
BA (FWIP)
...WE ENDED THIS!!!

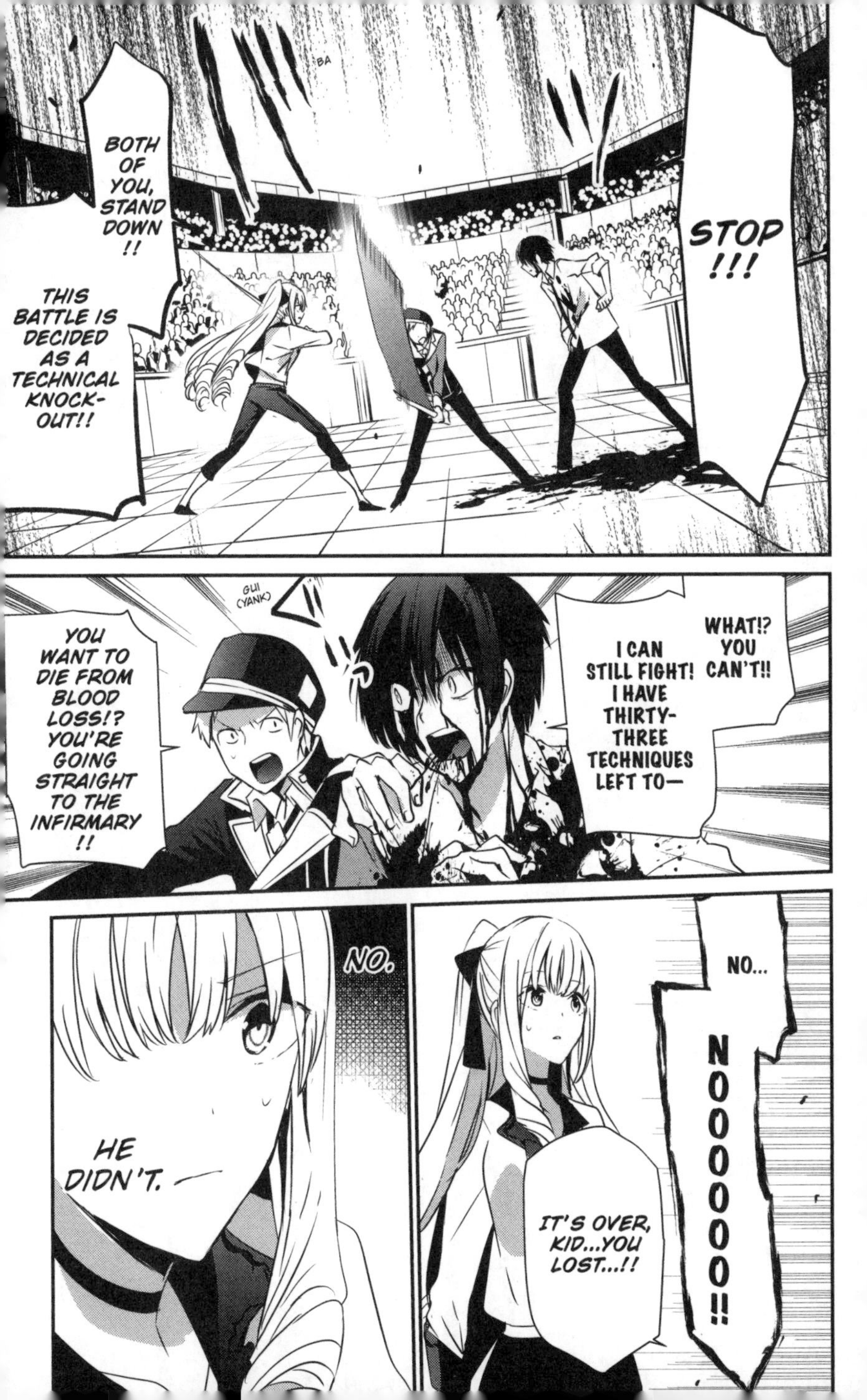
STOP!!!
BA
BOTH OF YOU, STAND DOWN!!
THIS BATTLE IS DECIDED AS A TECHNICAL KNOCK-OUT!!
WHAT!? YOU CAN'T!!
I CAN STILL FIGHT! I HAVE THIRTY-THREE TECHNIQUES LEFT TO—
GUI (YANK)
YOU WANT TO DIE FROM BLOOD LOSS!? YOU'RE GOING STRAIGHT TO THE INFIRMARY!!
NO...
NOOOOOOO!!
IT'S OVER, KID...YOU LOST...!!
NO.
HE DIDN'T.

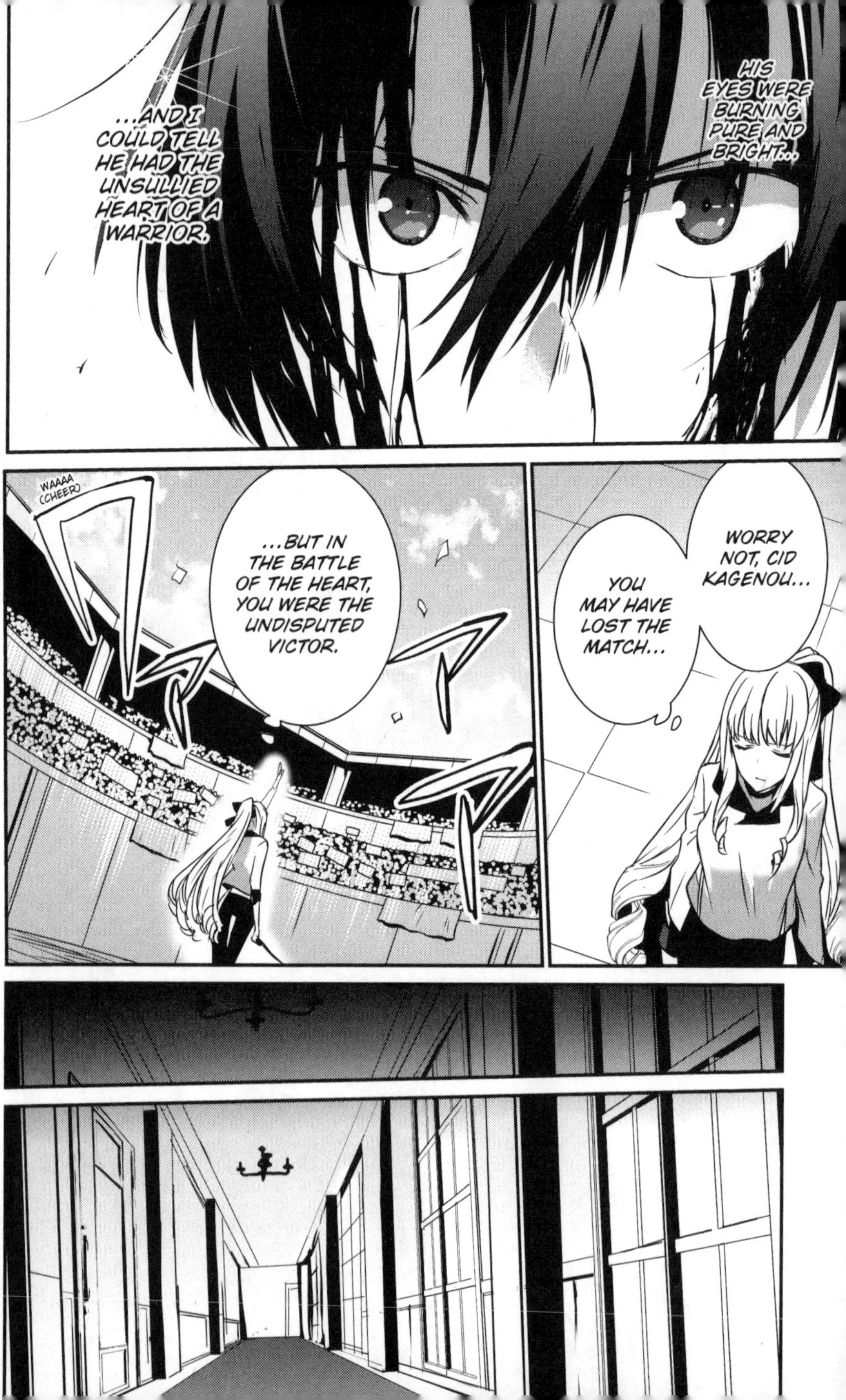

HIS EYES WERE BURNING PURE AND BRIGHT...
...AND I COULD TELL HE HAD THE UNSULLIED HEART OF A WARRIOR.
WORRY NOT, CID KAGENOU...
YOU MAY HAVE LOST THE MATCH...
...BUT IN THE BATTLE OF THE HEART, YOU WERE THE UNDISPUTED VICTOR.
WAAAA (CHEER)

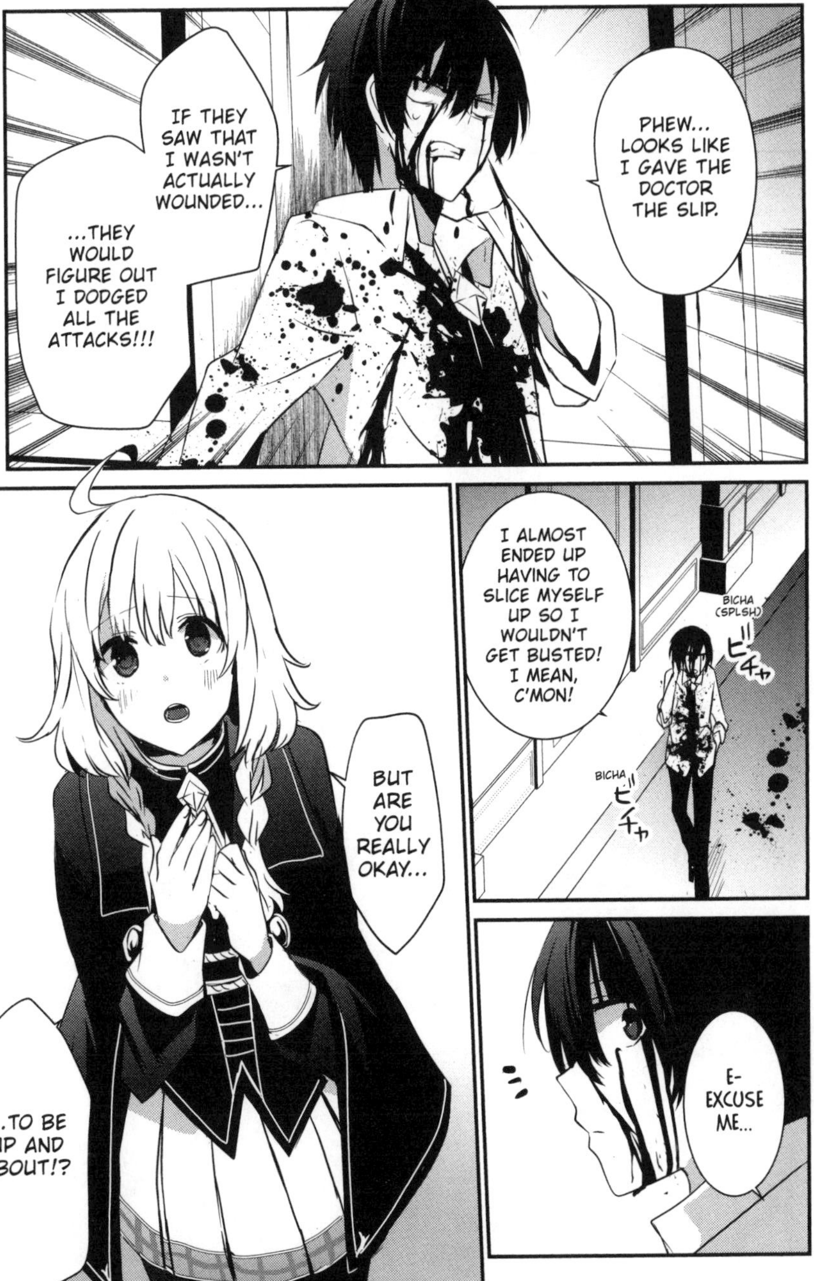
PHEW... LOOKS LIKE I GAVE THE DOCTOR THE SLIP.
IF THEY SAW THAT I WASN'T ACTUALLY WOUNDED...
...THEY WOULD FIGURE OUT I DODGED ALL THE ATTACKS!!!
I ALMOST ENDED UP HAVING TO SLICE MYSELF UP SO I WOULDN'T GET BUSTED! I MEAN, C'MON!
BICHA (SPLSH)
ビチャ
BICHA
ビチャ
E- EXCUSE ME...
BUT ARE YOU REALLY OKAY...
...TO BE UP AND ABOUT!?

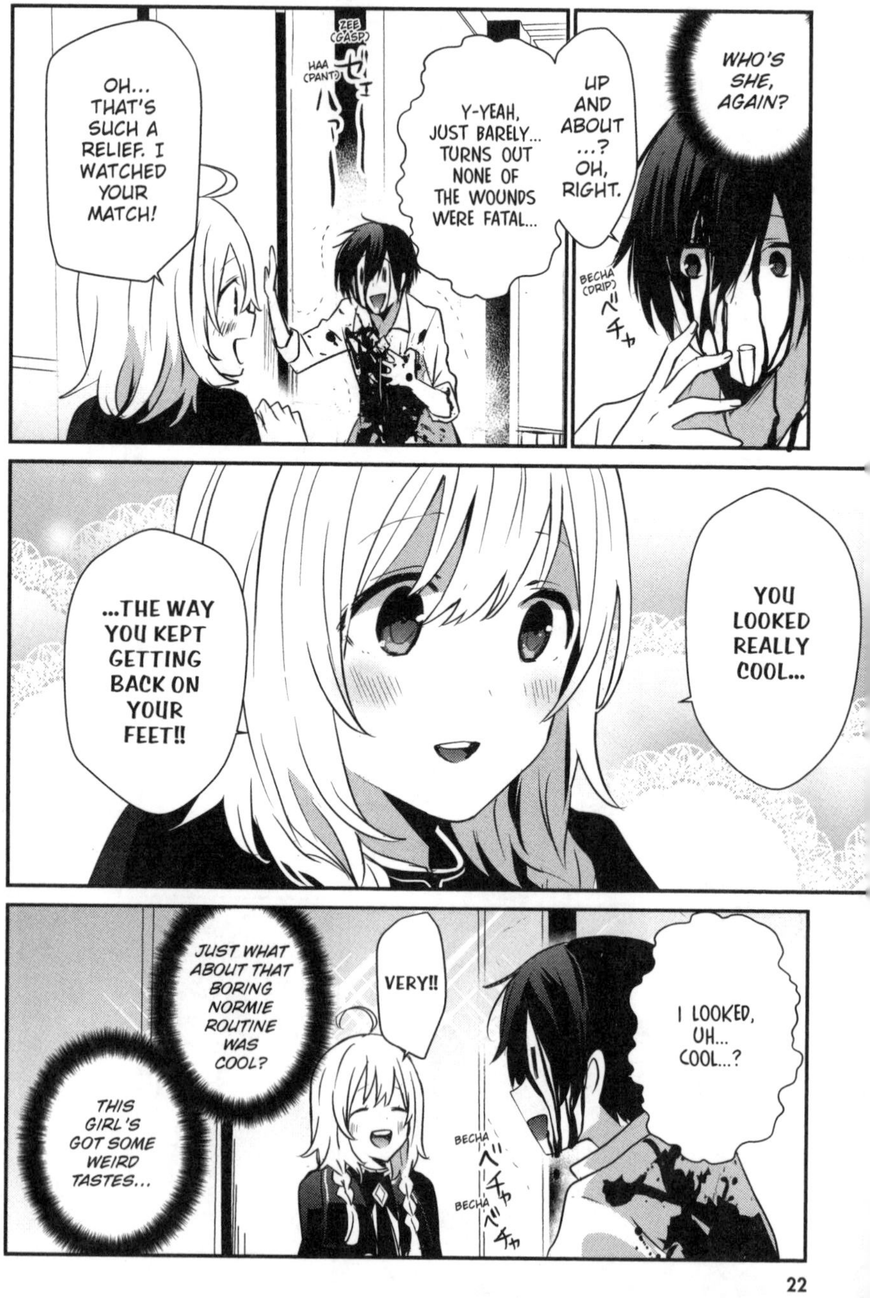
WHO'S SHE, AGAIN?
UP AND ABOUT...? OH, RIGHT.
BECHA (DRIP)
Y-YEAH, JUST BARELY... TURNS OUT NONE OF THE WOUNDS WERE FATAL...
ZEE (GASP)
HAA (PANT)
OH... THAT'S SUCH A RELIEF. I WATCHED YOUR MATCH!
YOU LOOKED REALLY COOL...
...THE WAY YOU KEPT GETTING BACK ON YOUR FEET!!
I LOOKED, UH... COOL...?
VERY!!
JUST WHAT ABOUT THAT BORING NORMIE ROUTINE WAS COOL?
THIS GIRL'S GOT SOME WEIRD TASTES...
BECHA
BECHA

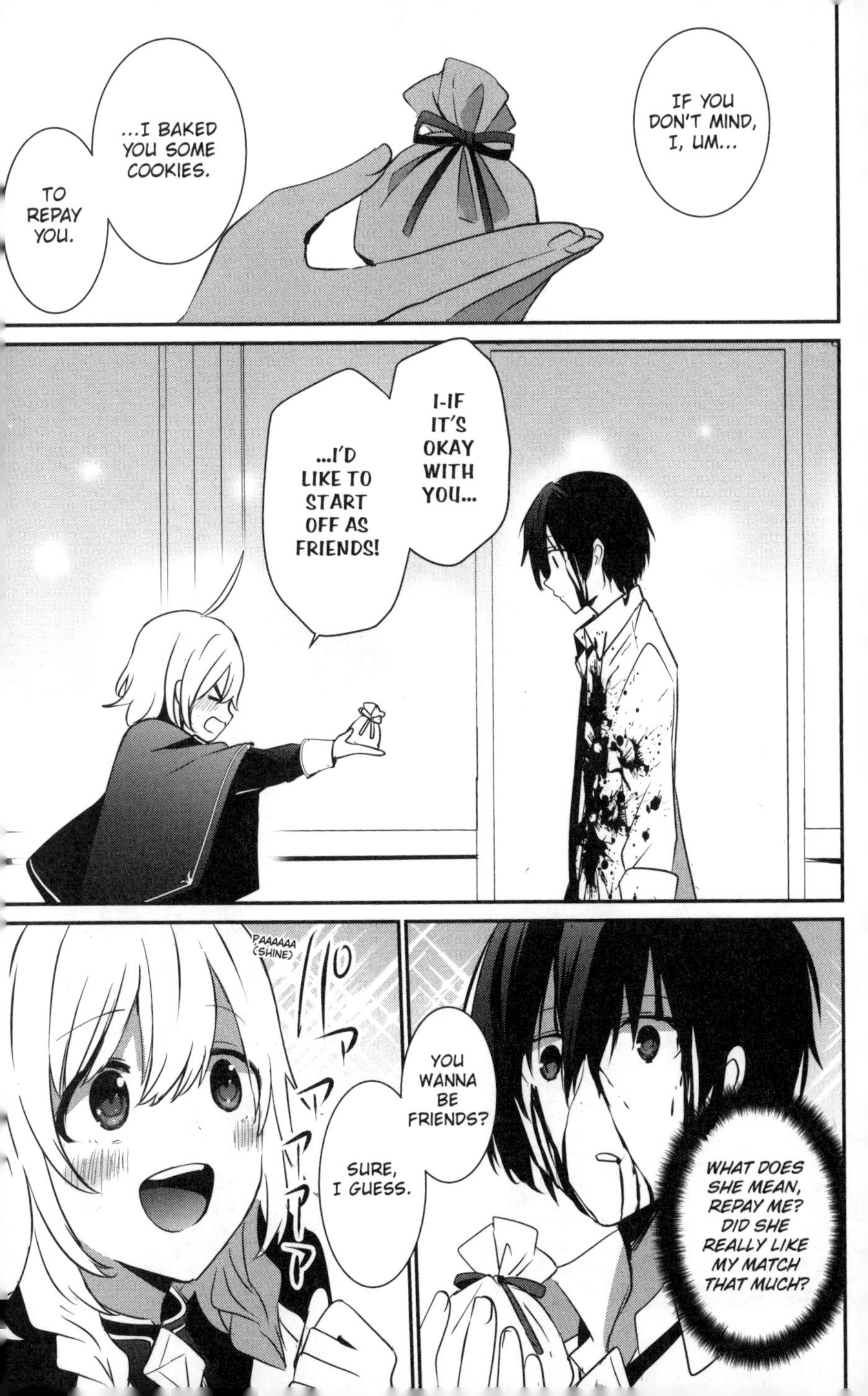
IF YOU DON'T MIND, I, UM...
...I BAKED YOU SOME COOKIES.
TO REPAY YOU.
I-IF IT'S OKAY WITH YOU...
...I'D LIKE TO START OFF AS FRIENDS!
WHAT DOES SHE MEAN, REPAY ME? DID SHE REALLY LIKE MY MATCH THAT MUCH?
YOU WANNA BE FRIENDS?
SURE, I GUESS.
PAAAAAA (SHINE)

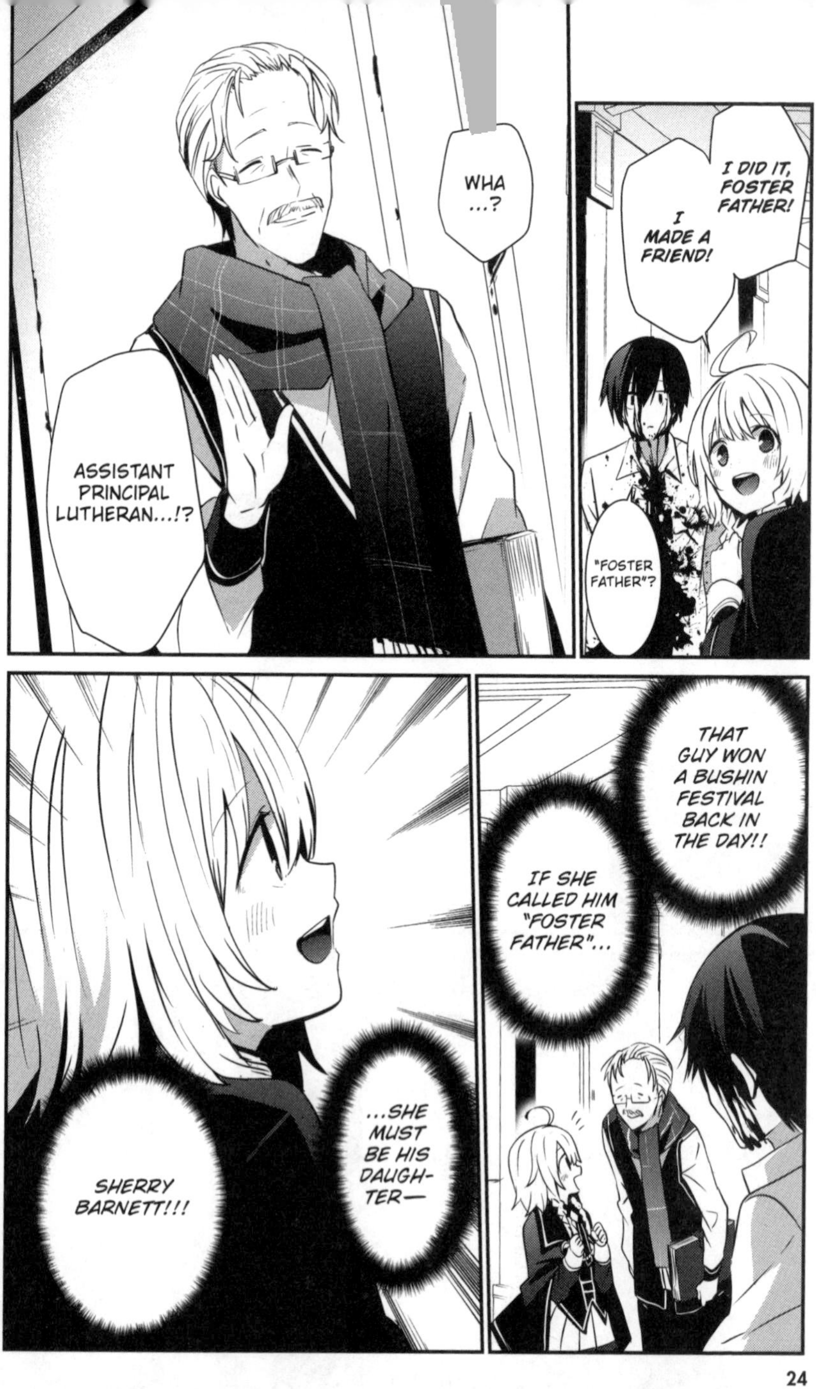
I DID IT, FOSTER FATHER!
I MADE A FRIEND!
"FOSTER FATHER"?
WHA ...?
ASSISTANT PRINCIPAL LUTHERAN...!?
THAT GUY WON A BUSHIN FESTIVAL BACK IN THE DAY!!
IF SHE CALLED HIM "FOSTER FATHER"...
...SHE MUST BE HIS DAUGH-TER—
SHERRY BARNETT!!!

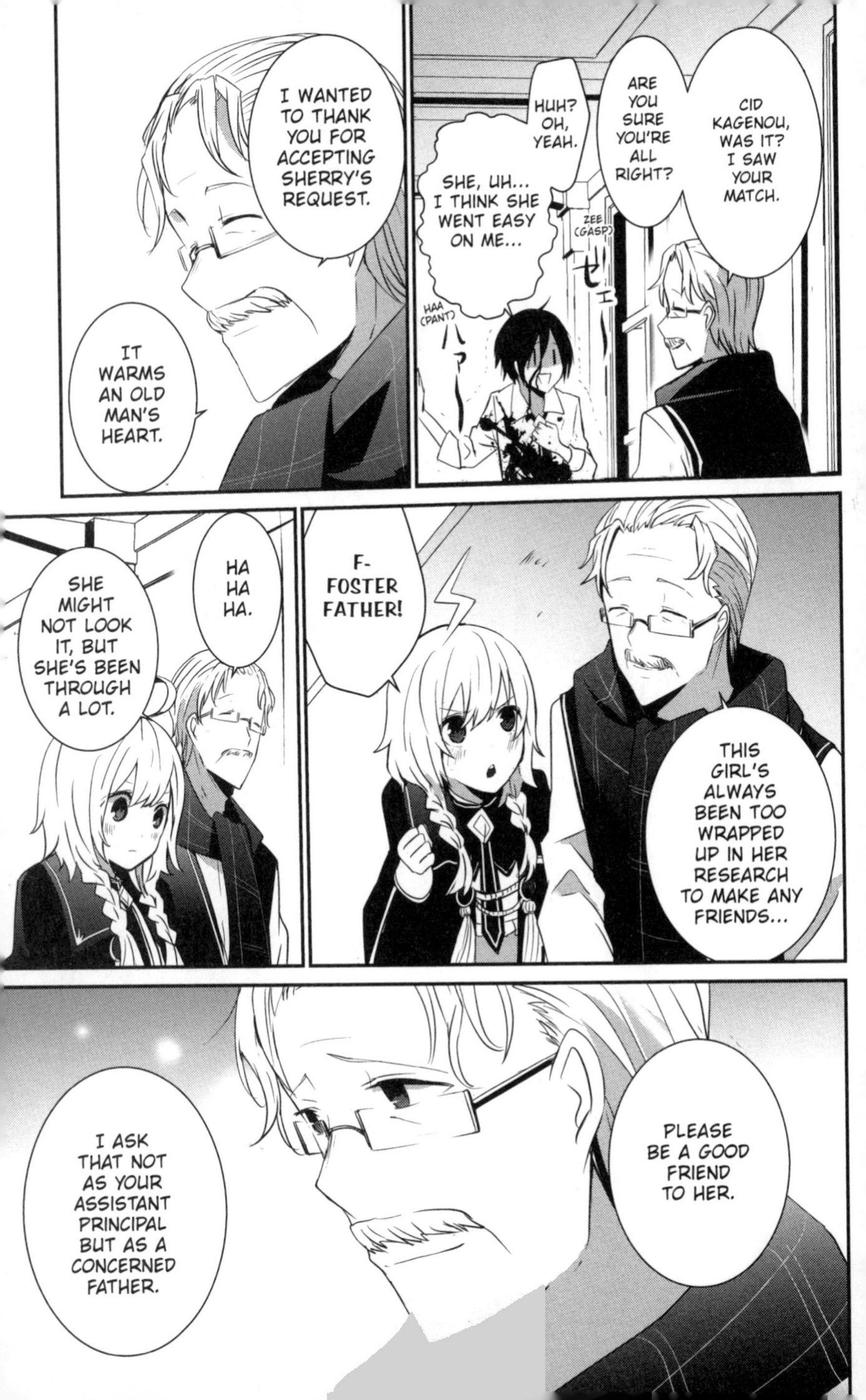
CID KAGENOU, WAS IT? I SAW YOUR MATCH.
ARE YOU SURE YOU'RE ALL RIGHT?
HUH? OH, YEAH.
ZEE (GASP)
SHE, UH... I THINK SHE WENT EASY ON ME...
HAA (PANT)
I WANTED TO THANK YOU FOR ACCEPTING SHERRY'S REQUEST.
IT WARMS AN OLD MAN'S HEART.
THIS GIRL'S ALWAYS BEEN TOO WRAPPED UP IN HER RESEARCH TO MAKE ANY FRIENDS...
F-FOSTER FATHER!
HA HA HA.
SHE MIGHT NOT LOOK IT, BUT SHE'S BEEN THROUGH A LOT.
PLEASE BE A GOOD FRIEND TO HER.
I ASK THAT NOT AS YOUR ASSISTANT PRINCIPAL BUT AS A CONCERNED FATHER.

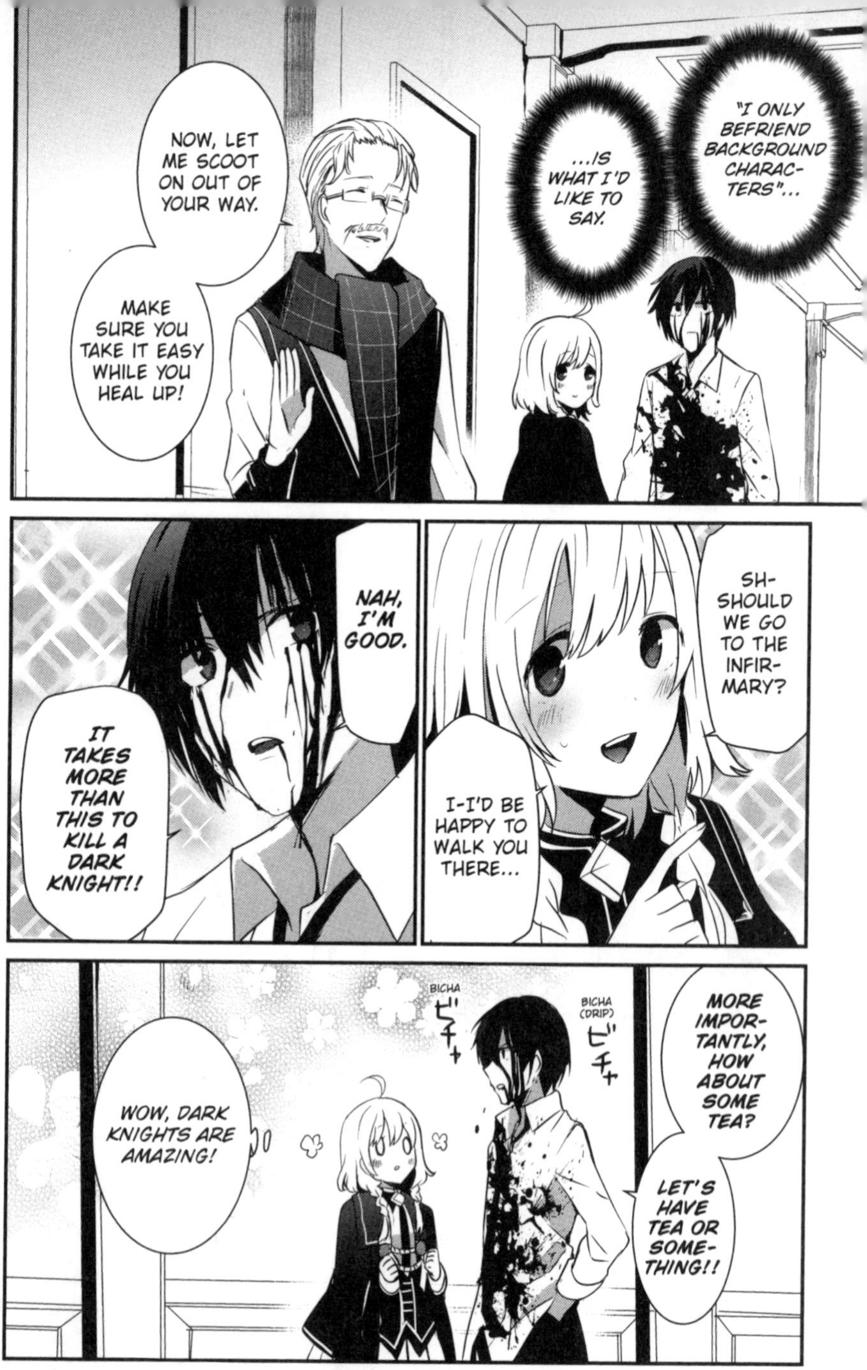
"I ONLY BEFRIEND BACKGROUND CHARACTERS"...
...IS WHAT I'D LIKE TO SAY.
NOW, LET ME SCOOT ON OUT OF YOUR WAY.
MAKE SURE YOU TAKE IT EASY WHILE YOU HEAL UP!
SH-SHOULD WE GO TO THE INFIRMARY?
I-I'D BE HAPPY TO WALK YOU THERE...
NAH, I'M GOOD.
IT TAKES MORE THAN THIS TO KILL A DARK KNIGHT!!
MORE IMPORTANTLY, HOW ABOUT SOME TEA?
BICHA (DRIP)
ビチャ
BICHA
ビチャ
LET'S HAVE TEA OR SOMETHING!!
WOW, DARK KNIGHTS ARE AMAZING!

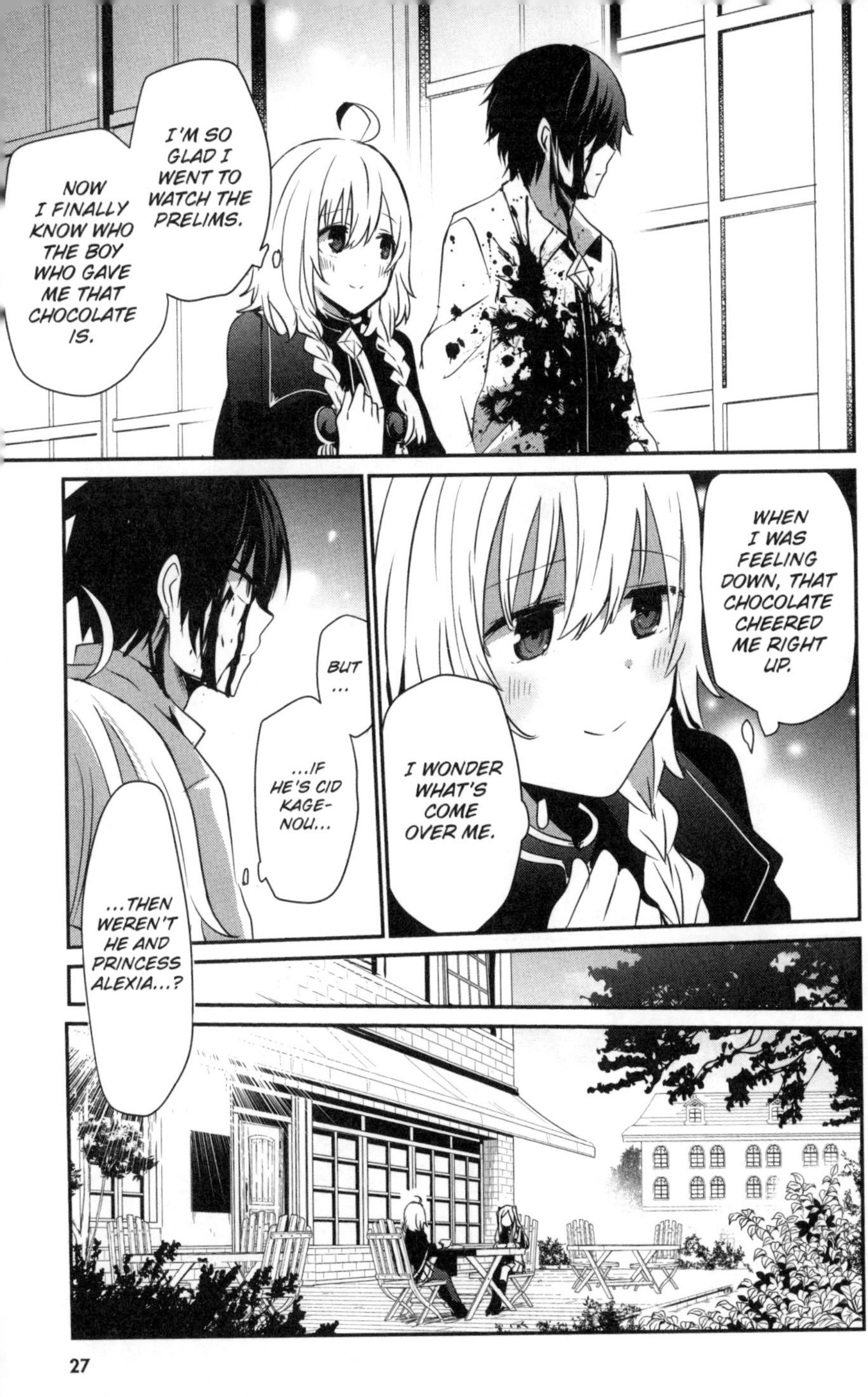
I'M SO GLAD I WENT TO WATCH THE PRELIMS.
NOW I FINALLY KNOW WHO THE BOY WHO GAVE ME THAT CHOCOLATE IS.
WHEN I WAS FEELING DOWN, THAT CHOCOLATE CHEERED ME RIGHT UP.
I WONDER WHAT'S COME OVER ME.
BUT...
...IF HE'S CID KAGE-NOU...
...THEN WEREN'T HE AND PRINCESS ALEXIA...?

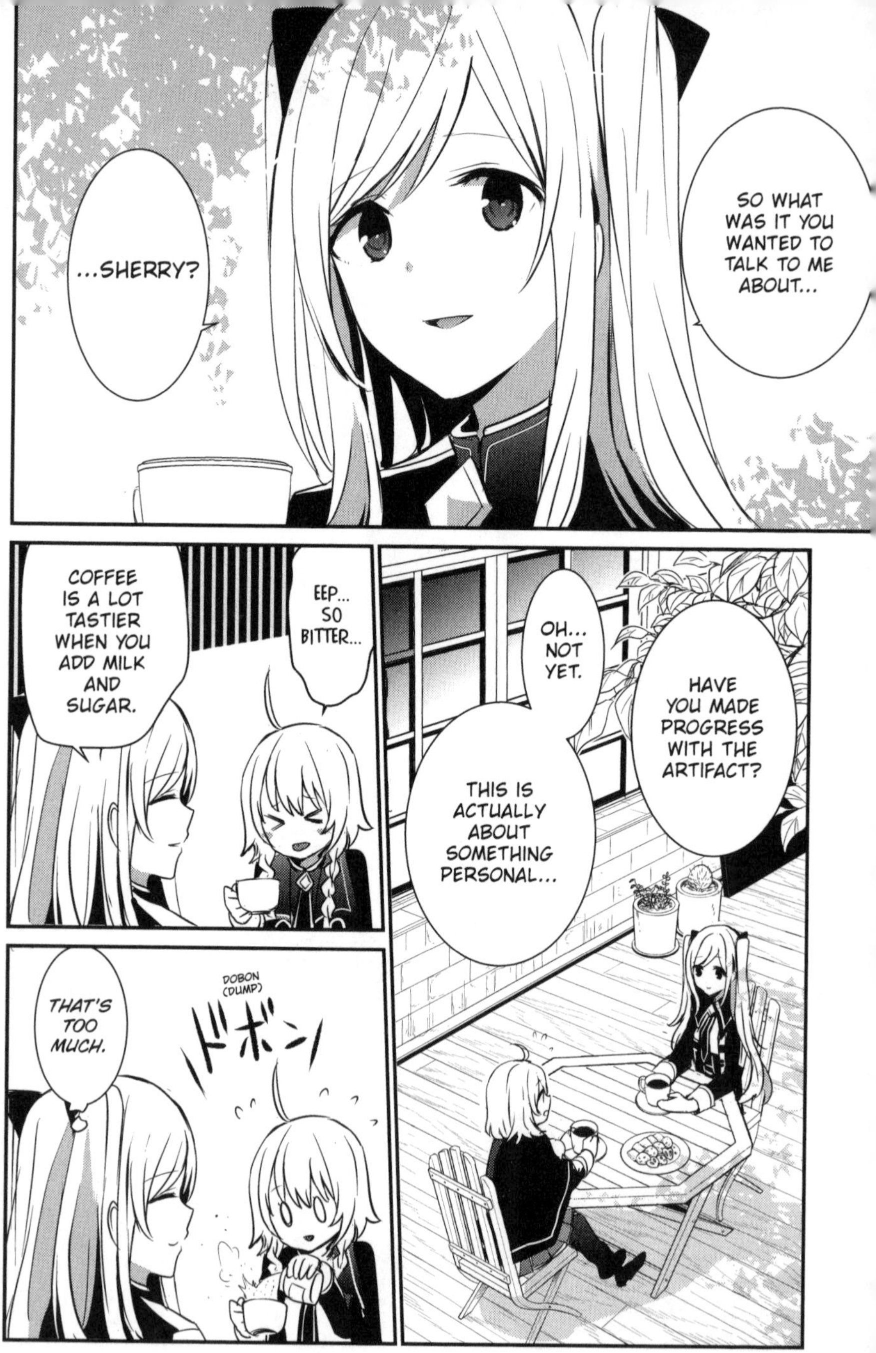
SO WHAT WAS IT YOU WANTED TO TALK TO ME ABOUT...
...SHERRY?
HAVE YOU MADE PROGRESS WITH THE ARTIFACT?
OH... NOT YET.
THIS IS ACTUALLY ABOUT SOMETHING PERSONAL...
EEP... SO BITTER...
COFFEE IS A LOT TASTIER WHEN YOU ADD MILK AND SUGAR.
ドボン
DOBON (DUMP)
THAT'S TOO MUCH.

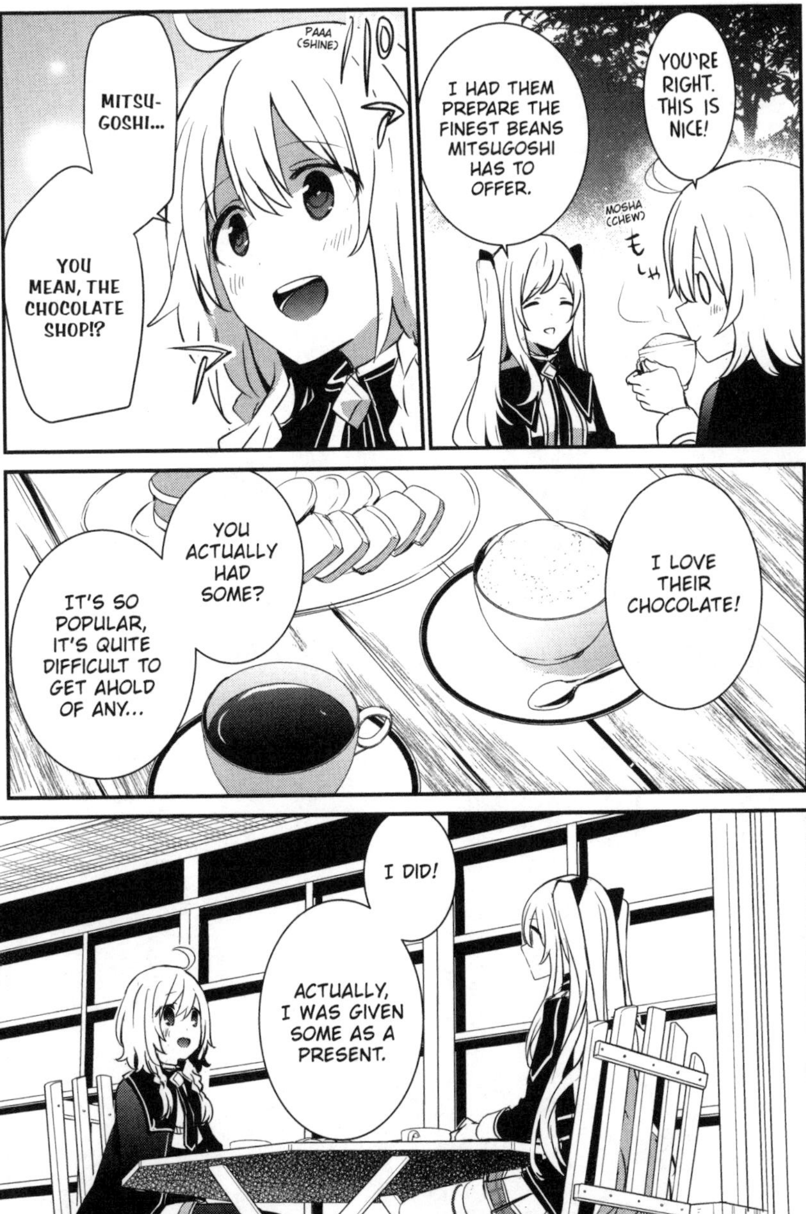
YOU'RE RIGHT. THIS IS NICE!
I HAD THEM PREPARE THE FINEST BEANS MITSUGOSHI HAS TO OFFER.
MOSHA (CHEW)
PAAA (SHINE)
MITSU-GOSHI...
YOU MEAN, THE CHOCOLATE SHOP!?
I LOVE THEIR CHOCOLATE!
YOU ACTUALLY HAD SOME?
IT'S SO POPULAR, IT'S QUITE DIFFICULT TO GET AHOLD OF ANY...
I DID!
ACTUALLY, I WAS GIVEN SOME AS A PRESENT.

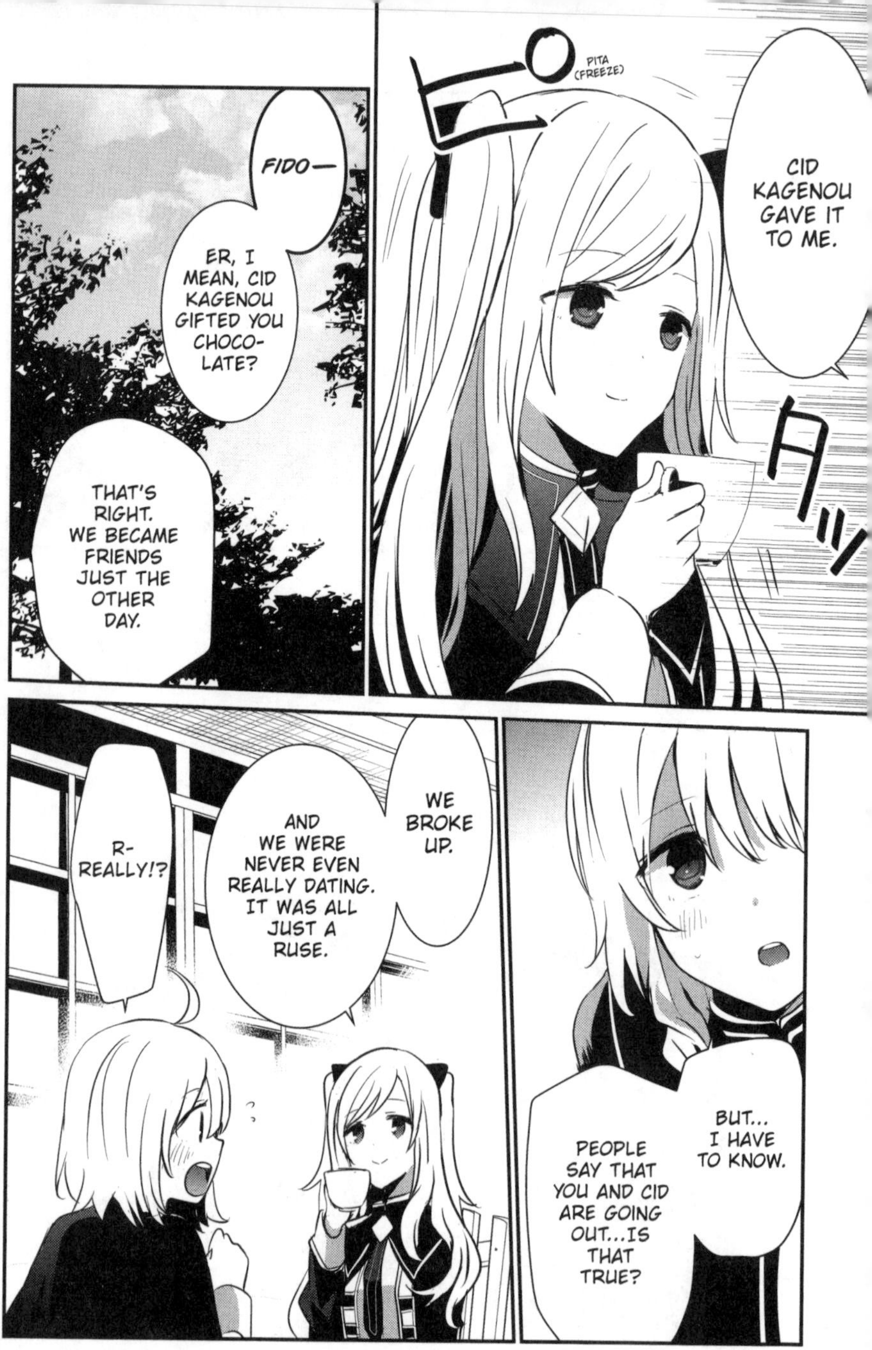
PITA (FREEZE)
CID KAGENOU GAVE IT TO ME.
FIDO—
ER, I MEAN, CID KAGENOU GIFTED YOU CHOCOLATE?
THAT'S RIGHT. WE BECAME FRIENDS JUST THE OTHER DAY.
BUT... I HAVE TO KNOW.
PEOPLE SAY THAT YOU AND CID ARE GOING OUT...IS THAT TRUE?
WE BROKE UP.
AND WE WERE NEVER EVEN REALLY DATING. IT WAS ALL JUST A RUSE.
R-REALLY!?

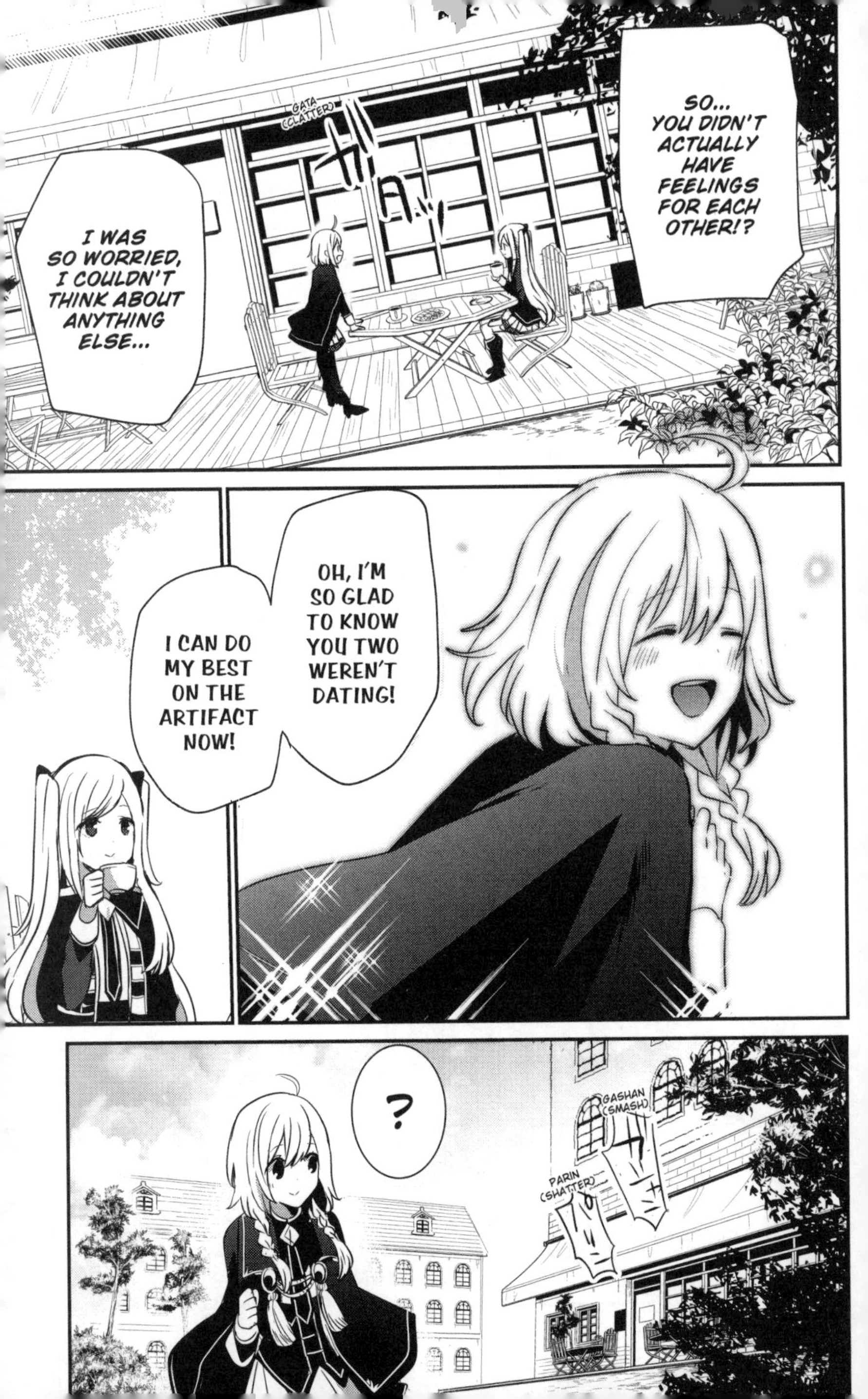
SO... YOU DIDN'T ACTUALLY HAVE FEELINGS FOR EACH OTHER!?
GATA (CLATTER)
I WAS SO WORRIED, I COULDN'T THINK ABOUT ANYTHING ELSE...
OH, I'M SO GLAD TO KNOW YOU TWO WEREN'T DATING!
I CAN DO MY BEST ON THE ARTIFACT NOW!
GASHAN (SMASH)
PARIN (SHATTER)
?

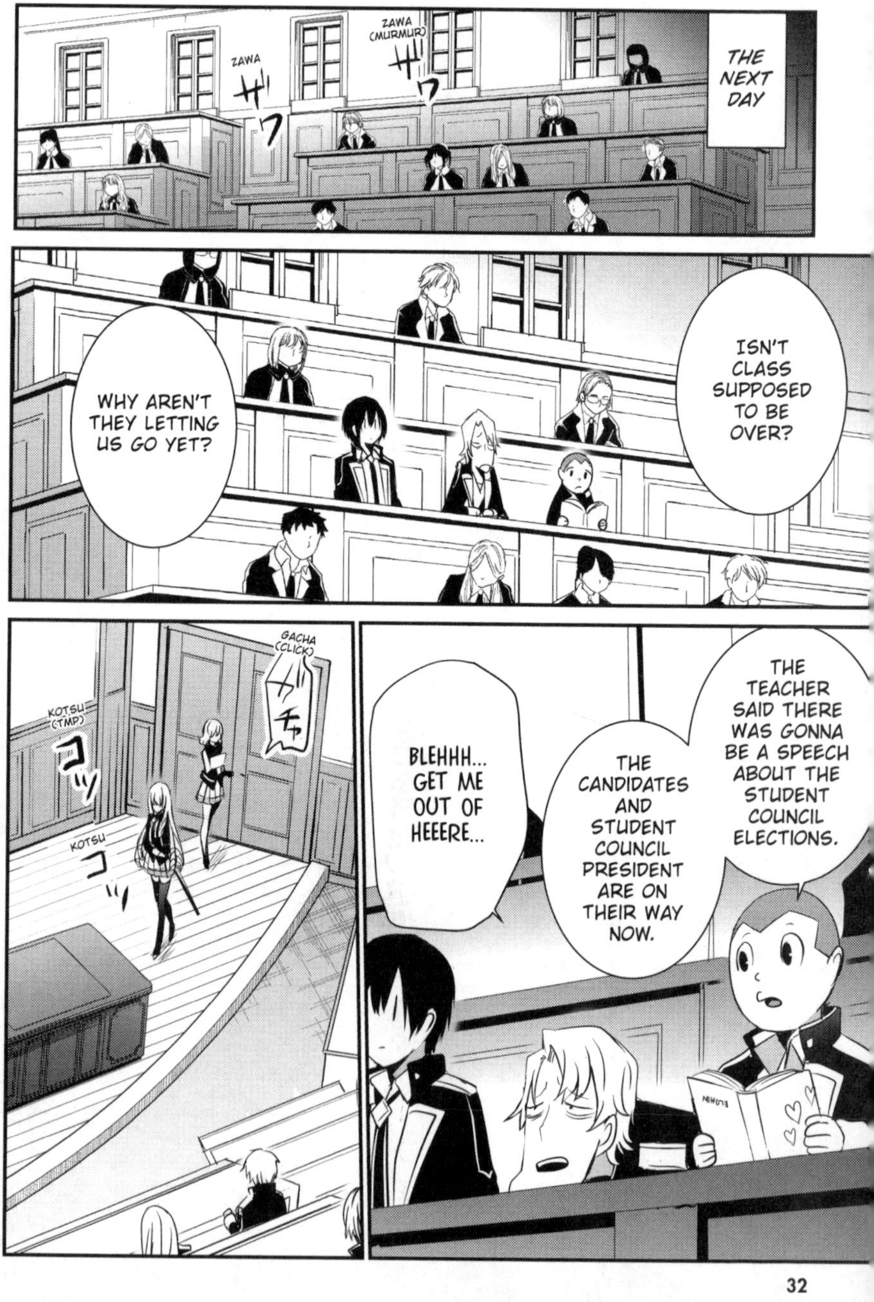
THE NEXT DAY
ZAWA (MURMUR)
ザワ
ZAWA
ザワ
ISN'T CLASS SUPPOSED TO BE OVER?
WHY AREN'T THEY LETTING US GO YET?
THE TEACHER SAID THERE WAS GONNA BE A SPEECH ABOUT THE STUDENT COUNCIL ELECTIONS.
THE CANDIDATES AND STUDENT COUNCIL PRESIDENT ARE ON THEIR WAY NOW.
BLEHHH... GET ME OUT OF HEEERE...
GACHA (CLICK)
ガチャ
KOTSU (TMP)
コツ
KOTSU
コツ

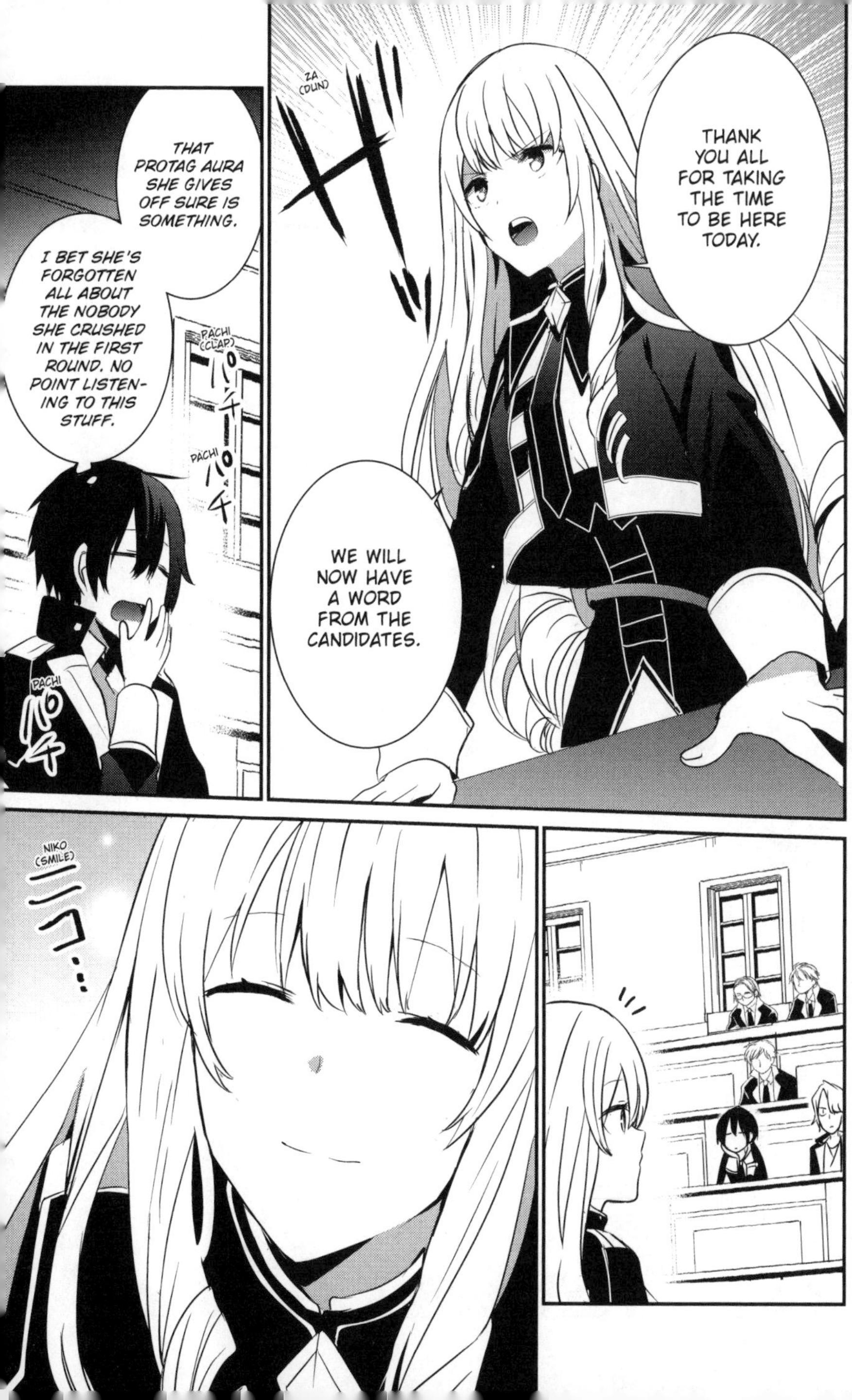
ZA (DUN)
THANK YOU ALL FOR TAKING THE TIME TO BE HERE TODAY.
WE WILL NOW HAVE A WORD FROM THE CANDIDATES.
THAT PROTAG AURA SHE GIVES OFF SURE IS SOMETHING.
I BET SHE'S FORGOTTEN ALL ABOUT THE NOBODY SHE CRUSHED IN THE FIRST ROUND. NO POINT LISTENING TO THIS STUFF.
PACHI (CLAP)
PACHI
PACHI
NIKO (SMILE)

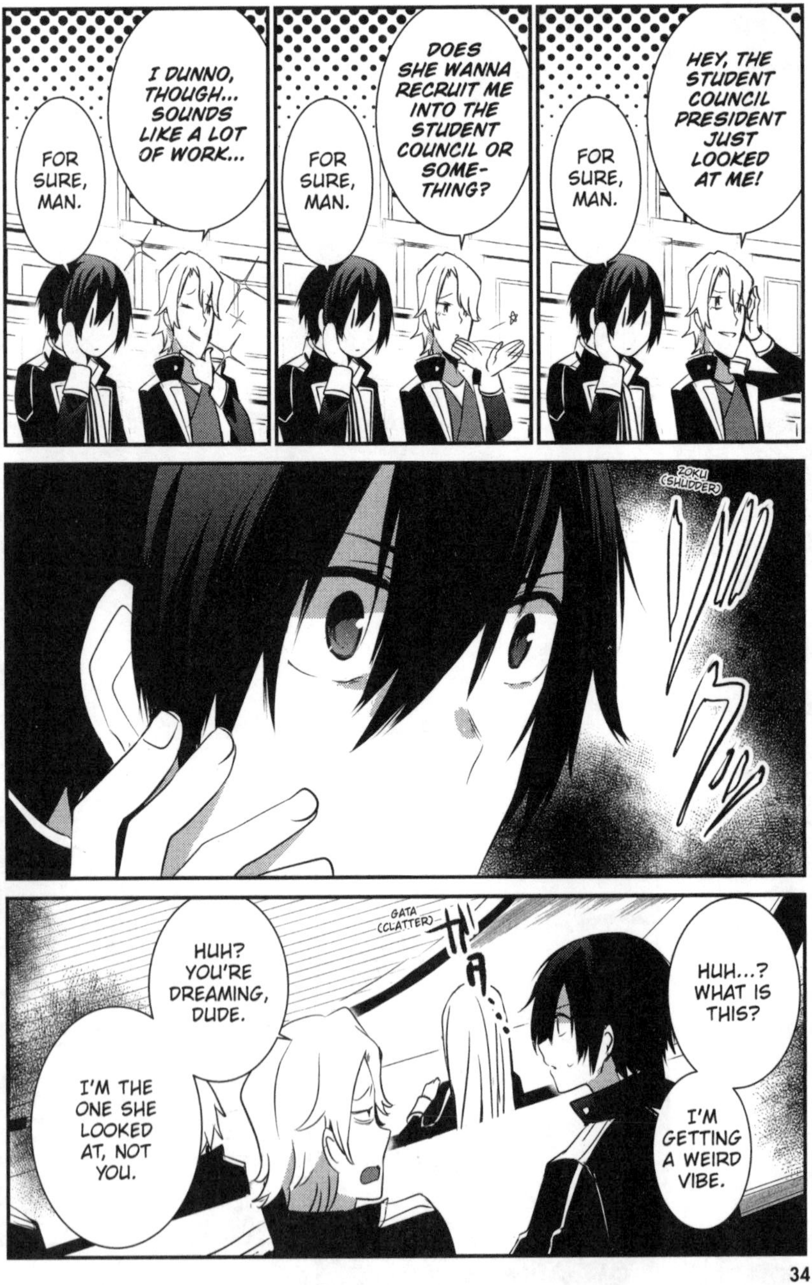
HEY, THE STUDENT COUNCIL PRESIDENT JUST LOOKED AT ME!
FOR SURE, MAN.
DOES SHE WANNA RECRUIT ME INTO THE STUDENT COUNCIL OR SOME-THING?
FOR SURE, MAN.
I DUNNO, THOUGH... SOUNDS LIKE A LOT OF WORK...
FOR SURE, MAN.
ZOKU (SHUDDER)
GATA (CLATTER)
HUH...? WHAT IS THIS?
I'M GETTING A WEIRD VIBE.
HUH? YOU'RE DREAMING, DUDE.
I'M THE ONE SHE LOOKED AT, NOT YOU.

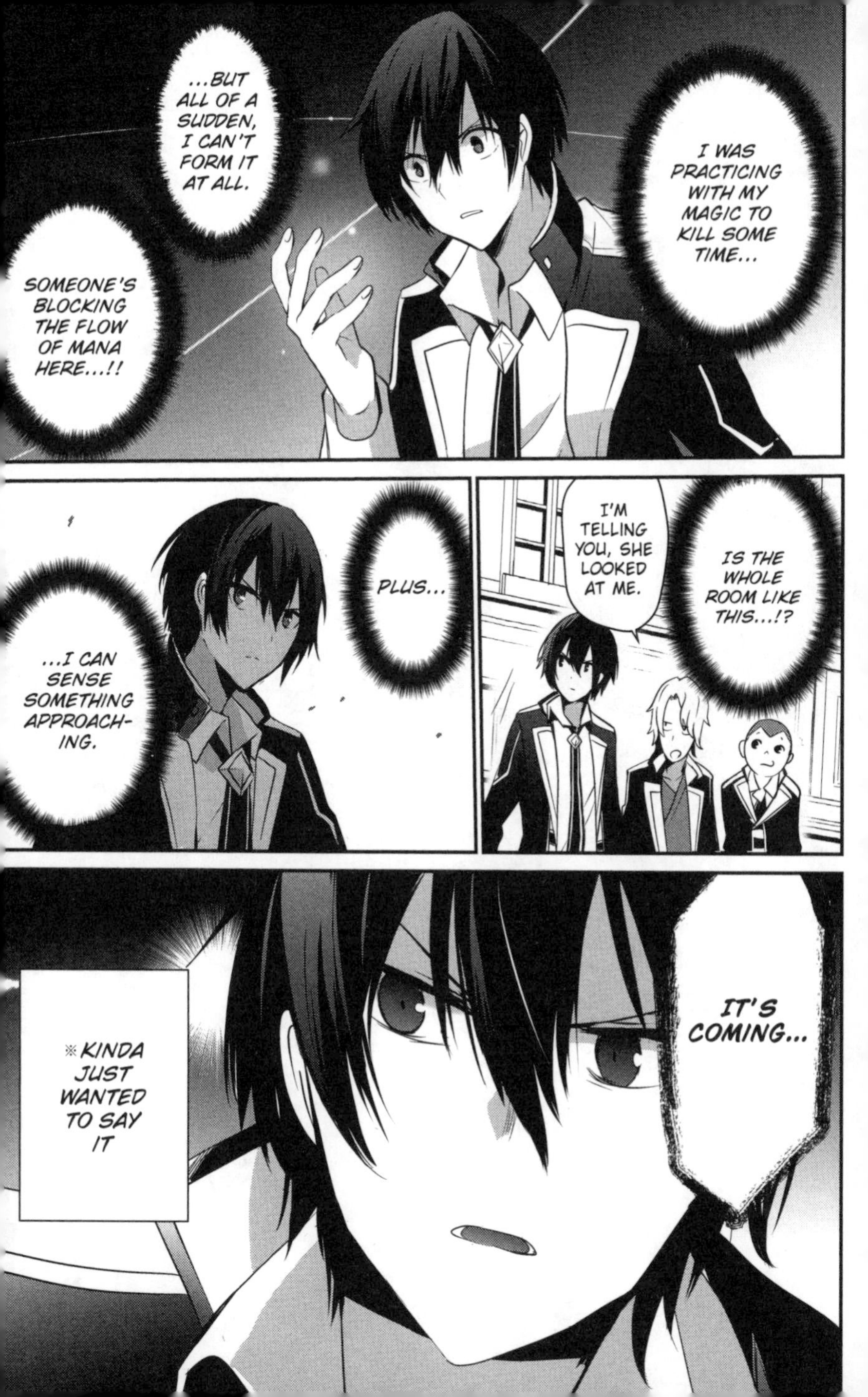
I WAS PRACTICING WITH MY MAGIC TO KILL SOME TIME...
...BUT ALL OF A SUDDEN, I CAN'T FORM IT AT ALL.
SOMEONE'S BLOCKING THE FLOW OF MANA HERE...!!
IS THE WHOLE ROOM LIKE THIS...!?
I'M TELLING YOU, SHE LOOKED AT ME.
PLUS...
...I CAN SENSE SOMETHING APPROACHING.
IT'S COMING...
※KINDA JUST WANTED TO SAY IT

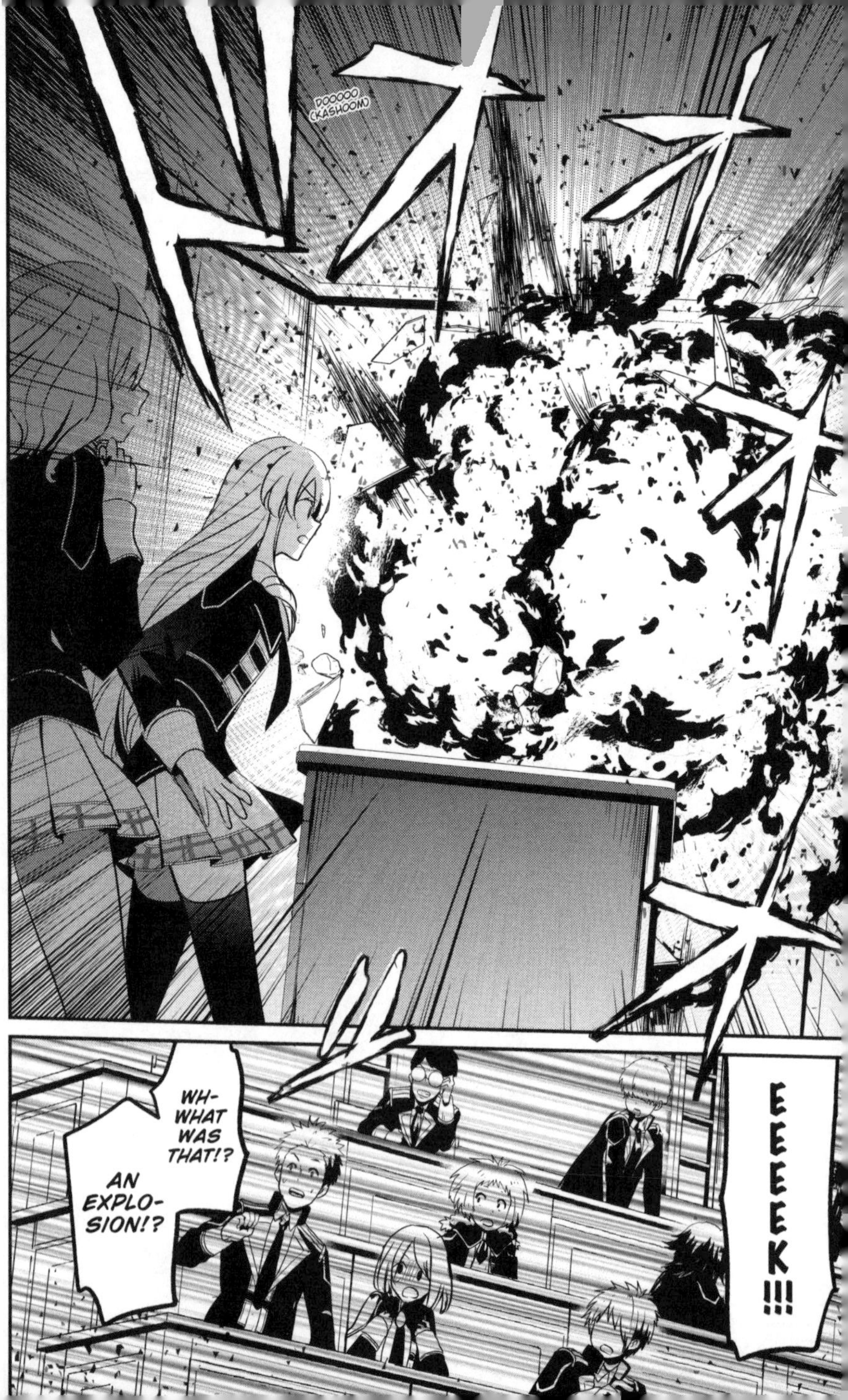
DOOOOO
(KASHOOM)
EEEEEK!!!
WH-WHAT WAS THAT!? AN EXPLOSION!?

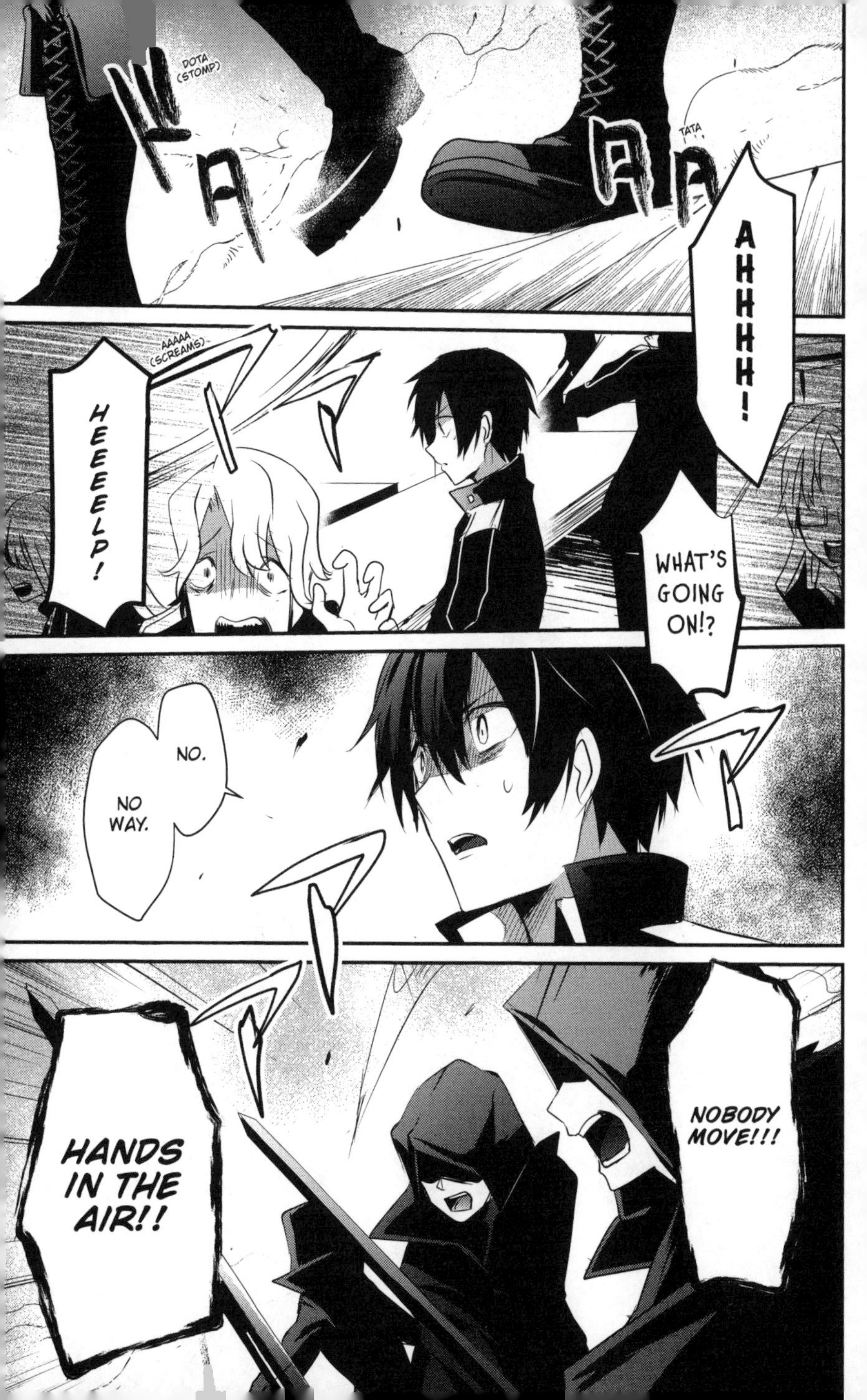
TATA
AHHHHH!
DOTA (STOMP)
WHAT'S GOING ON!?
AAAAA (SCREAMS)
HEEEEELP!
NO.
NO WAY.
NOBODY MOVE!!!
HANDS IN THE AIR!!

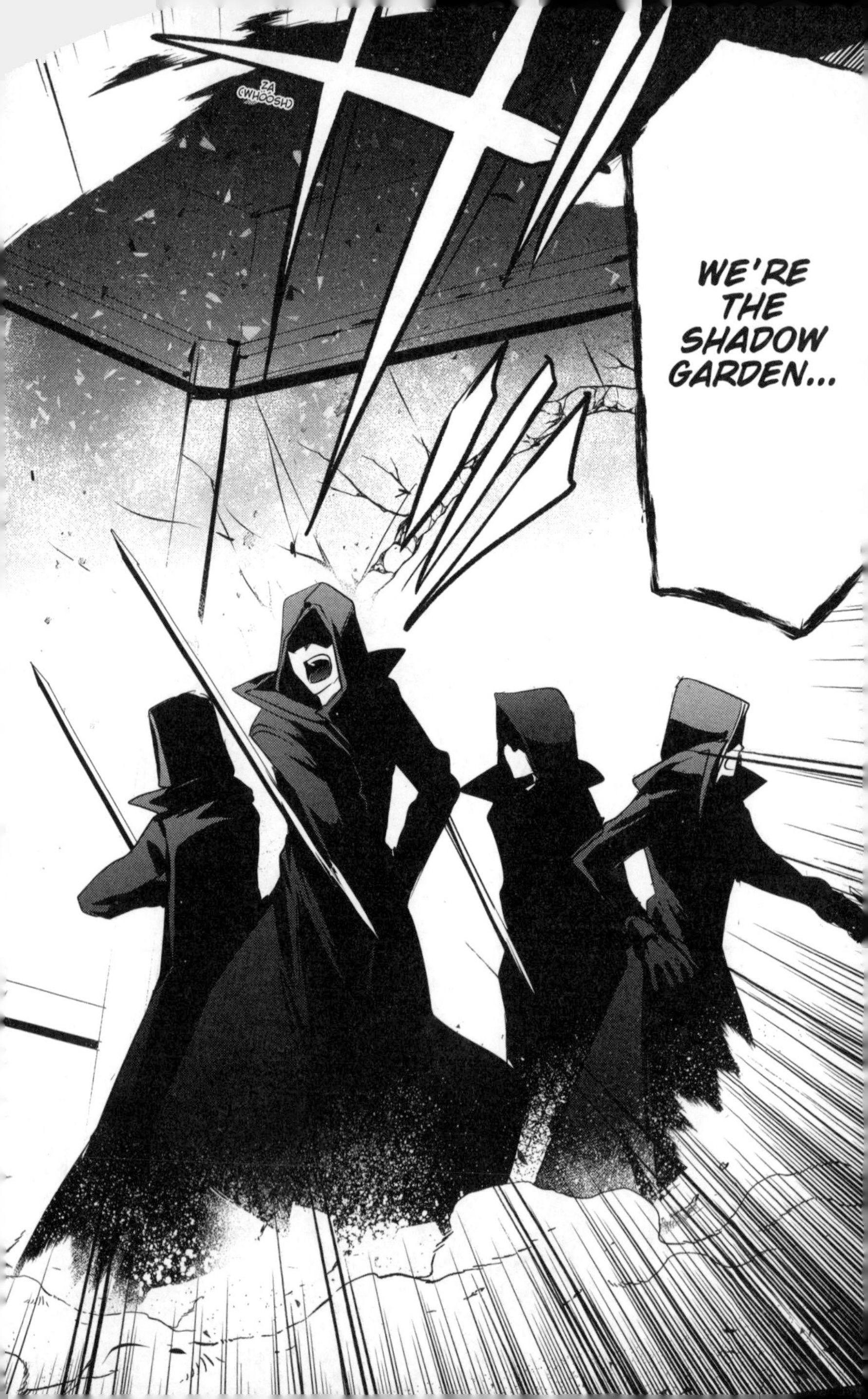
WE'RE THE SHADOW GARDEN...
ZA (WHOOSH)

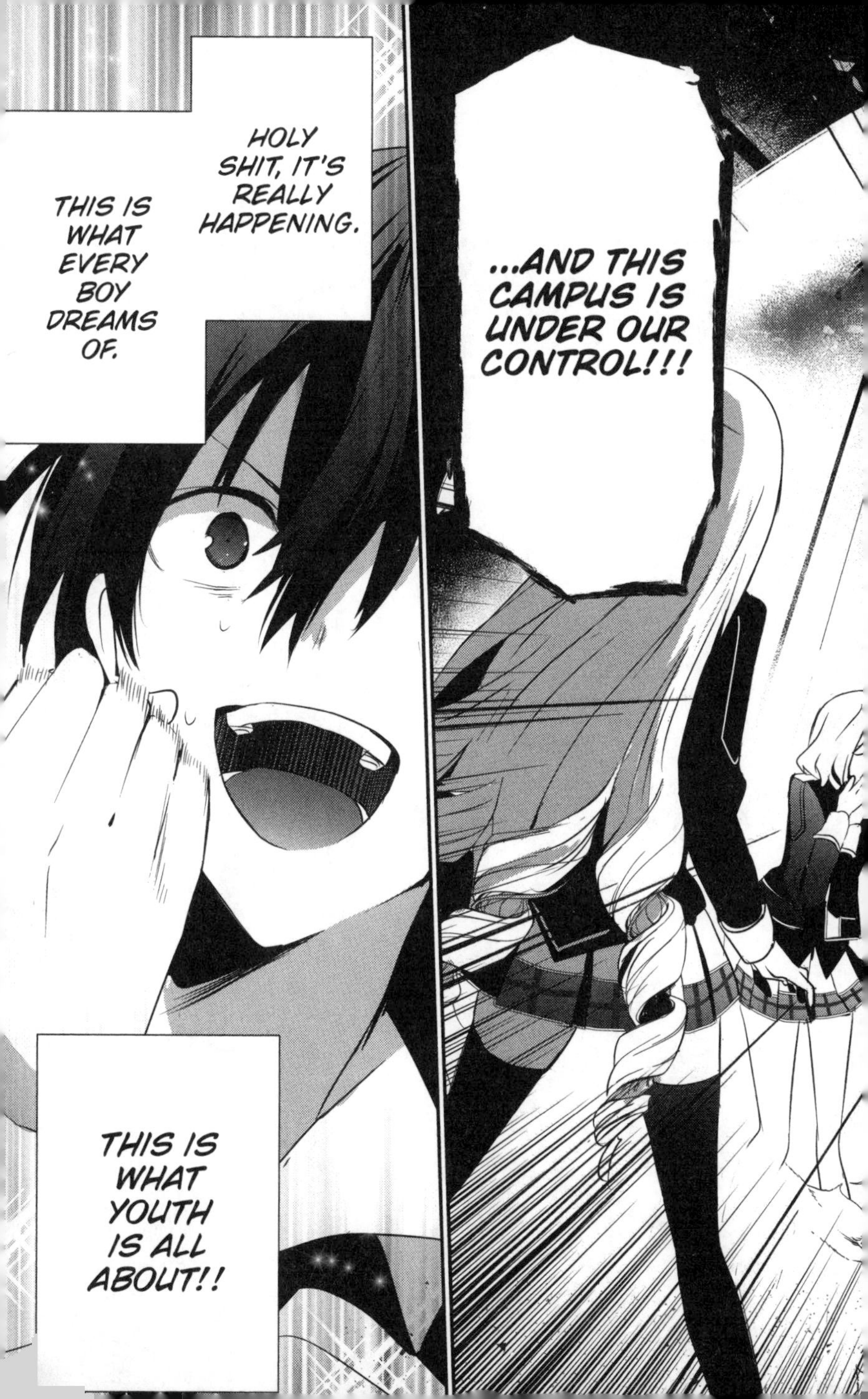
...AND THIS CAMPUS IS UNDER OUR CONTROL!!!
HOLY SHIT, IT'S REALLY HAPPENING.
THIS IS WHAT EVERY BOY DREAMS OF.
THIS IS WHAT YOUTH IS ALL ABOUT!!

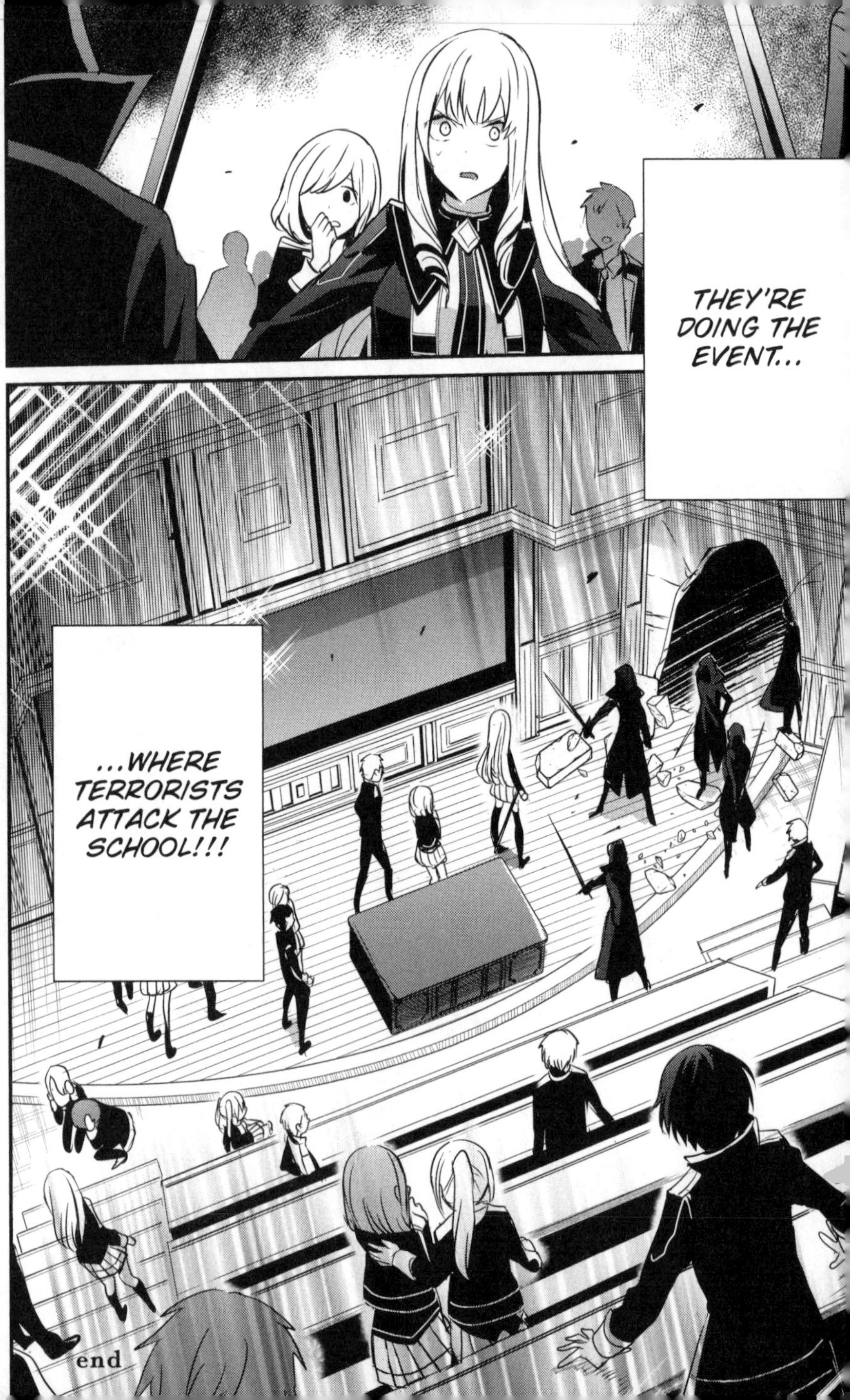
THEY'RE DOING THE EVENT...
...WHERE TERRORISTS ATTACK THE SCHOOL!!!
end

The Eminence in Shadow

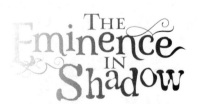

Episode. 10-1

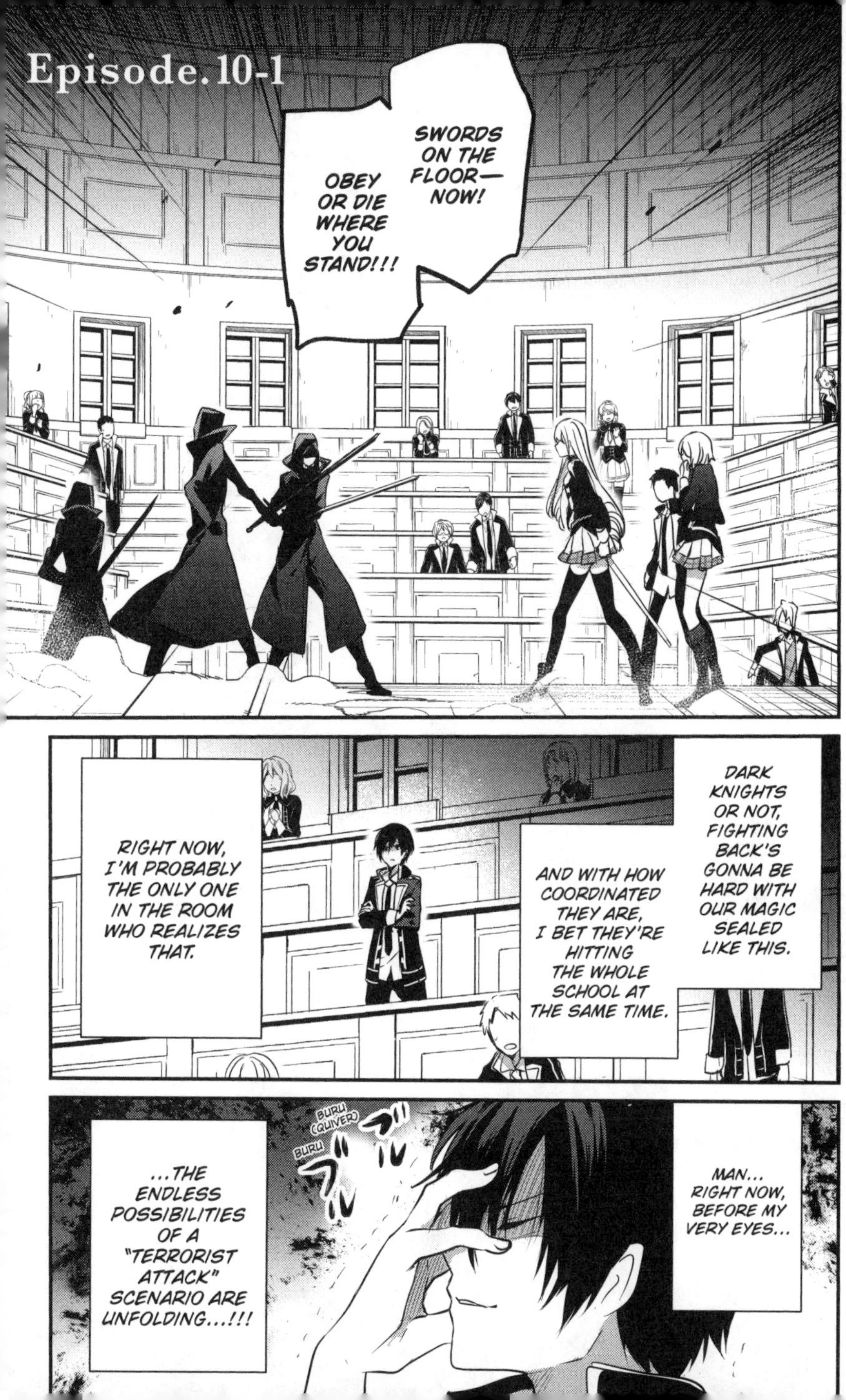

SWORDS ON THE FLOOR—NOW!
OBEY OR DIE WHERE YOU STAND!!!
DARK KNIGHTS OR NOT, FIGHTING BACK'S GONNA BE HARD WITH OUR MAGIC SEALED LIKE THIS.
AND WITH HOW COORDINATED THEY ARE, I BET THEY'RE HITTING THE WHOLE SCHOOL AT THE SAME TIME.
RIGHT NOW, I'M PROBABLY THE ONLY ONE IN THE ROOM WHO REALIZES THAT.
MAN... RIGHT NOW, BEFORE MY VERY EYES...
BURU (QUIVER)
BURU
...THE ENDLESS POSSIBILITIES OF A "TERRORIST ATTACK" SCENARIO ARE UNFOLDING...!!!

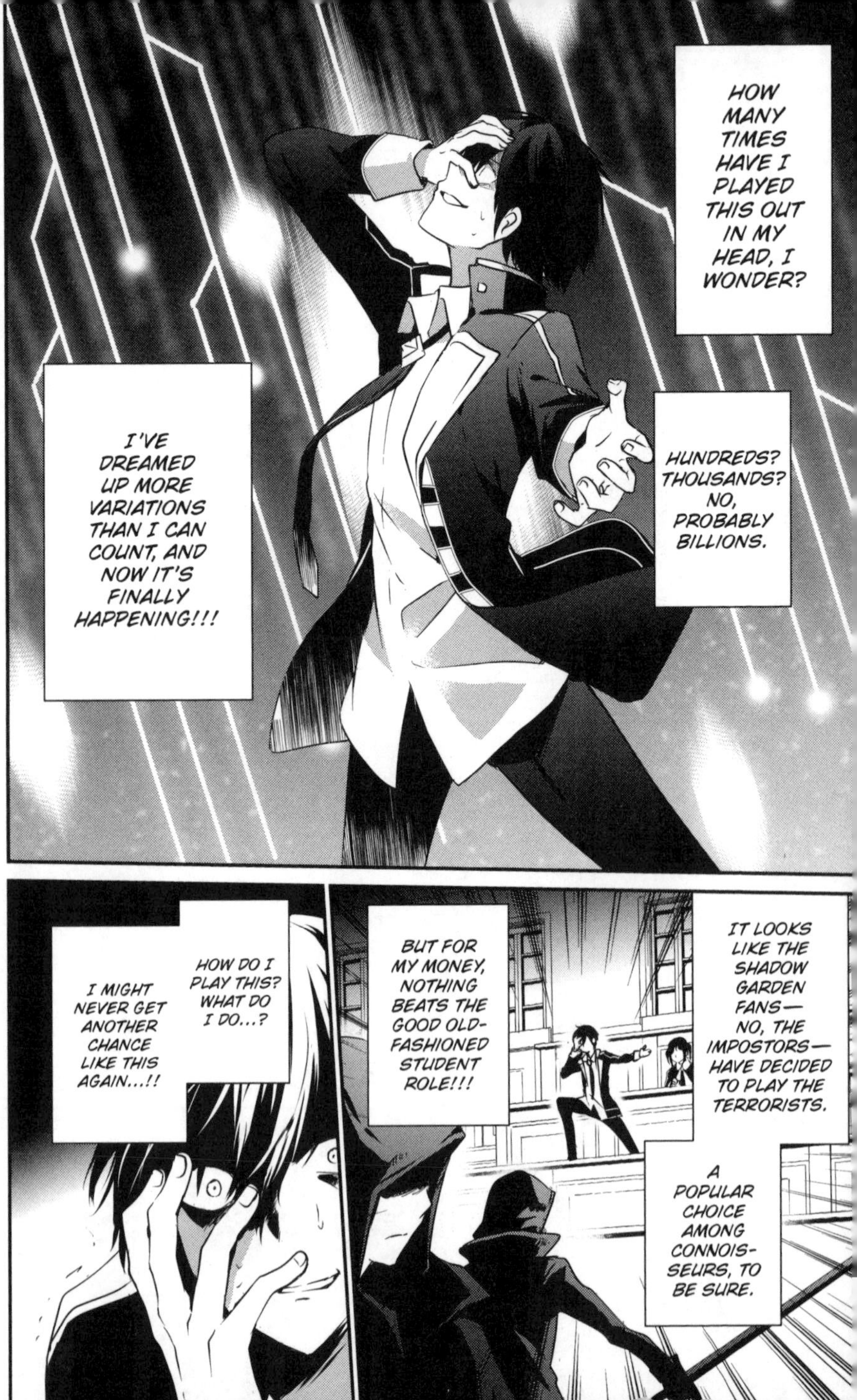
HOW MANY TIMES HAVE I PLAYED THIS OUT IN MY HEAD, I WONDER?
HUNDREDS? THOUSANDS? NO, PROBABLY BILLIONS.
I'VE DREAMED UP MORE VARIATIONS THAN I CAN COUNT, AND NOW IT'S FINALLY HAPPENING!!!
IT LOOKS LIKE THE SHADOW GARDEN FANS—NO, THE IMPOSTORS—HAVE DECIDED TO PLAY THE TERRORISTS.
A POPULAR CHOICE AMONG CONNOIS-SEURS, TO BE SURE.
BUT FOR MY MONEY, NOTHING BEATS THE GOOD OLD-FASHIONED STUDENT ROLE!!!
HOW DO I PLAY THIS? WHAT DO I DO...?
I MIGHT NEVER GET ANOTHER CHANCE LIKE THIS AGAIN...!!

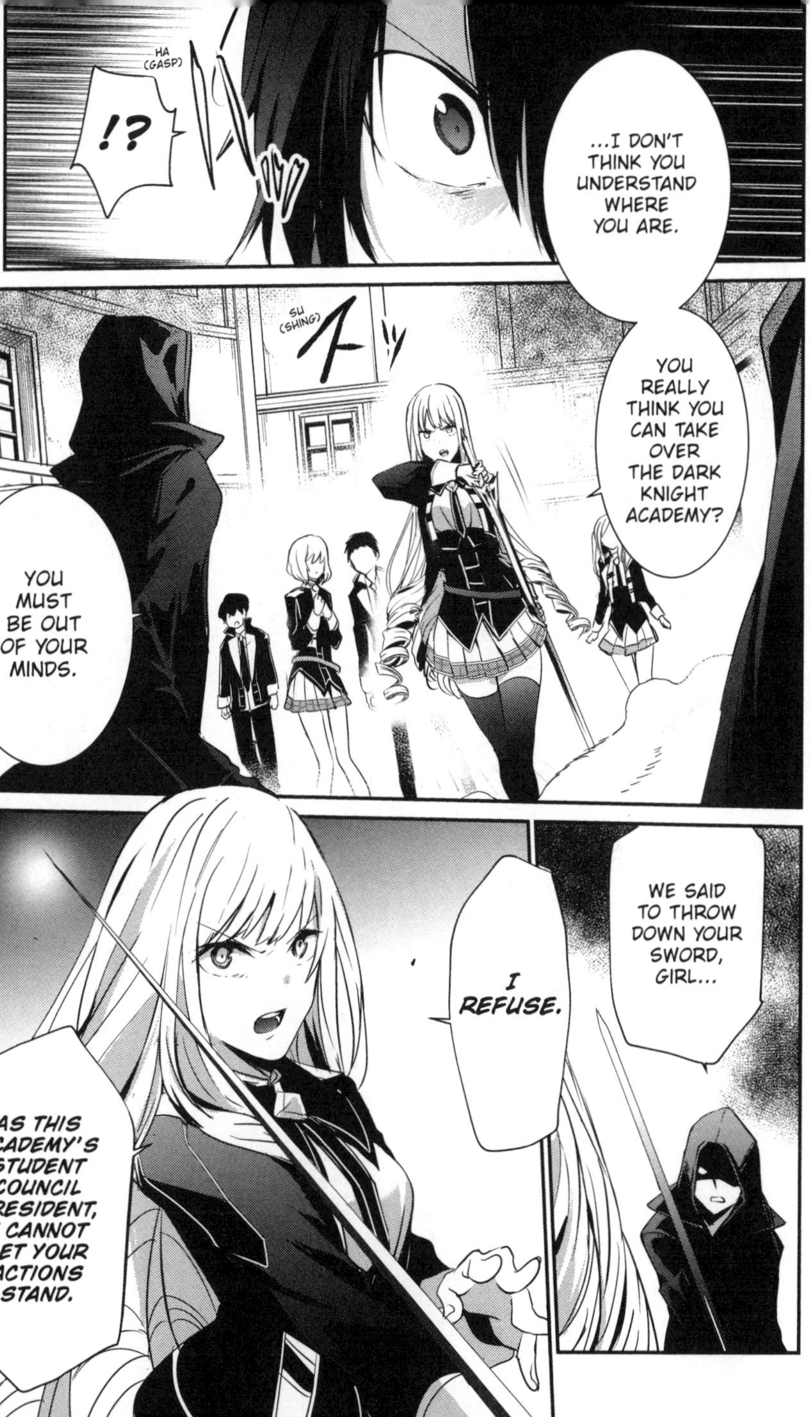
...I DON'T THINK YOU UNDERSTAND WHERE YOU ARE.
HA (GASP)
!?
YOU REALLY THINK YOU CAN TAKE OVER THE DARK KNIGHT ACADEMY?
SU (SHING)
YOU MUST BE OUT OF YOUR MINDS.
WE SAID TO THROW DOWN YOUR SWORD, GIRL...
I REFUSE.
AS THIS ACADEMY'S STUDENT COUNCIL PRESIDENT, I CANNOT LET YOUR ACTIONS STAND.

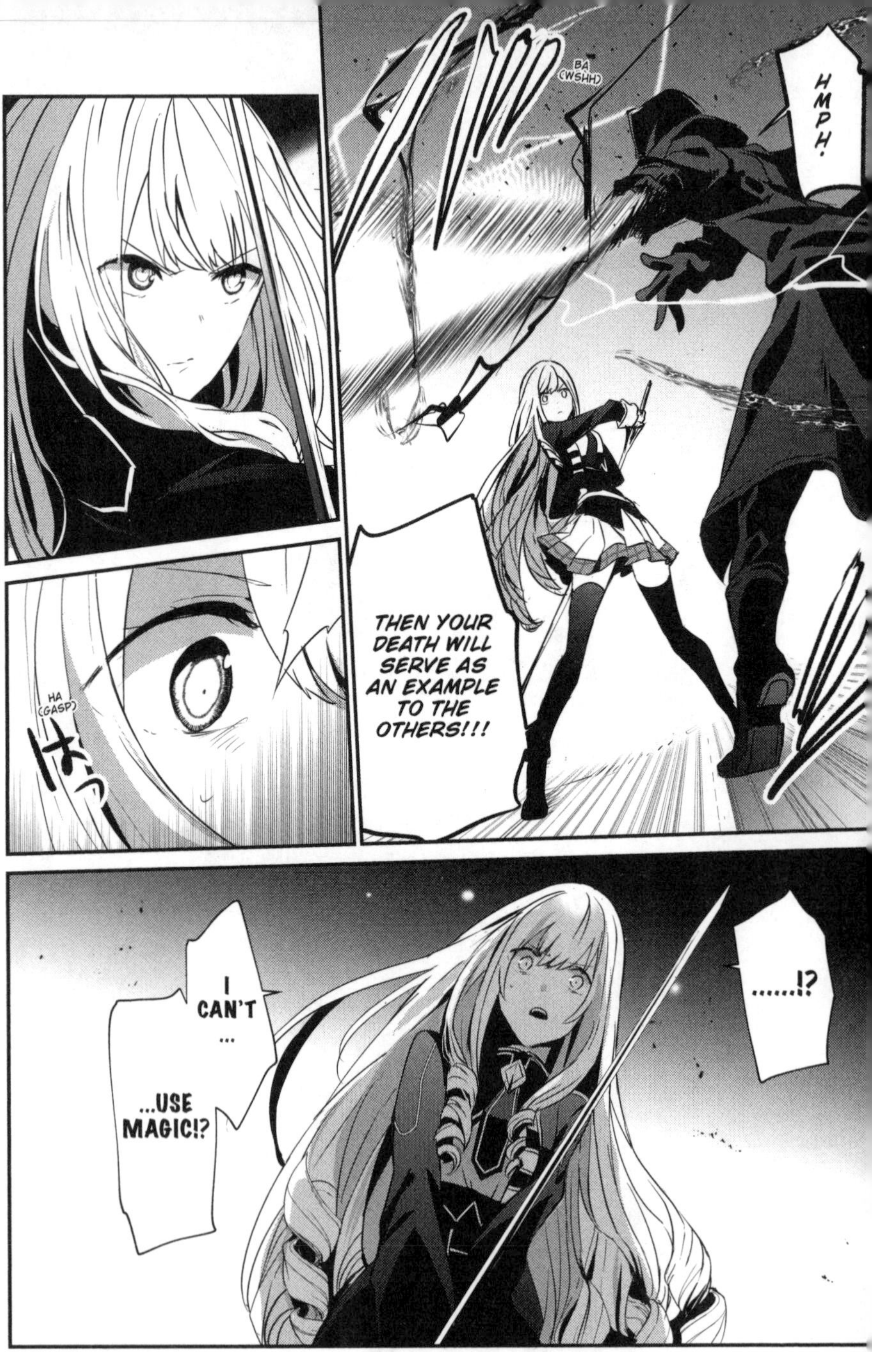
HMPH!
BA (WSHH)
THEN YOUR DEATH WILL SERVE AS AN EXAMPLE TO THE OTHERS!!!
HA (GASP)
はっ
......!?
I CAN'T ...
...USE MAGIC!?

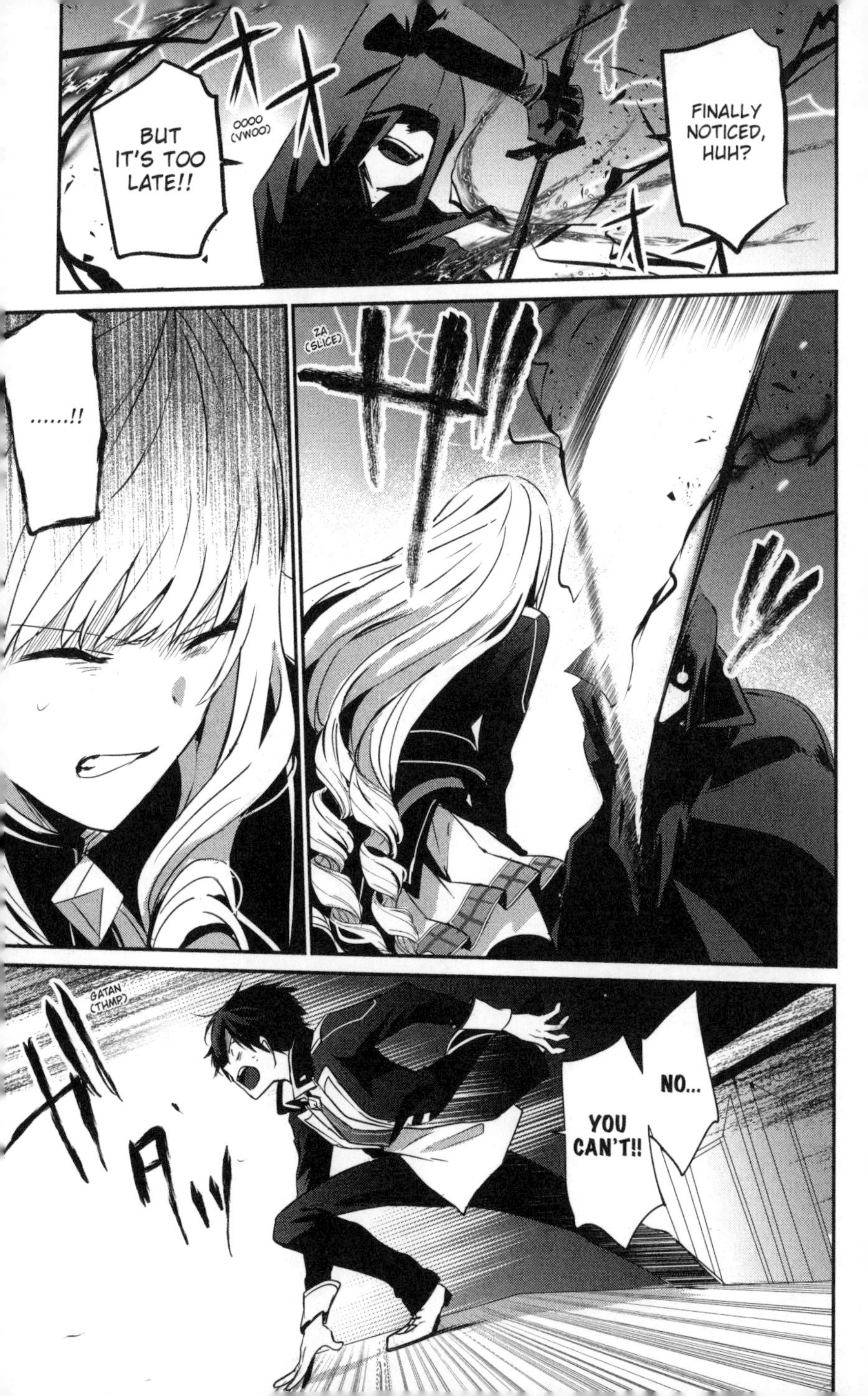
FINALLY NOTICED, HUH?
OOOO (VWOO)
BUT IT'S TOO LATE!!
ZA (SLICE)
......!!
NO...
YOU CAN'T!!
GATAN (THMP)

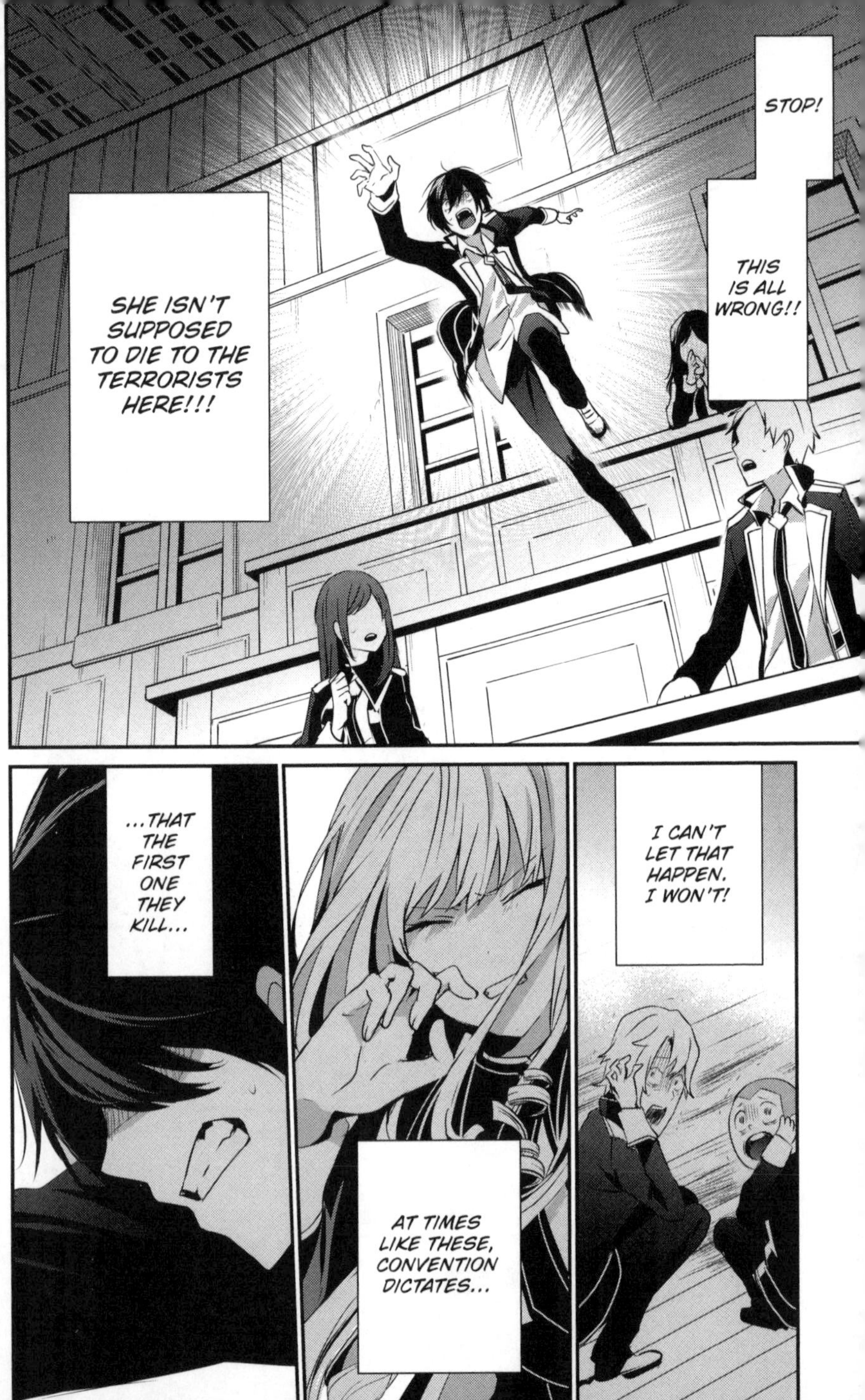
STOP!
THIS IS ALL WRONG!!
SHE ISN'T SUPPOSED TO DIE TO THE TERRORISTS HERE!!!
I CAN'T LET THAT HAPPEN. I WON'T!
AT TIMES LIKE THESE, CONVENTION DICTATES...
...THAT THE FIRST ONE THEY KILL...

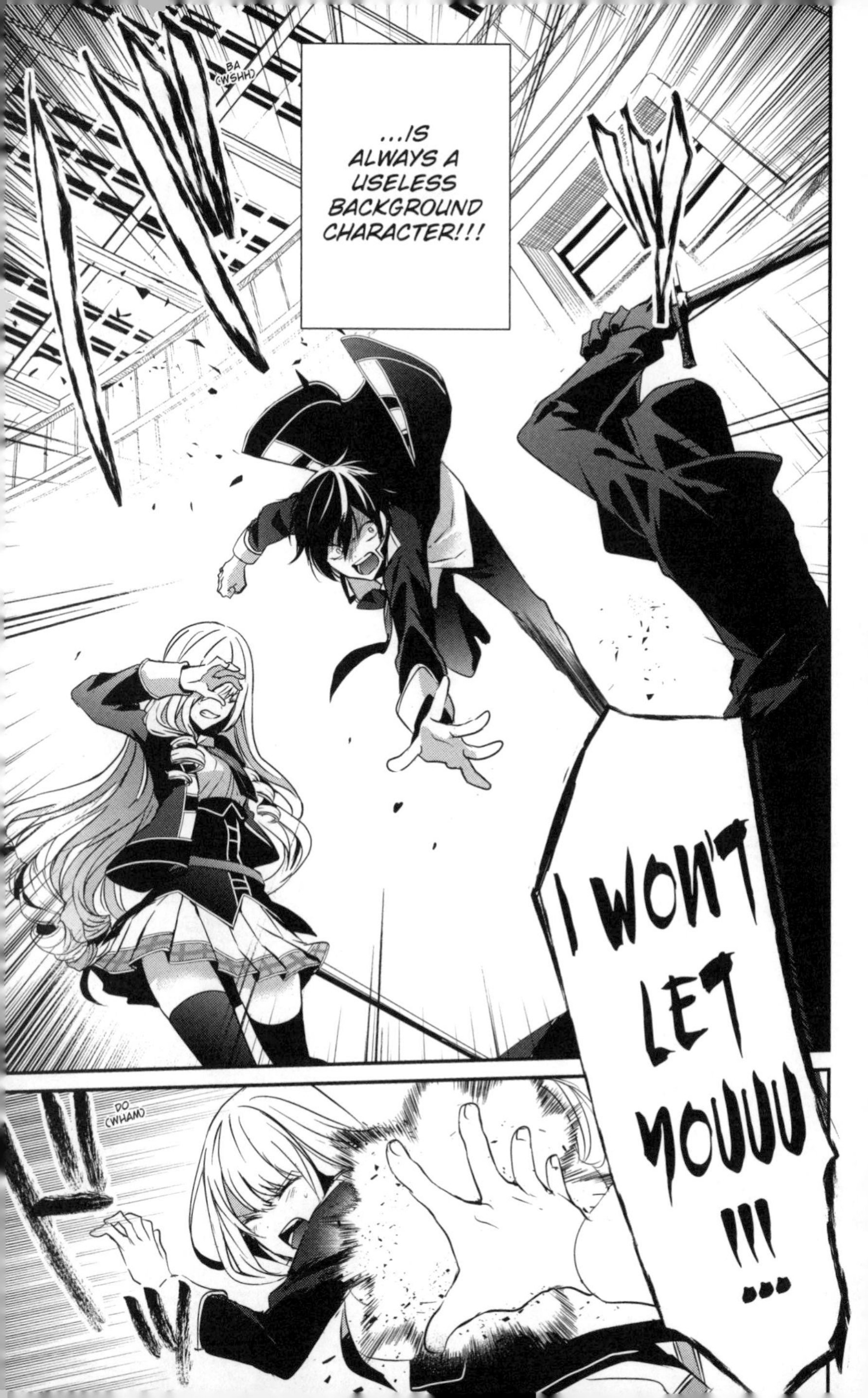
...IS ALWAYS A USELESS BACKGROUND CHARACTER!!!
BA (WSHH)
I WON'T LET YOUUU!!!...
DO (WHAM)

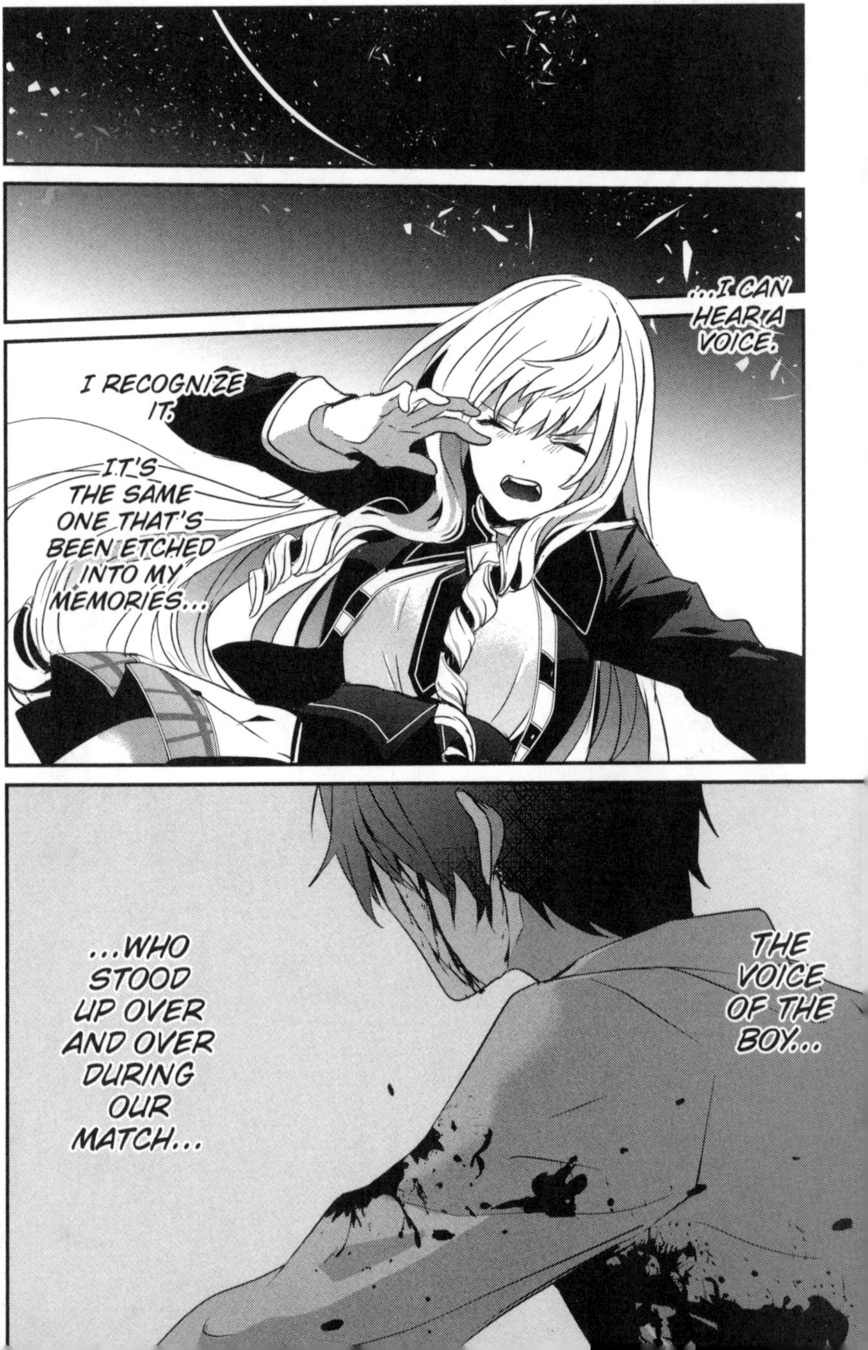
...I CAN HEAR A VOICE.
I RECOGNIZE IT.
IT'S THE SAME ONE THAT'S BEEN ETCHED INTO MY MEMORIES...
THE VOICE OF THE BOY...
...WHO STOOD UP OVER AND OVER DURING OUR MATCH...

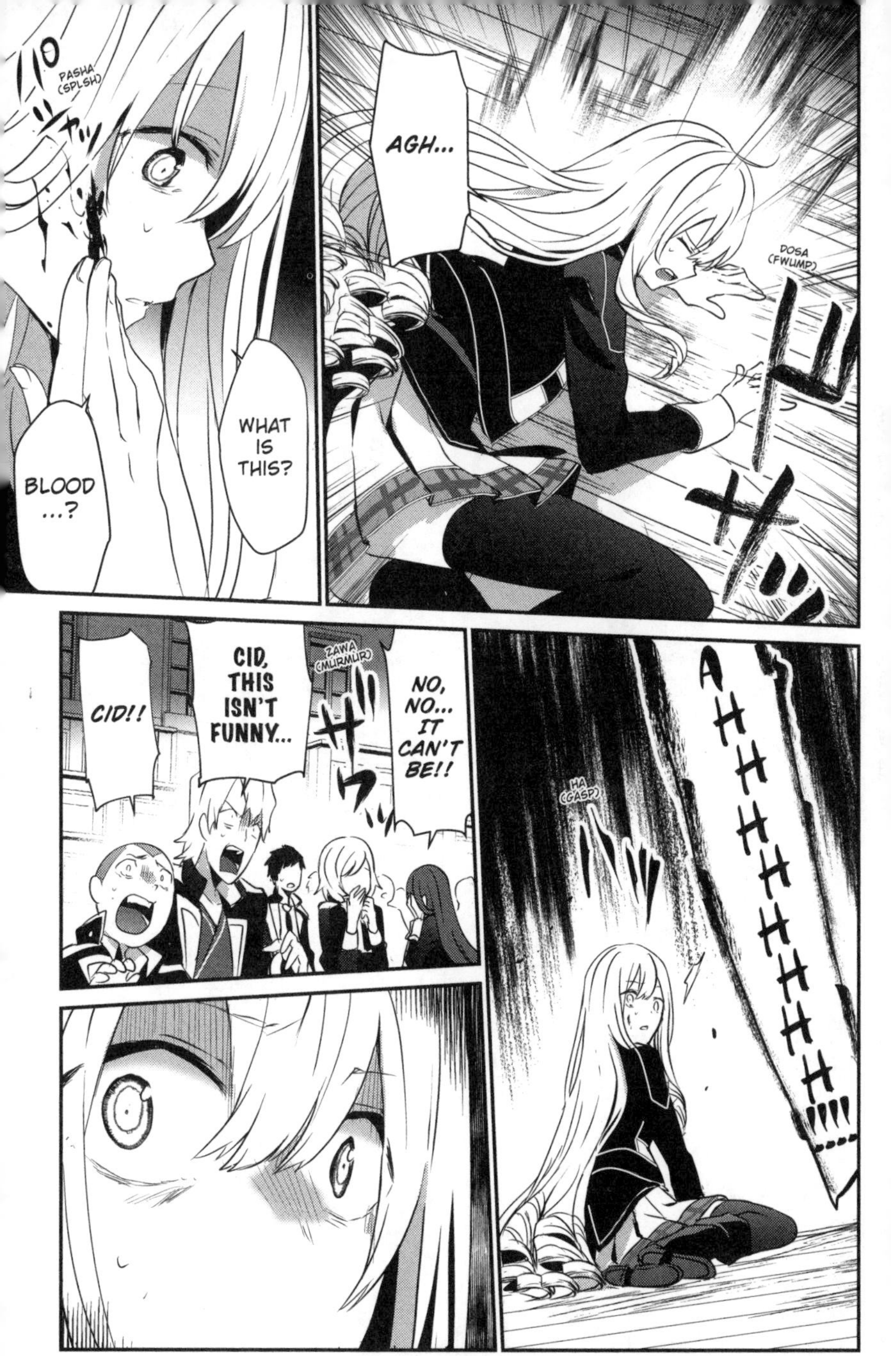
AGH...
DOSA (FWUMP)
PASHA (SPLSH)
WHAT IS THIS?
BLOOD ...?
AHHHHHHHHHH!!!!
HA (GASP)
NO, NO... IT CAN'T BE!!
ZAWA (MURMUR)
CID, THIS ISN'T FUNNY...
CID!!

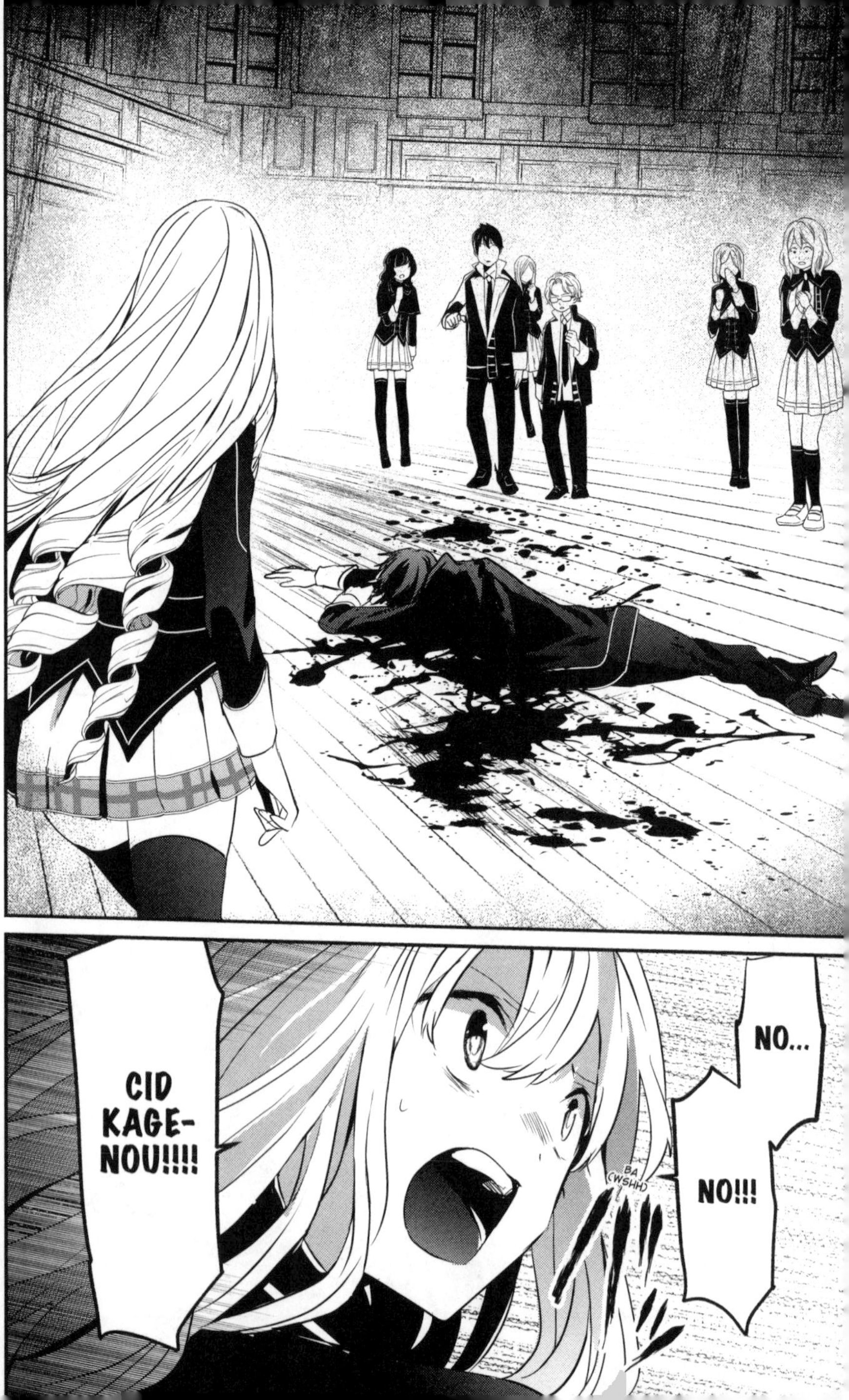
NO...
BA (WSHH)
NO!!!
CID KAGE-NOU!!!!

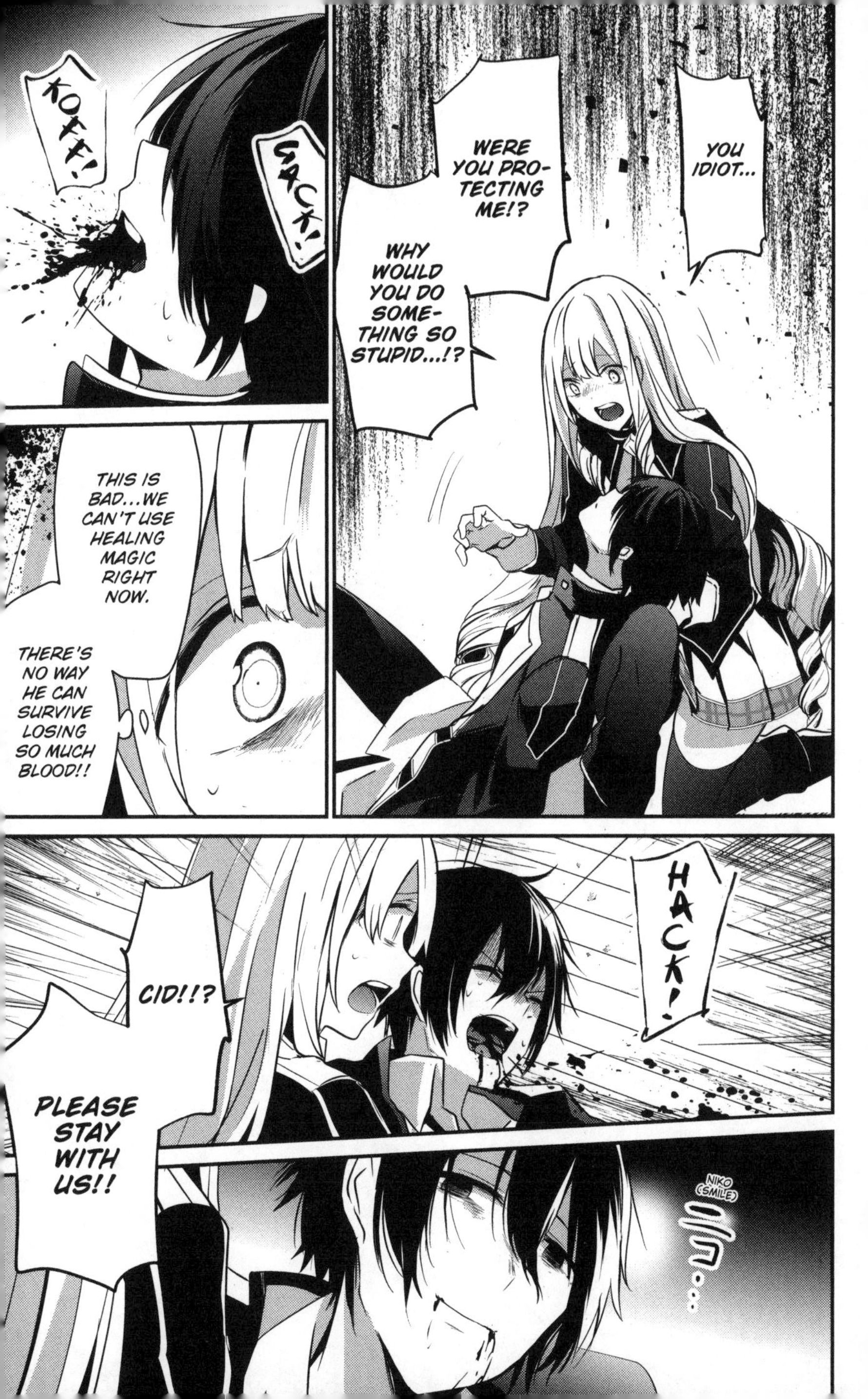
YOU IDIOT...
WERE YOU PRO-TECTING ME!?
WHY WOULD YOU DO SOME-THING SO STUPID...!?
GACK!
KOFF!
THIS IS BAD...WE CAN'T USE HEALING MAGIC RIGHT NOW.
THERE'S NO WAY HE CAN SURVIVE LOSING SO MUCH BLOOD!!
HACK!
CID!!?
PLEASE STAY WITH US!!
NIKO (SMILE)

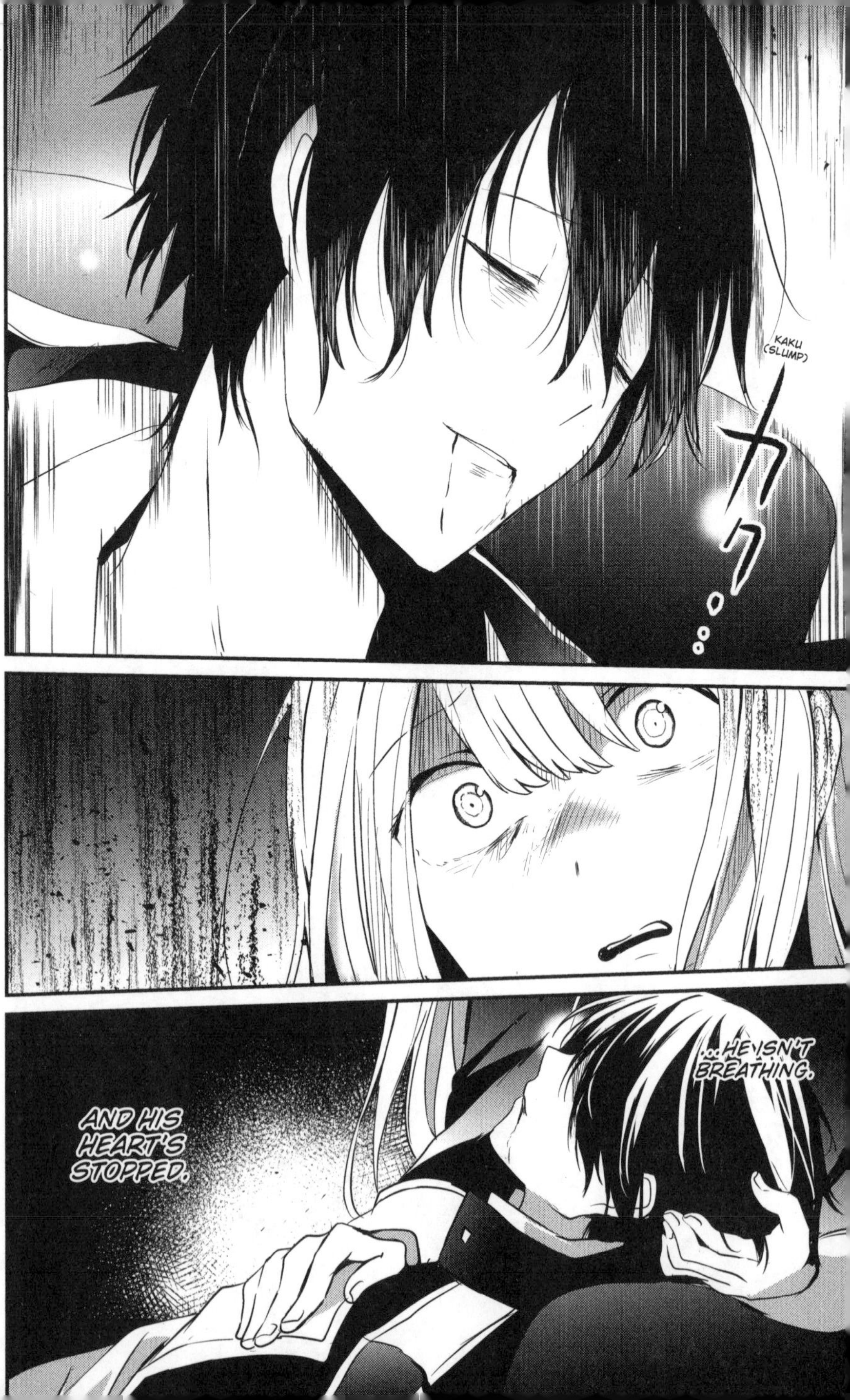
KAKU (SLUMP)
...HE ISN'T BREATHING.
AND HIS HEART'S STOPPED.

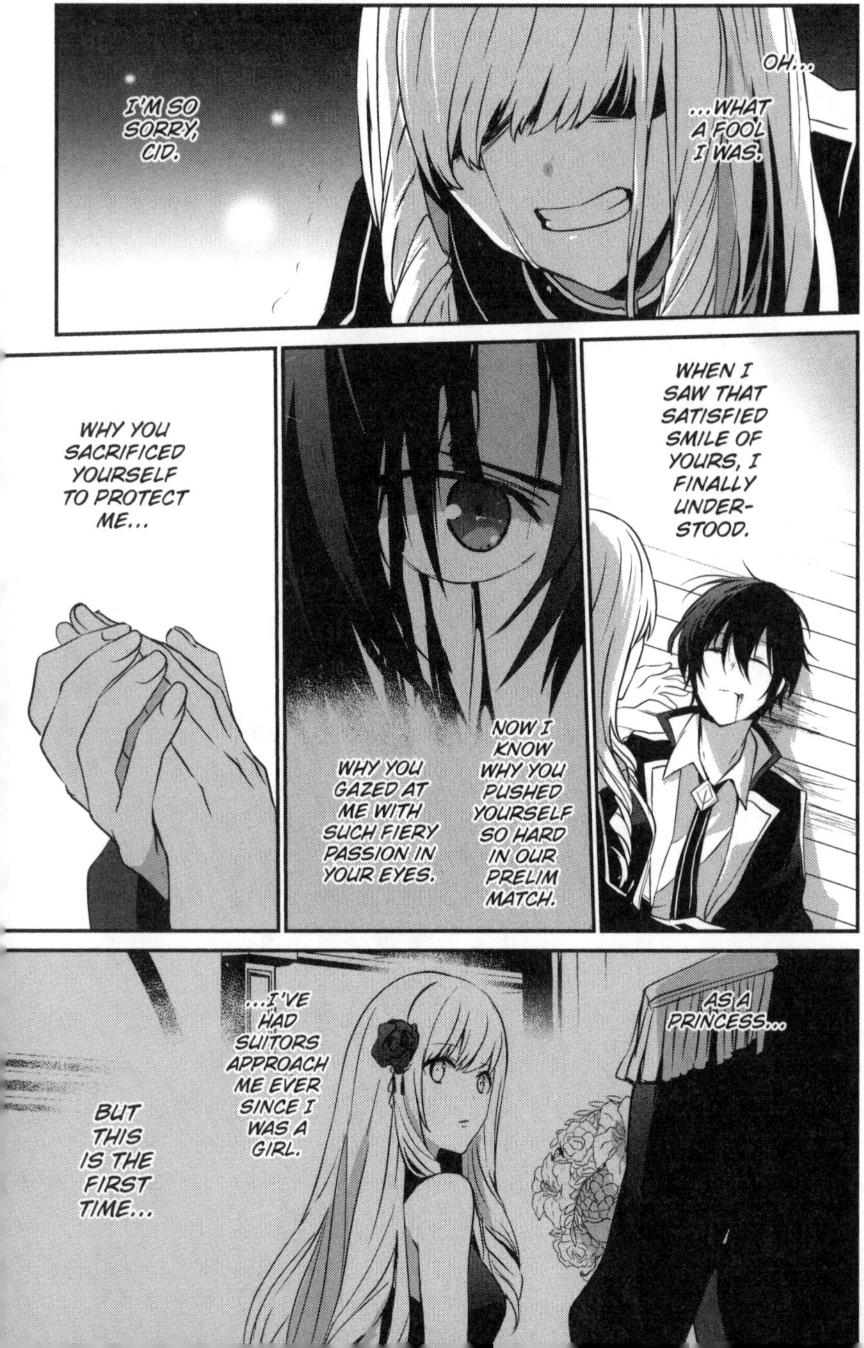
OH...
...WHAT A FOOL I WAS.
I'M SO SORRY, CID.
WHEN I SAW THAT SATISFIED SMILE OF YOURS, I FINALLY UNDER-STOOD.
NOW I KNOW WHY YOU PUSHED YOURSELF SO HARD IN OUR PRELIM MATCH.
WHY YOU GAZED AT ME WITH SUCH FIERY PASSION IN YOUR EYES.
WHY YOU SACRIFICED YOURSELF TO PROTECT ME...
AS A PRINCESS...
...I'VE HAD SUITORS APPROACH ME EVER SINCE I WAS A GIRL.
BUT THIS IS THE FIRST TIME...

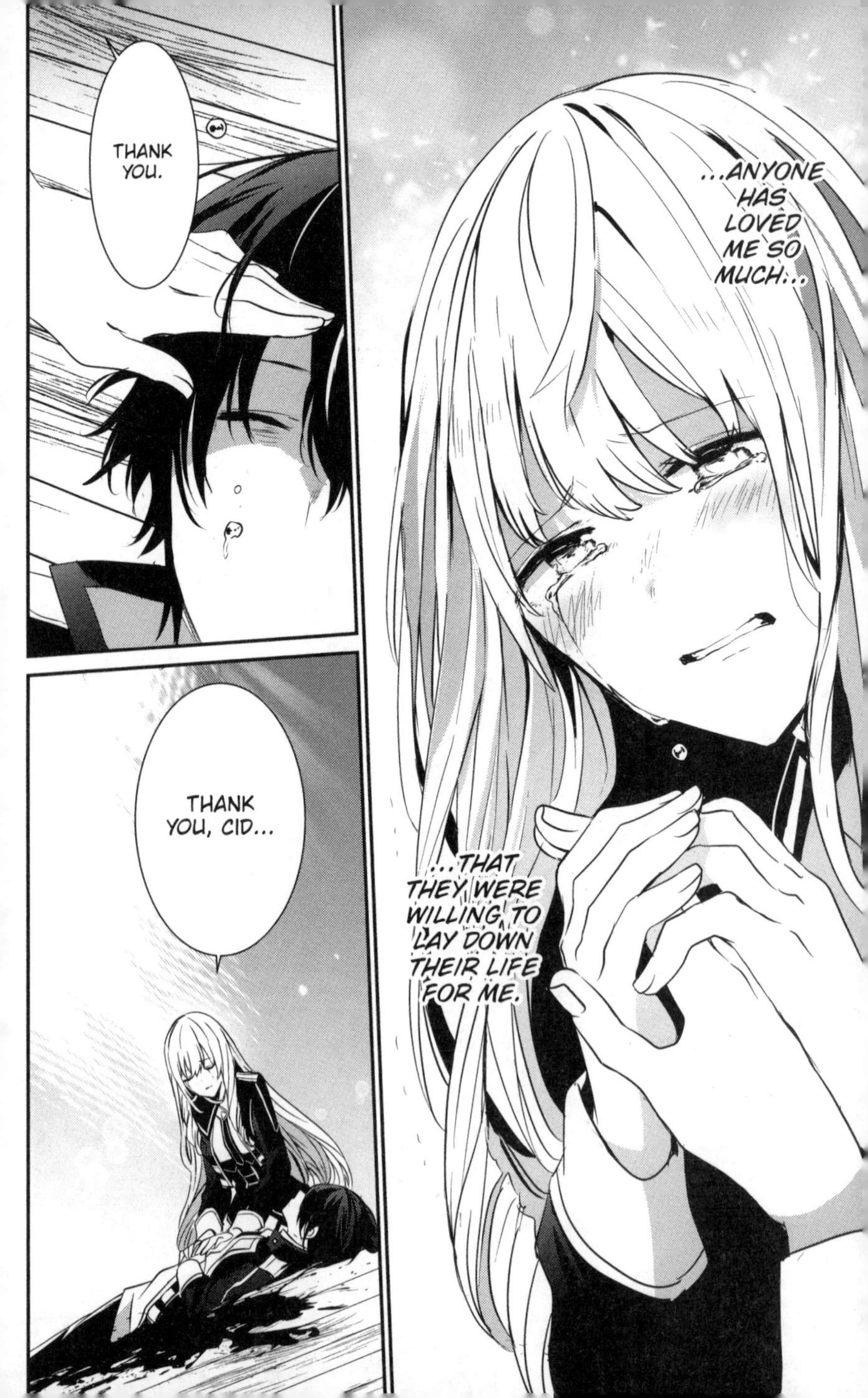
...ANYONE HAS LOVED ME SO MUCH...
...THAT THEY WERE WILLING TO LAY DOWN THEIR LIFE FOR ME.
THANK YOU.
THANK YOU, CID...

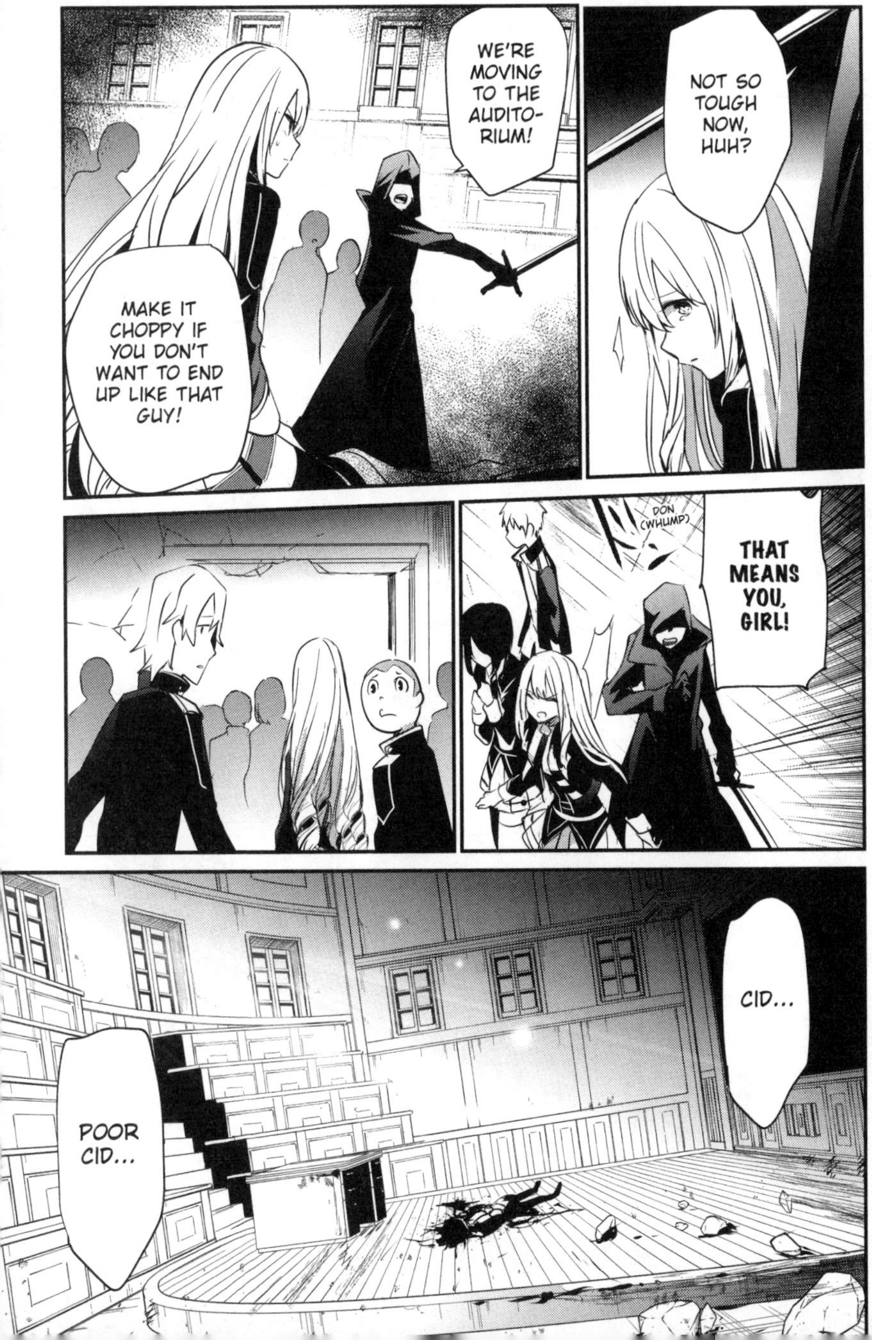
NOT SO TOUGH NOW, HUH?
WE'RE MOVING TO THE AUDITO-RIUM!
MAKE IT CHOPPY IF YOU DON'T WANT TO END UP LIKE THAT GUY!
THAT MEANS YOU, GIRL!
DON (WHUMP)
CID...
POOR CID...

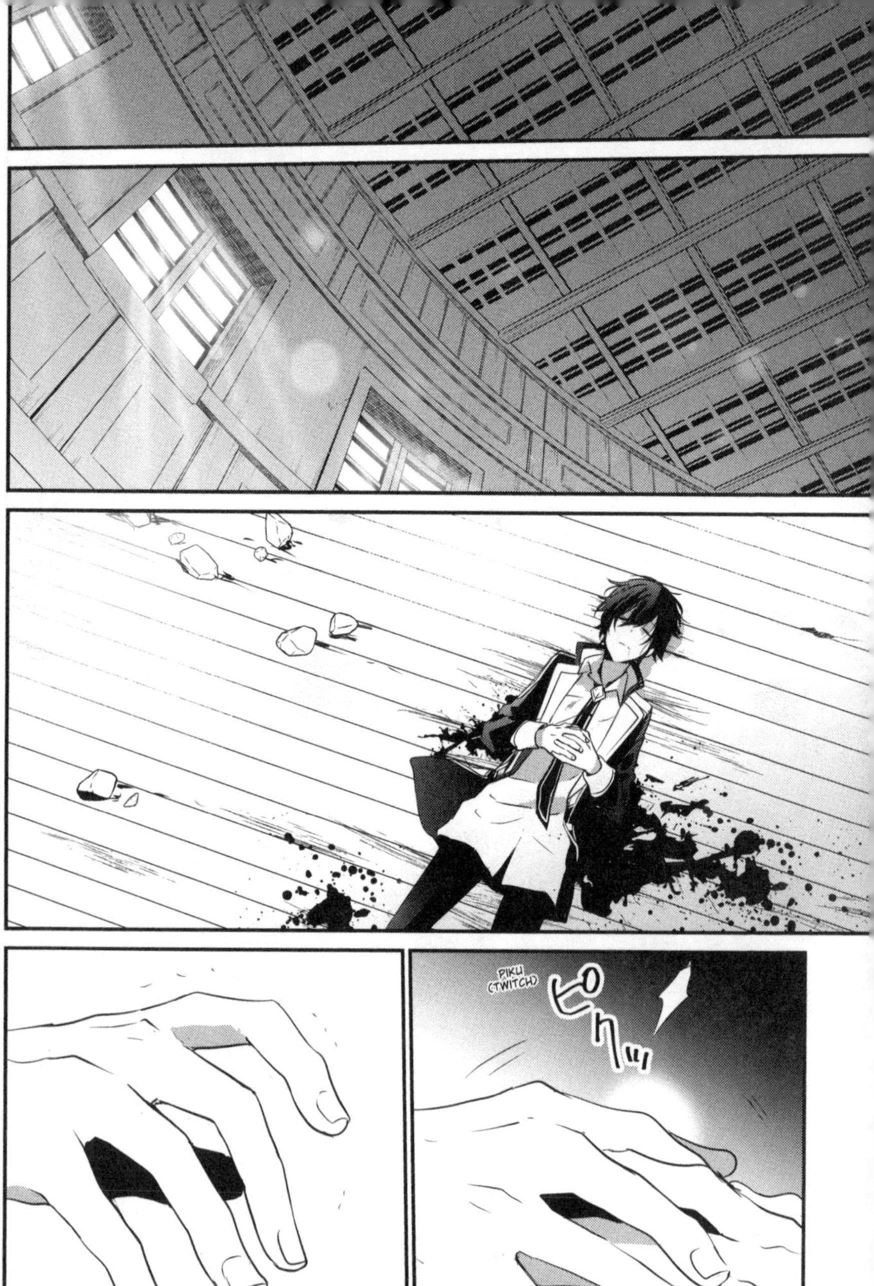
PIKU (TWITCH)
ピクッ

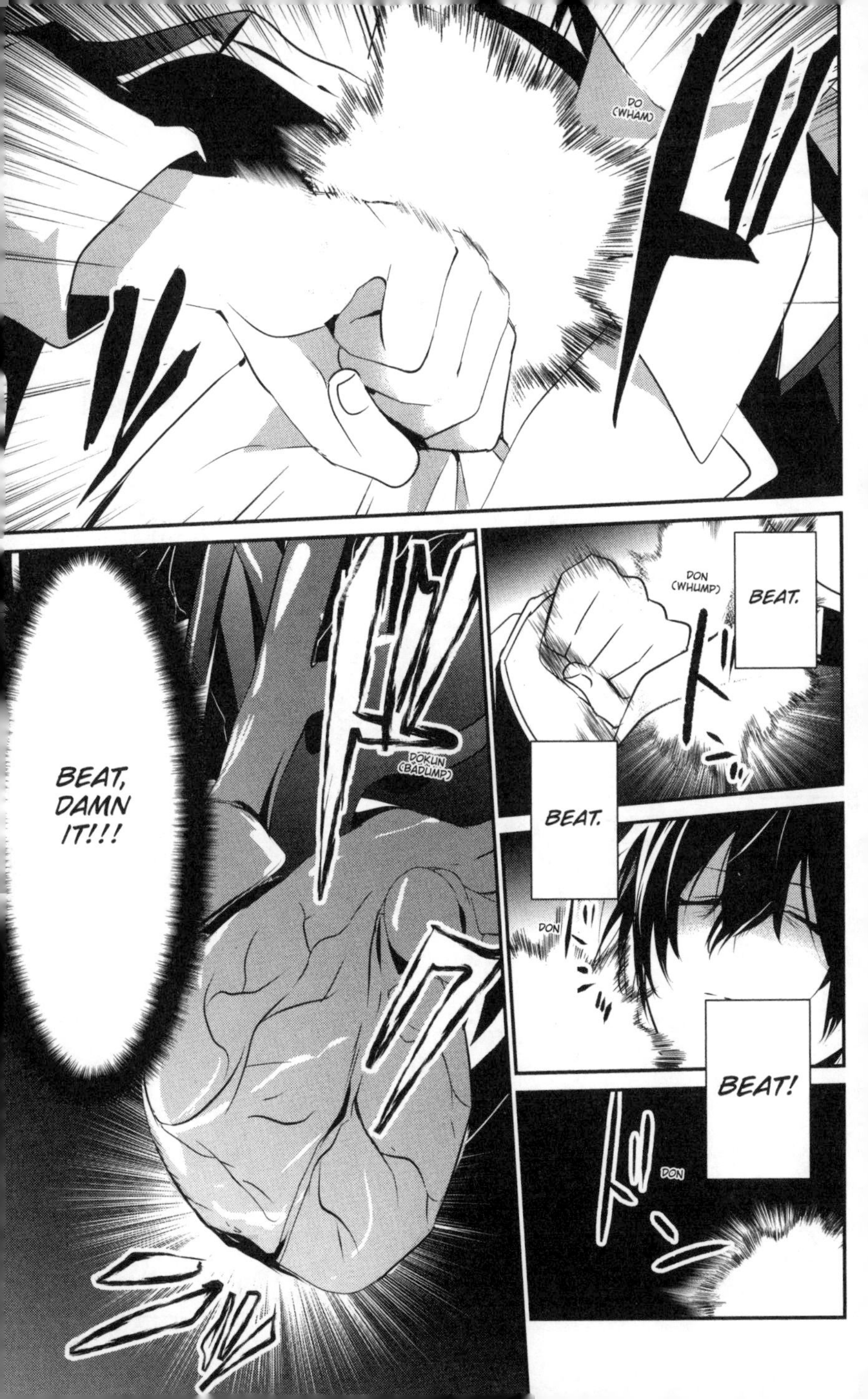
DO
(WHAM)
BEAT.
DON
(WHUMP)
BEAT.
DON
BEAT!
DON
DOKUN
(BADUMP)
BEAT, DAMN IT!!!

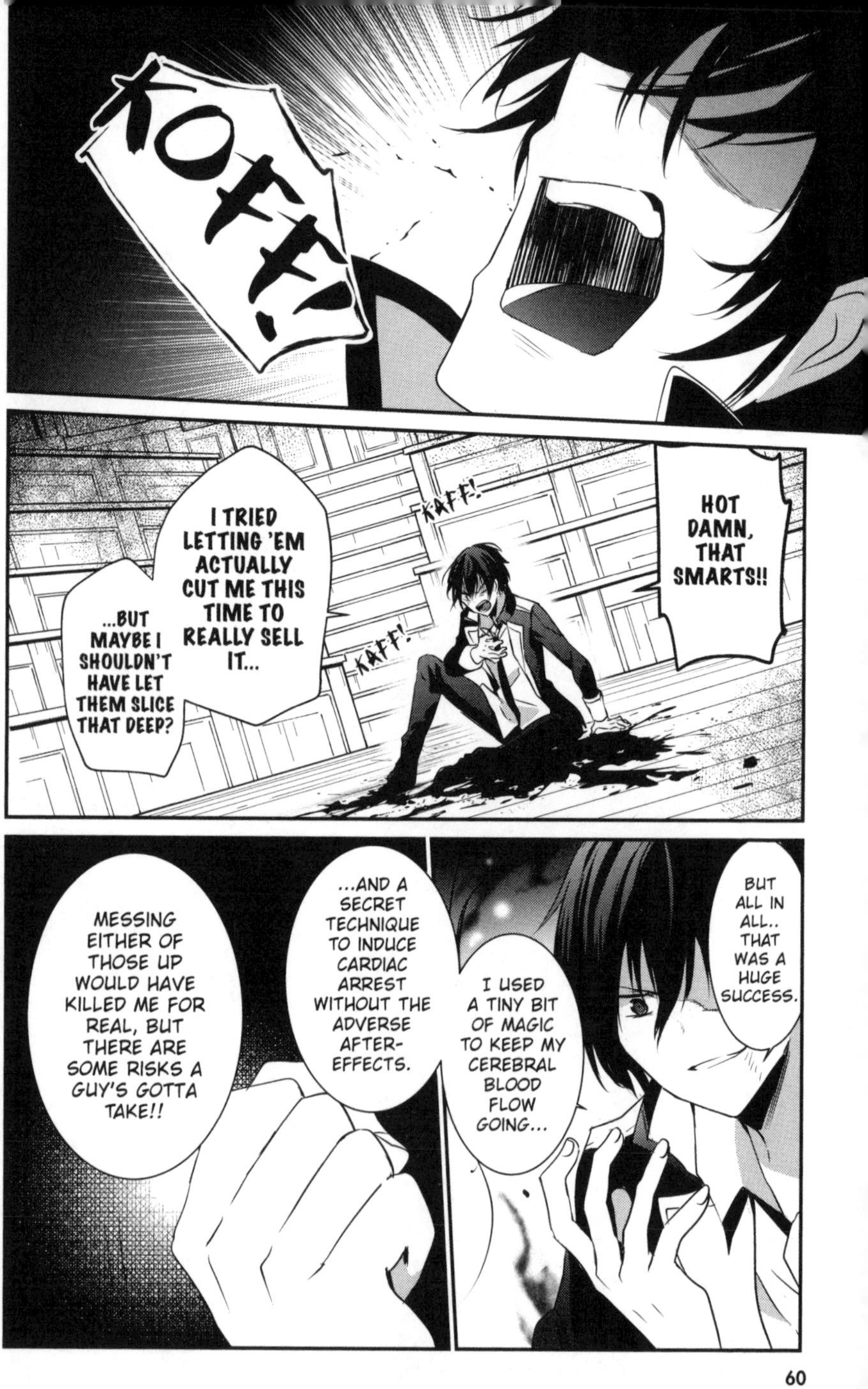
KOFF!!
HOT DAMN, THAT SMARTS!!
KAFF!
KAFF!
I TRIED LETTING 'EM ACTUALLY CUT ME THIS TIME TO REALLY SELL IT...
...BUT MAYBE I SHOULDN'T HAVE LET THEM SLICE THAT DEEP?
BUT ALL IN ALL.. THAT WAS A HUGE SUCCESS.
I USED A TINY BIT OF MAGIC TO KEEP MY CEREBRAL BLOOD FLOW GOING...
...AND A SECRET TECHNIQUE TO INDUCE CARDIAC ARREST WITHOUT THE ADVERSE AFTER-EFFECTS.
MESSING EITHER OF THOSE UP WOULD HAVE KILLED ME FOR REAL, BUT THERE ARE SOME RISKS A GUY'S GOTTA TAKE!!

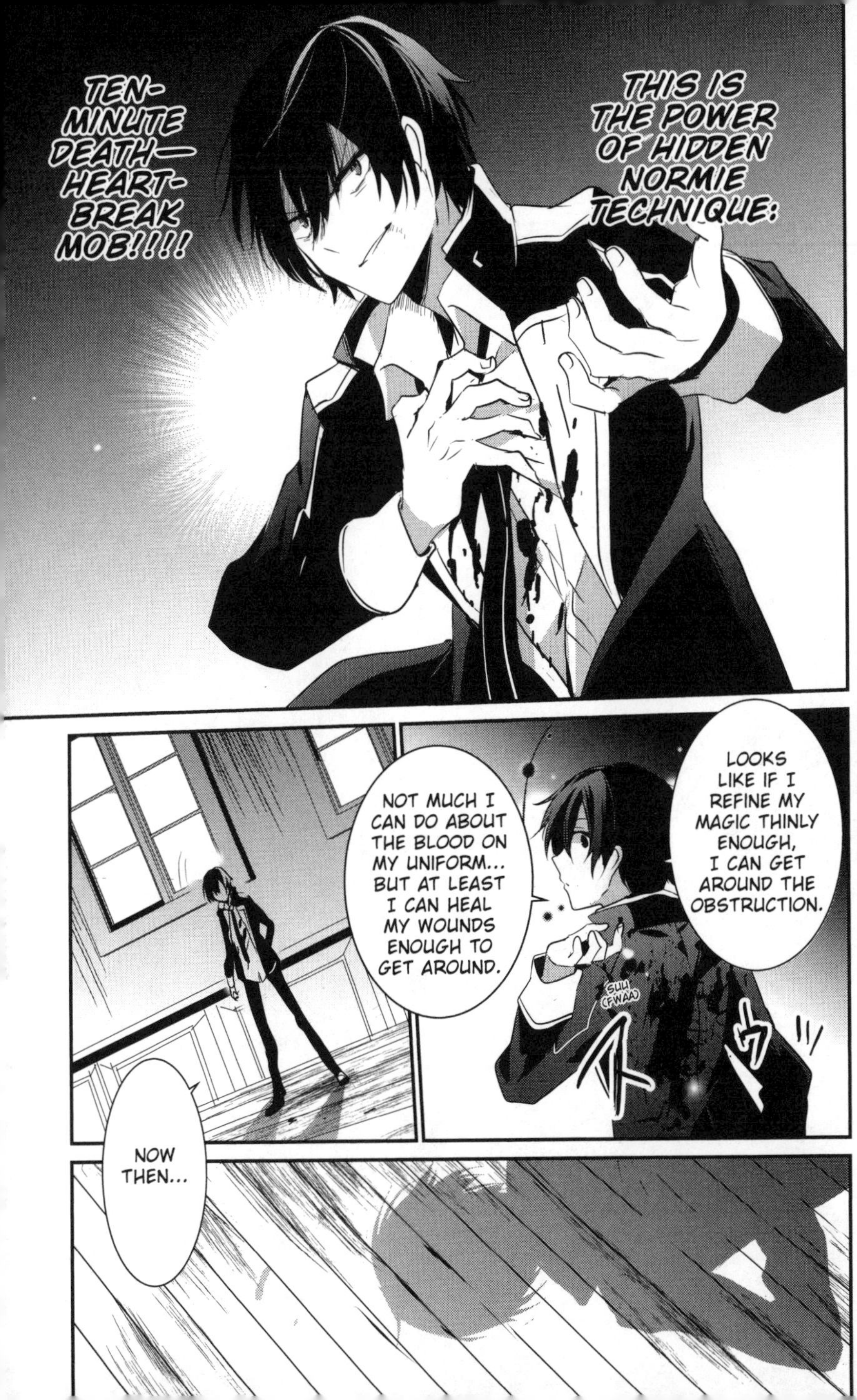
THIS IS THE POWER OF HIDDEN NORMIE TECHNIQUE:
TEN-MINUTE DEATH—HEARTBREAK MOB!!!!
LOOKS LIKE IF I REFINE MY MAGIC THINLY ENOUGH, I CAN GET AROUND THE OBSTRUCTION.
NOT MUCH I CAN DO ABOUT THE BLOOD ON MY UNIFORM... BUT AT LEAST I CAN HEAL MY WOUNDS ENOUGH TO GET AROUND.
SUU (FWAA)
NOW THEN...

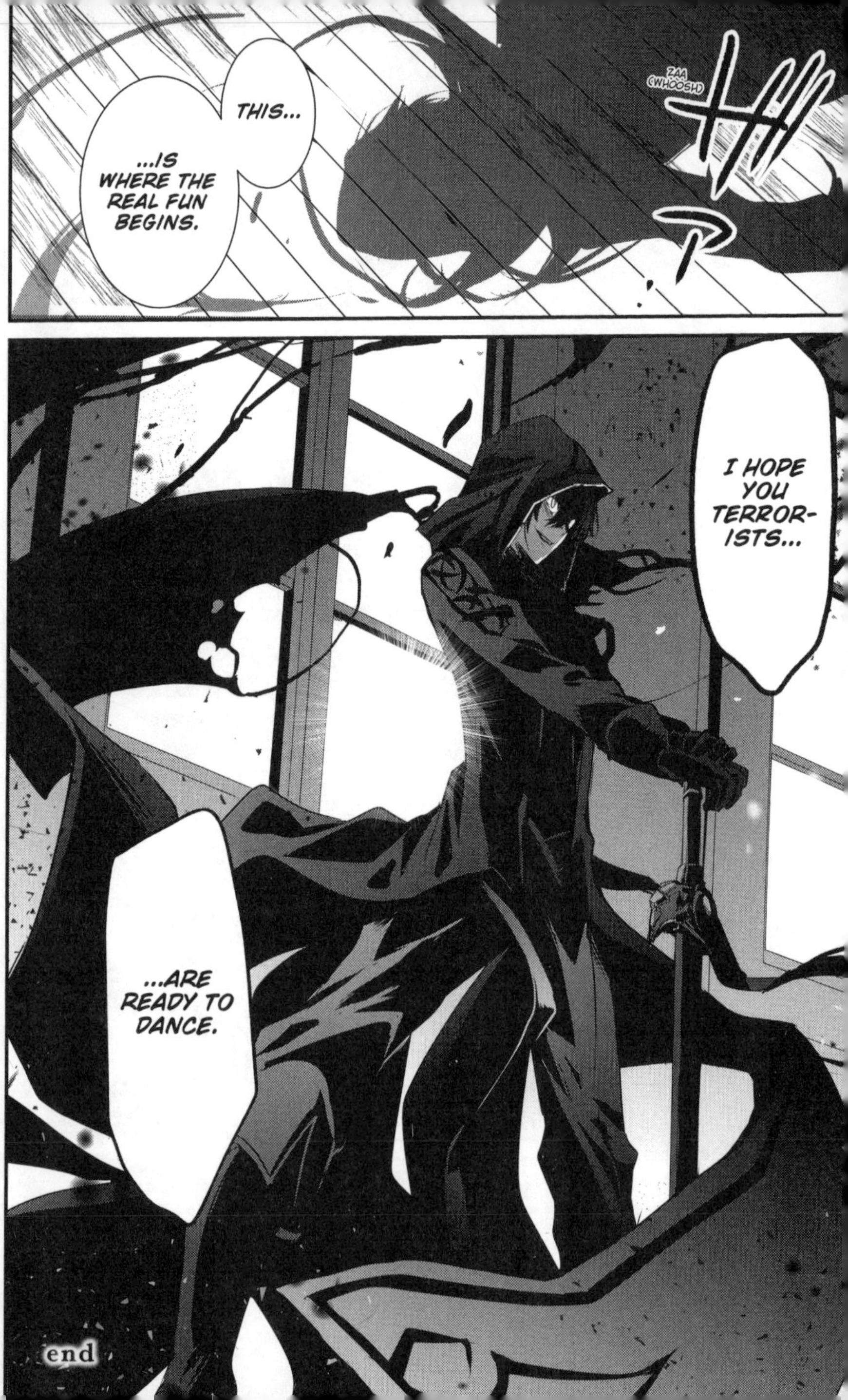
ZAA (WHOOSH)
THIS...
...IS WHERE THE REAL FUN BEGINS.
I HOPE YOU TERROR-ISTS...
...ARE READY TO DANCE.
end

The Eminence in Shadow

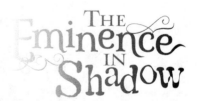

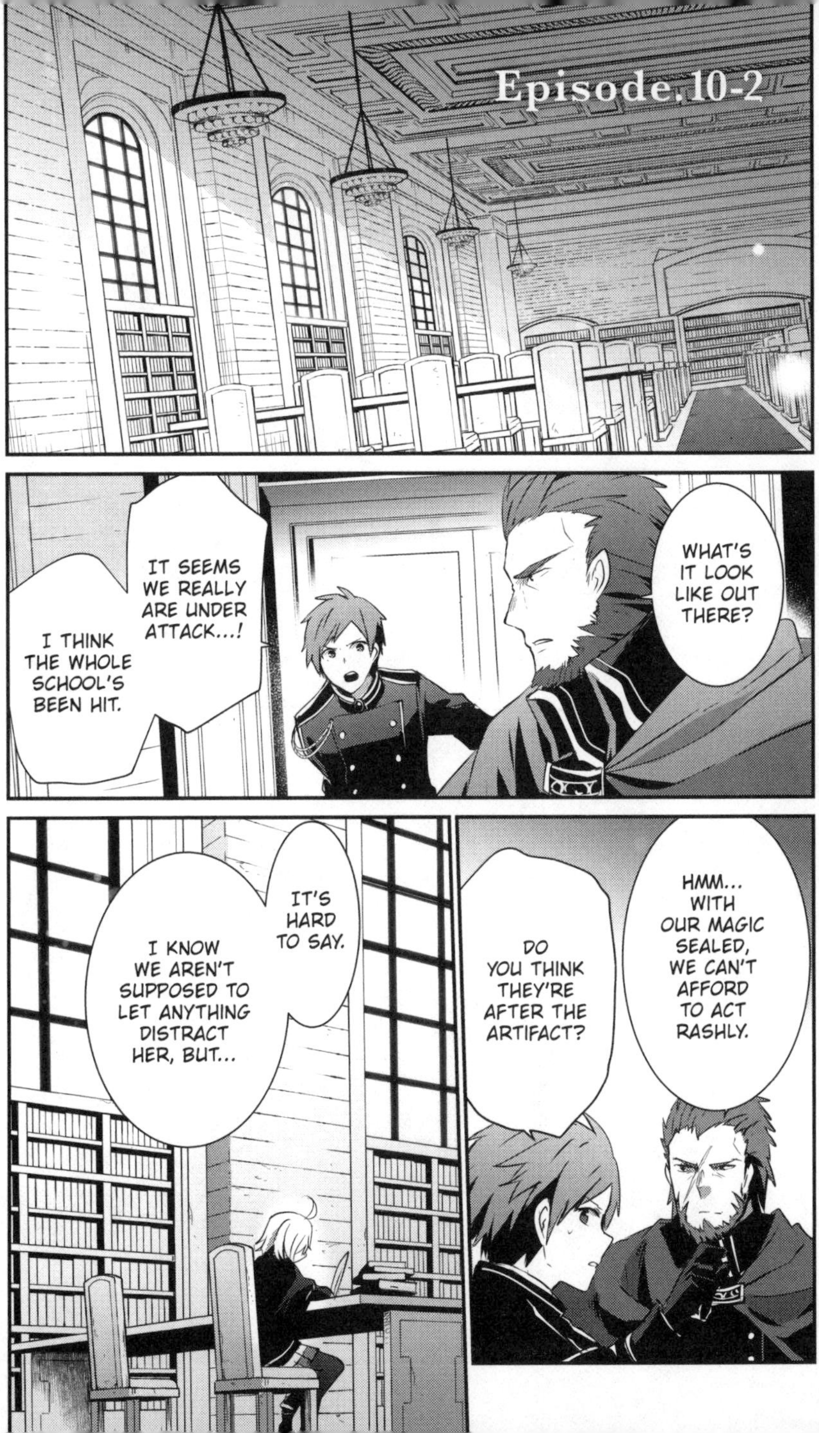
Episode.10-2
WHAT'S IT LOOK LIKE OUT THERE?
IT SEEMS WE REALLY ARE UNDER ATTACK...!
I THINK THE WHOLE SCHOOL'S BEEN HIT.
HMM... WITH OUR MAGIC SEALED, WE CAN'T AFFORD TO ACT RASHLY.
DO YOU THINK THEY'RE AFTER THE ARTIFACT?
IT'S HARD TO SAY.
I KNOW WE AREN'T SUPPOSED TO LET ANYTHING DISTRACT HER, BUT...

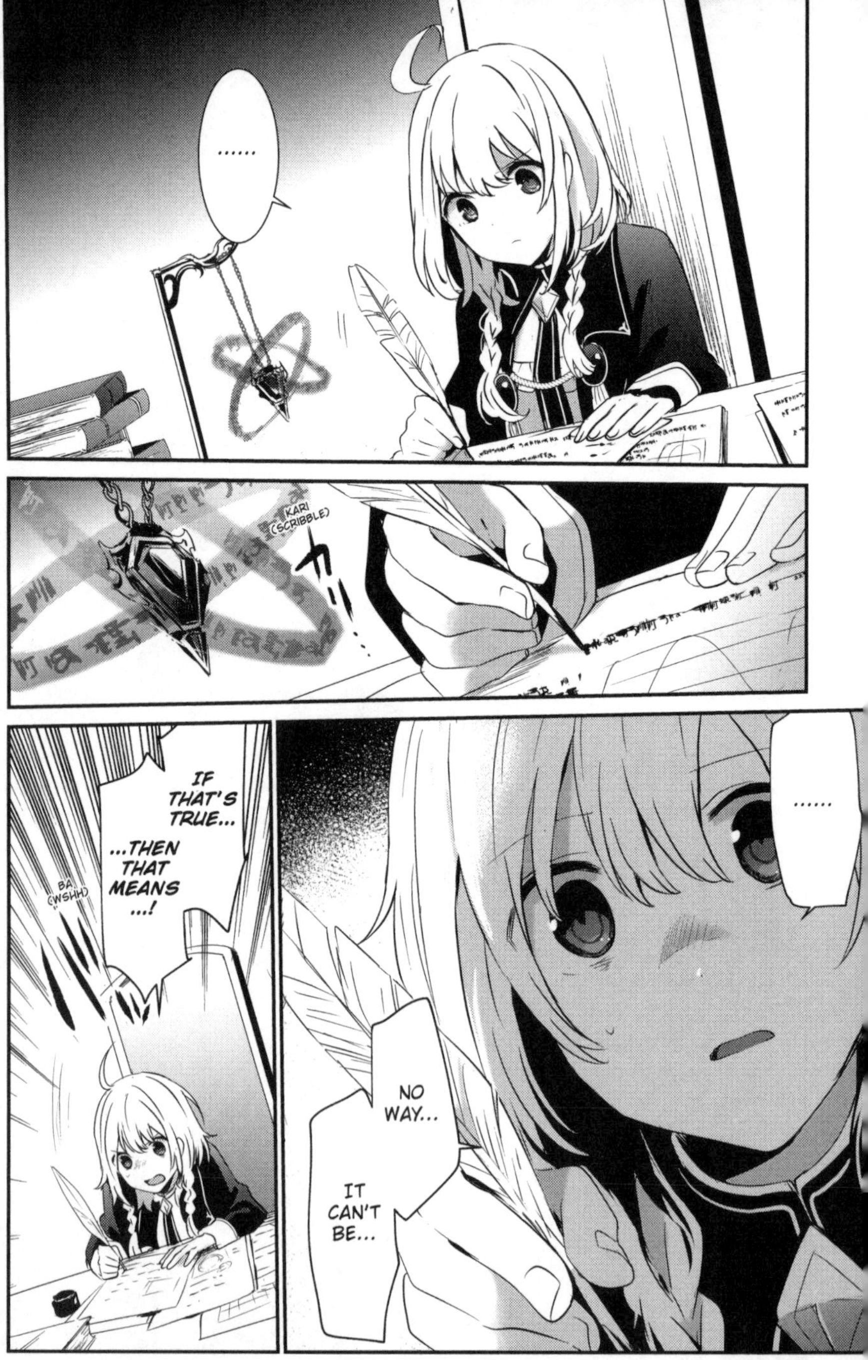
......
KARI (SCRIBBLE)
......
IF THAT'S TRUE...
...THEN THAT MEANS ...!
BA (WSHH)
NO WAY...
IT CAN'T BE...

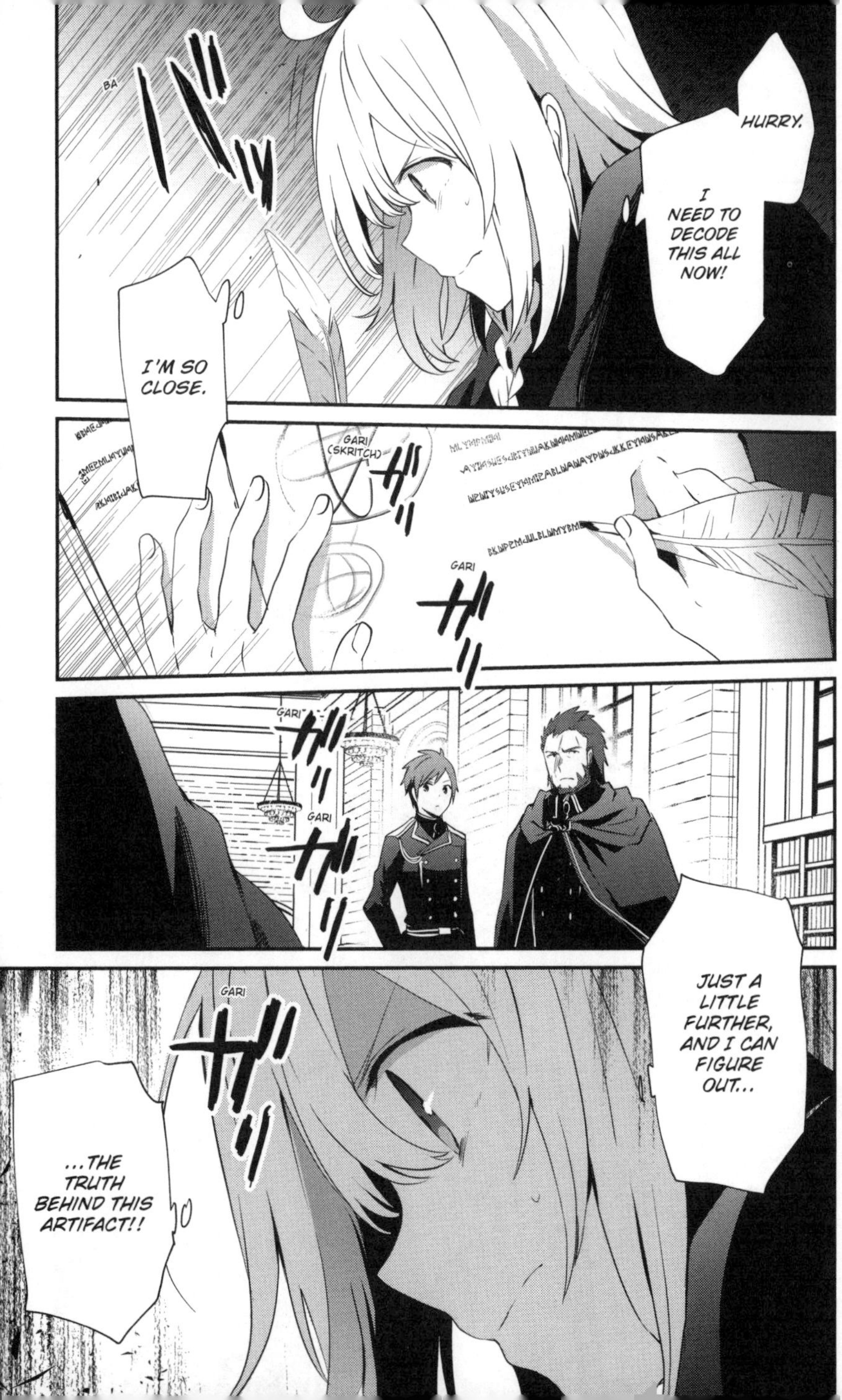
HURRY.
I NEED TO DECODE THIS ALL NOW!
BA
I'M SO CLOSE.
GARI (SKRITCH)
GARI
GARI
GARI
JUST A LITTLE FURTHER, AND I CAN FIGURE OUT...
GARI
...THE TRUTH BEHIND THIS ARTIFACT!!

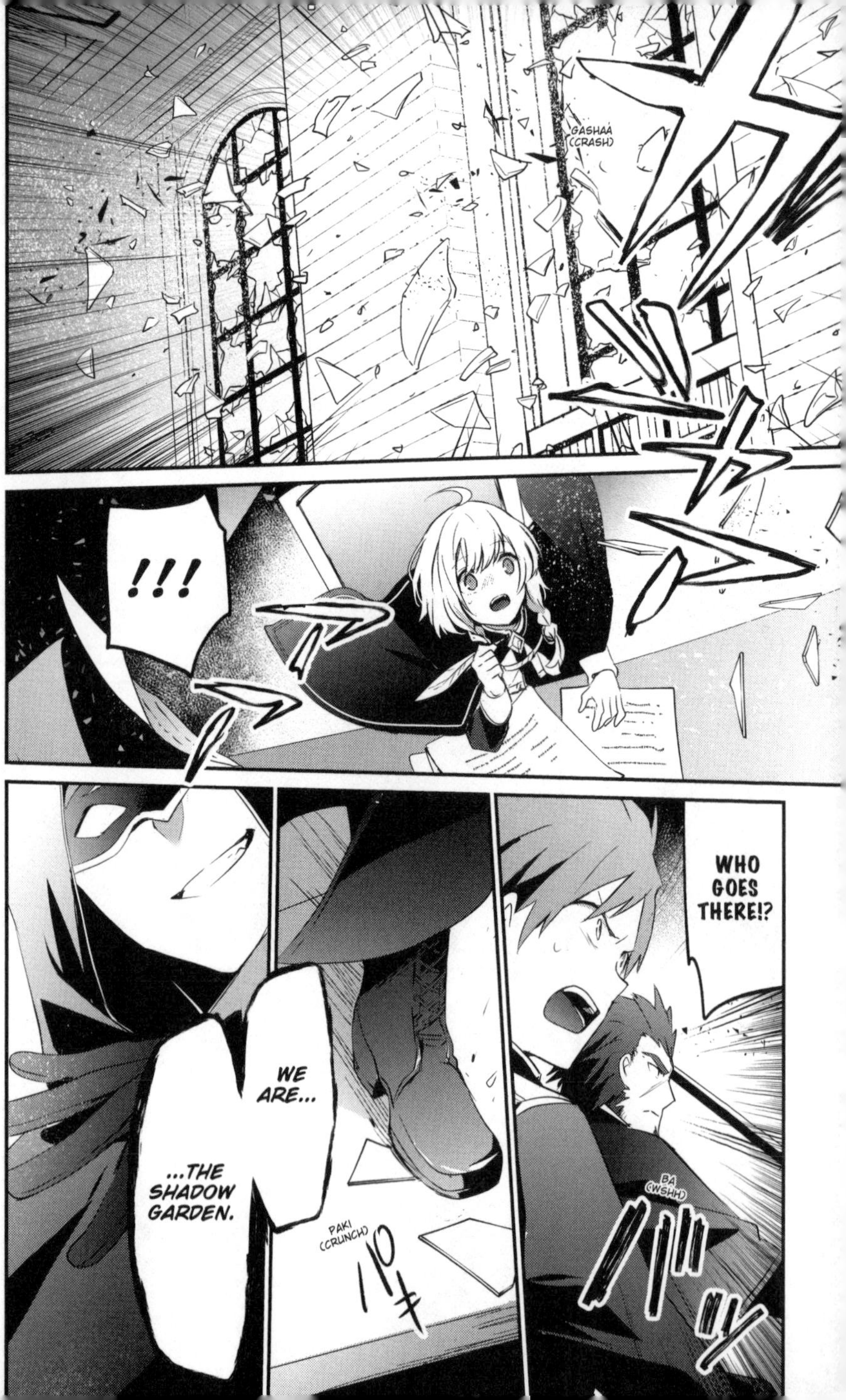
GASHAA (CRASH)
!!!
WHO GOES THERE!?
BA (WSHH)
PAKI (CRUNCH)
WE ARE...
...THE SHADOW GARDEN.

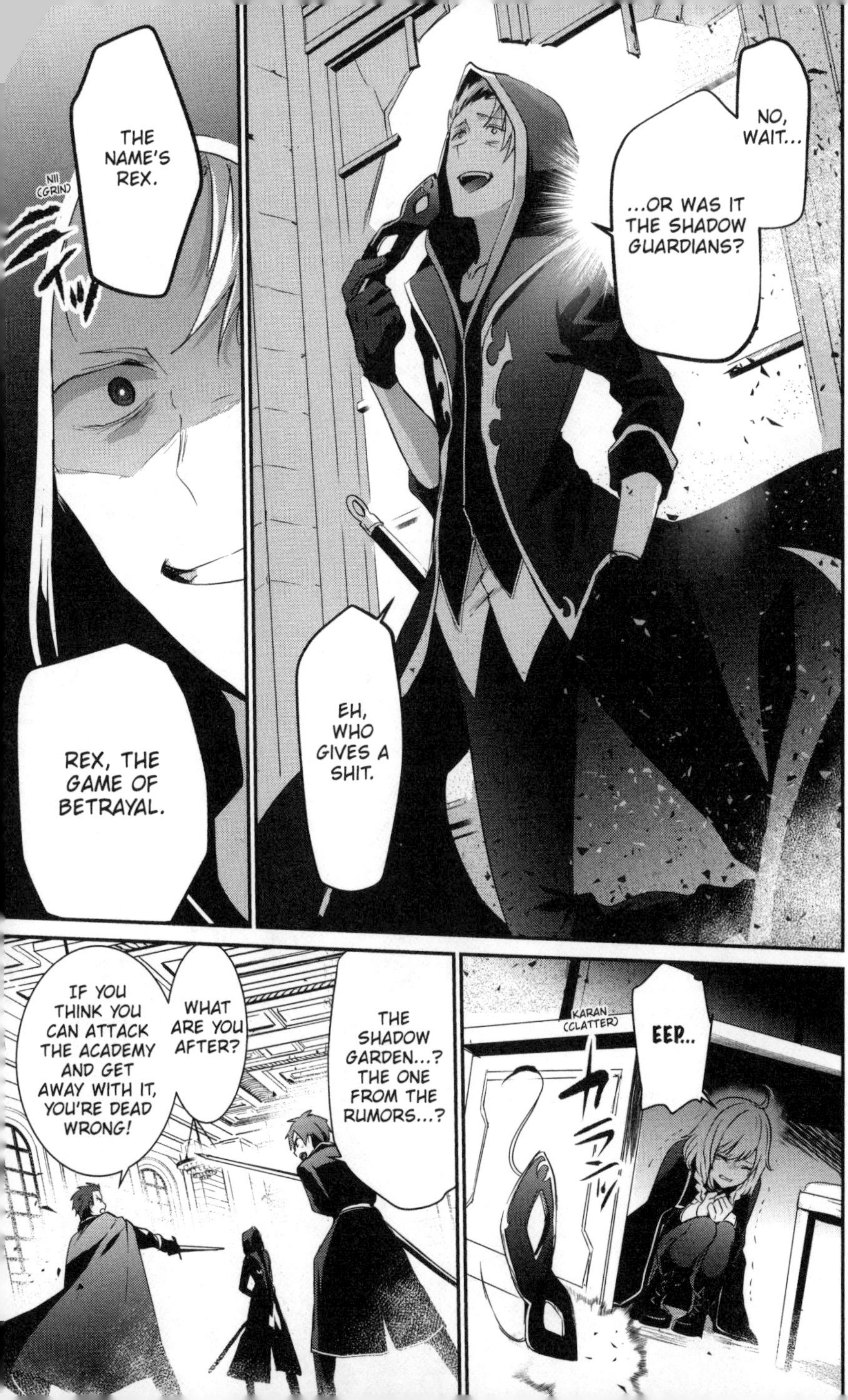
NO, WAIT...
...OR WAS IT THE SHADOW GUARDIANS?
EH, WHO GIVES A SHIT.
NII (GRIN)
THE NAME'S REX.
REX, THE GAME OF BETRAYAL.
KARAN (CLATTER)
EEP...
THE SHADOW GARDEN...? THE ONE FROM THE RUMORS...?
WHAT ARE YOU AFTER?
IF YOU THINK YOU CAN ATTACK THE ACADEMY AND GET AWAY WITH IT, YOU'RE DEAD WRONG!

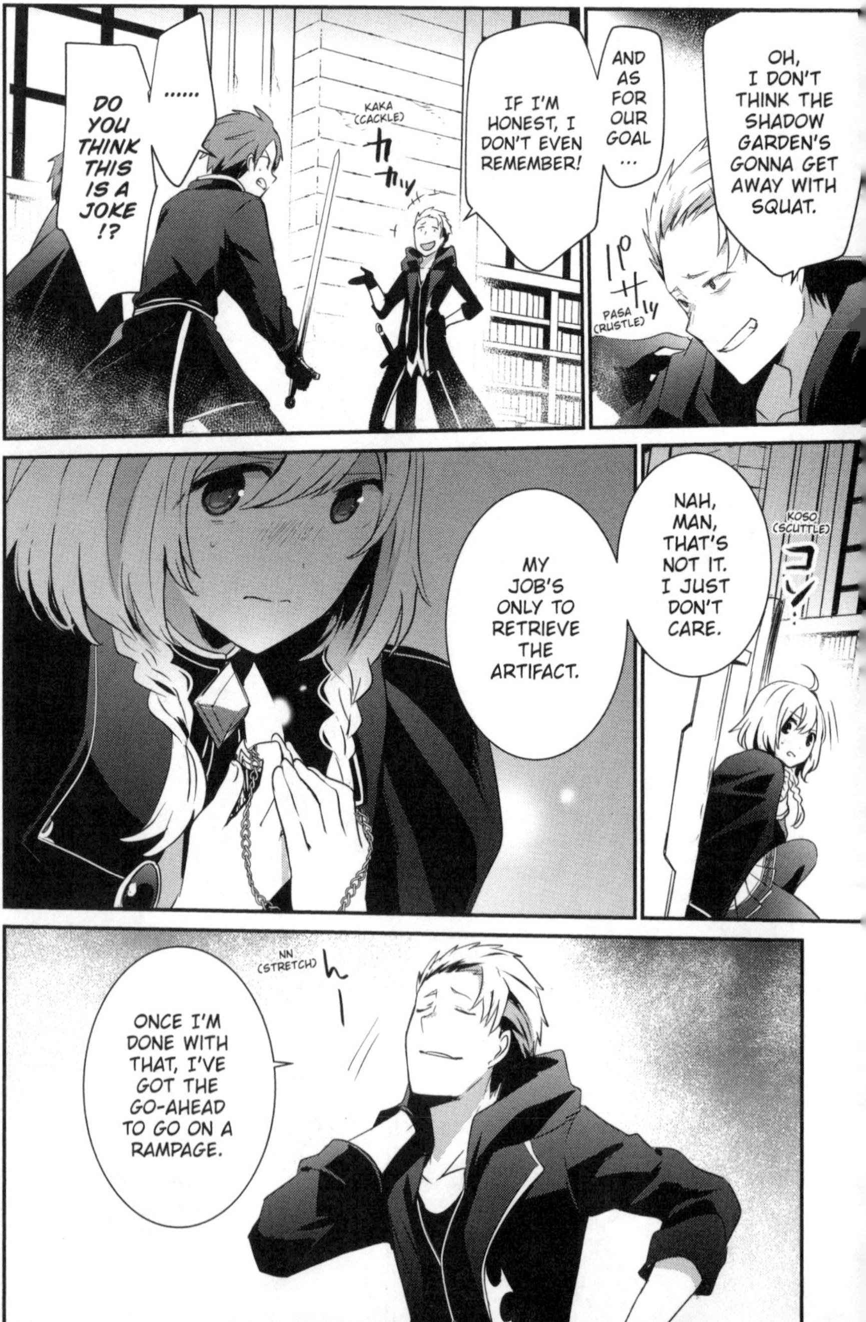
OH, I DON'T THINK THE SHADOW GARDEN'S GONNA GET AWAY WITH SQUAT.
PASA (RUSTLE)
AND AS FOR OUR GOAL...
IF I'M HONEST, I DON'T EVEN REMEMBER!
KAKA (CACKLE)
......
DO YOU THINK THIS IS A JOKE!?
KOSO (SCUTTLE)
NAH, MAN, THAT'S NOT IT. I JUST DON'T CARE.
MY JOB'S ONLY TO RETRIEVE THE ARTIFACT.
NN (STRETCH)
ONCE I'M DONE WITH THAT, I'VE GOT THE GO-AHEAD TO GO ON A RAMPAGE.

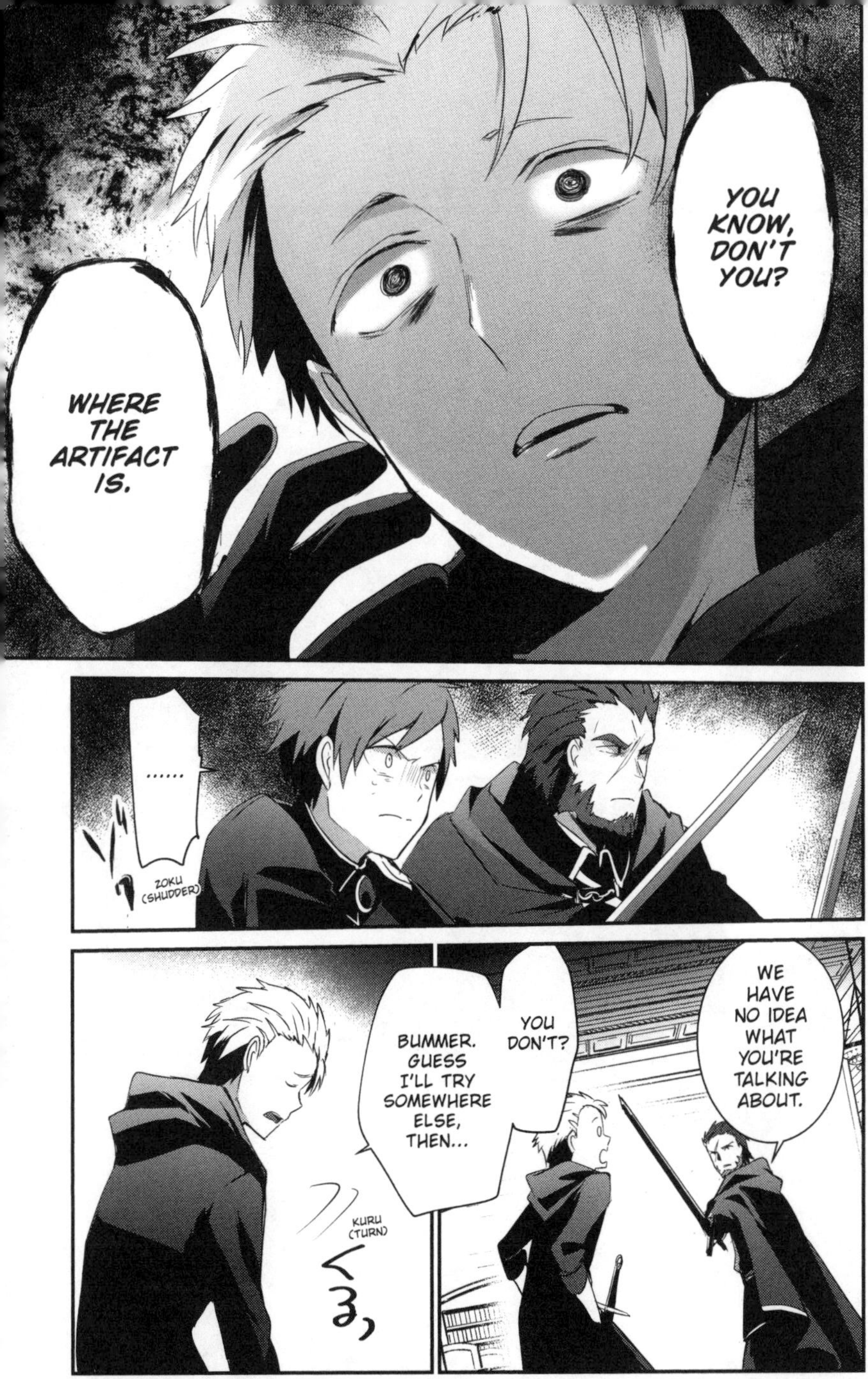
YOU KNOW, DON'T YOU?
WHERE THE ARTIFACT IS.
......
ZOKU (SHUDDER)
WE HAVE NO IDEA WHAT YOU'RE TALKING ABOUT.
YOU DON'T?
BUMMER. GUESS I'LL TRY SOMEWHERE ELSE, THEN...
KURU (TURN)
くるっ

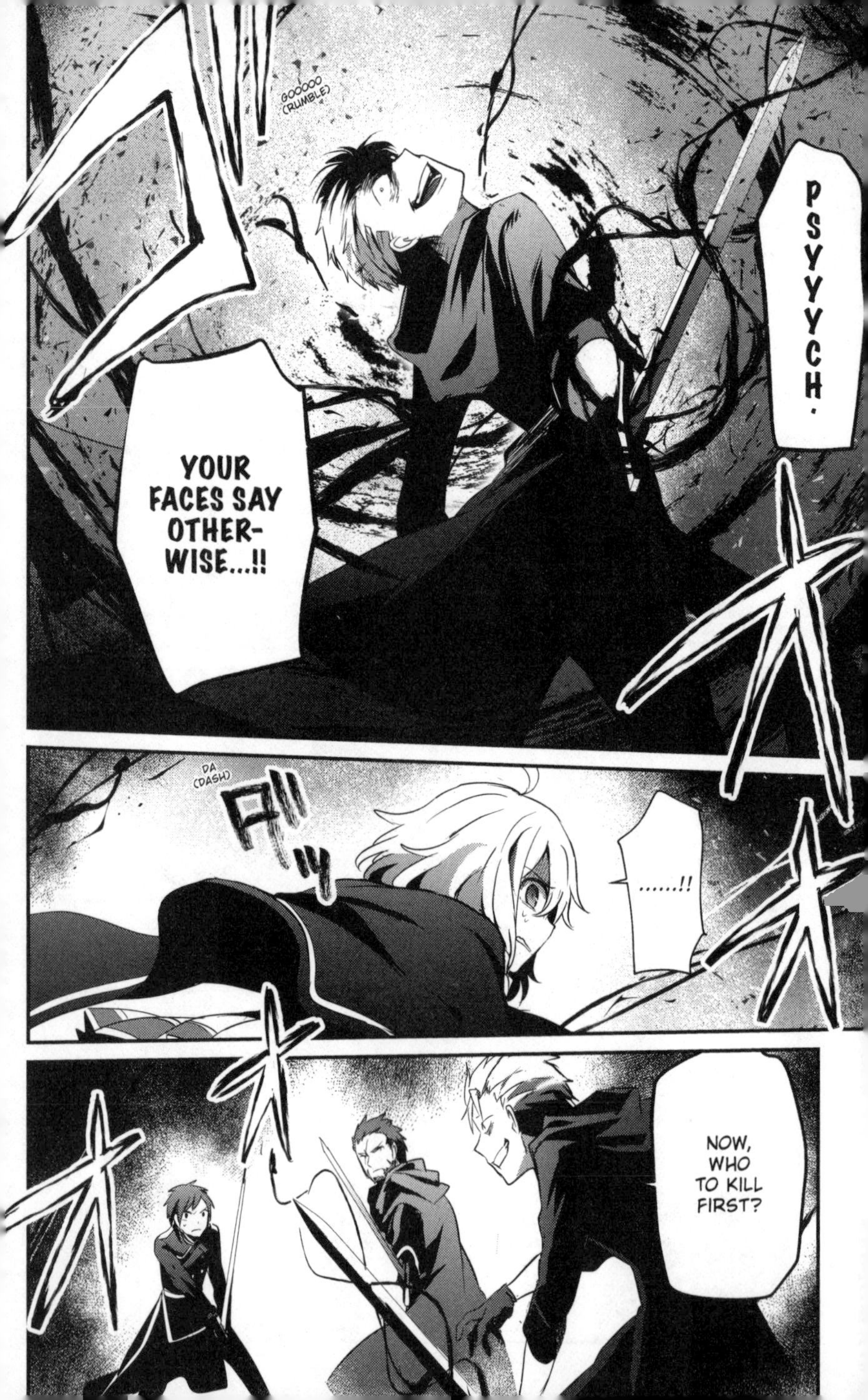
PSYYYCH.
GOOOOO (RUMBLE)
YOUR FACES SAY OTHER-WISE...!!
......!!
DA (DASH)
NOW, WHO TO KILL FIRST?

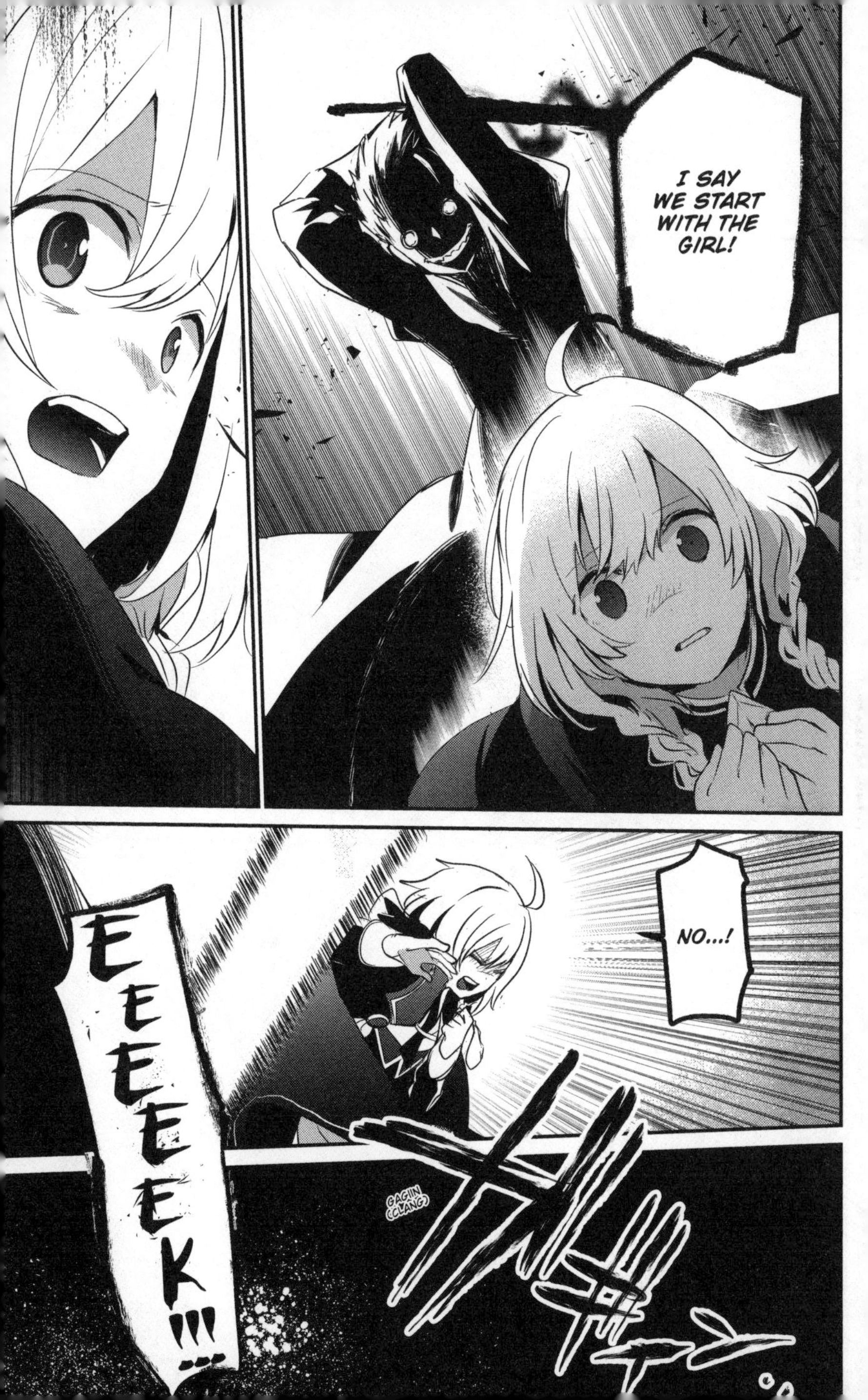
I SAY WE START WITH THE GIRL!
NO...!
EEEEEEK!!!...
GAGIIN (CLANG)

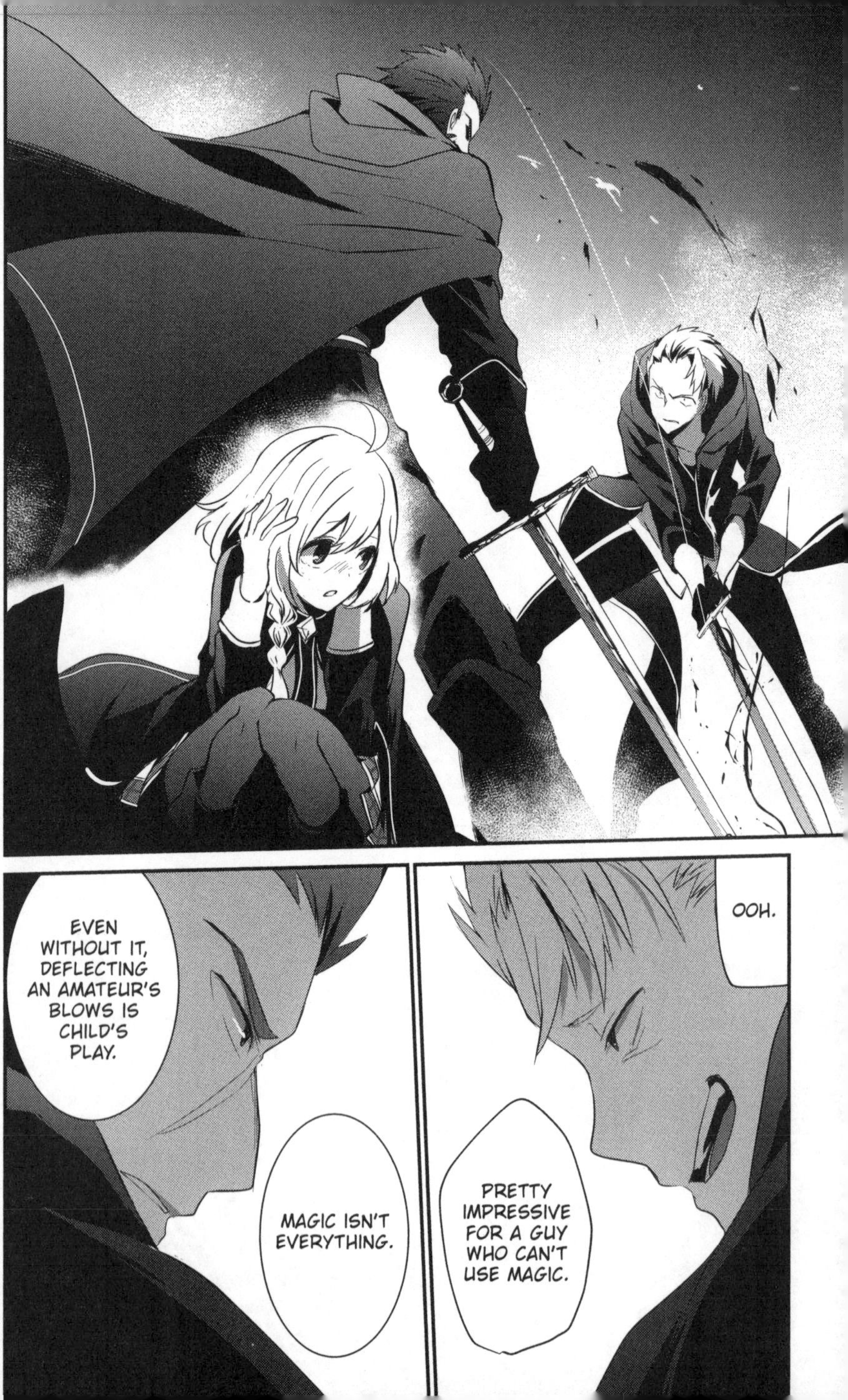
OOH.
PRETTY IMPRESSIVE FOR A GUY WHO CAN'T USE MAGIC.
MAGIC ISN'T EVERYTHING.
EVEN WITHOUT IT, DEFLECTING AN AMATEUR'S BLOWS IS CHILD'S PLAY.

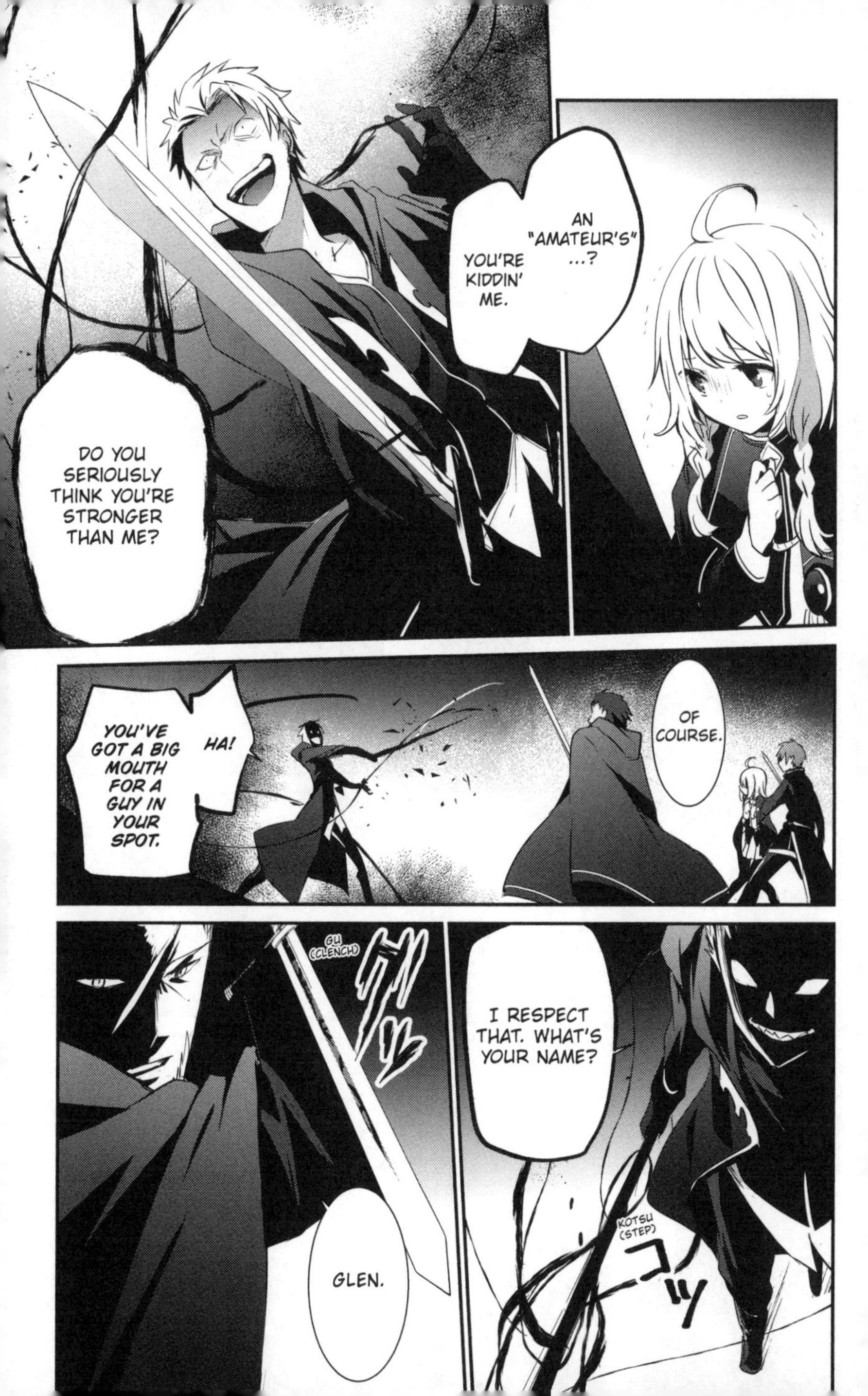
AN "AMATEUR'S" ...?
YOU'RE KIDDIN' ME.
DO YOU SERIOUSLY THINK YOU'RE STRONGER THAN ME?
OF COURSE.
HA!
YOU'VE GOT A BIG MOUTH FOR A GUY IN YOUR SPOT.
I RESPECT THAT. WHAT'S YOUR NAME?
KOTSU (STEP)
GU (CLENCH)
GLEN.

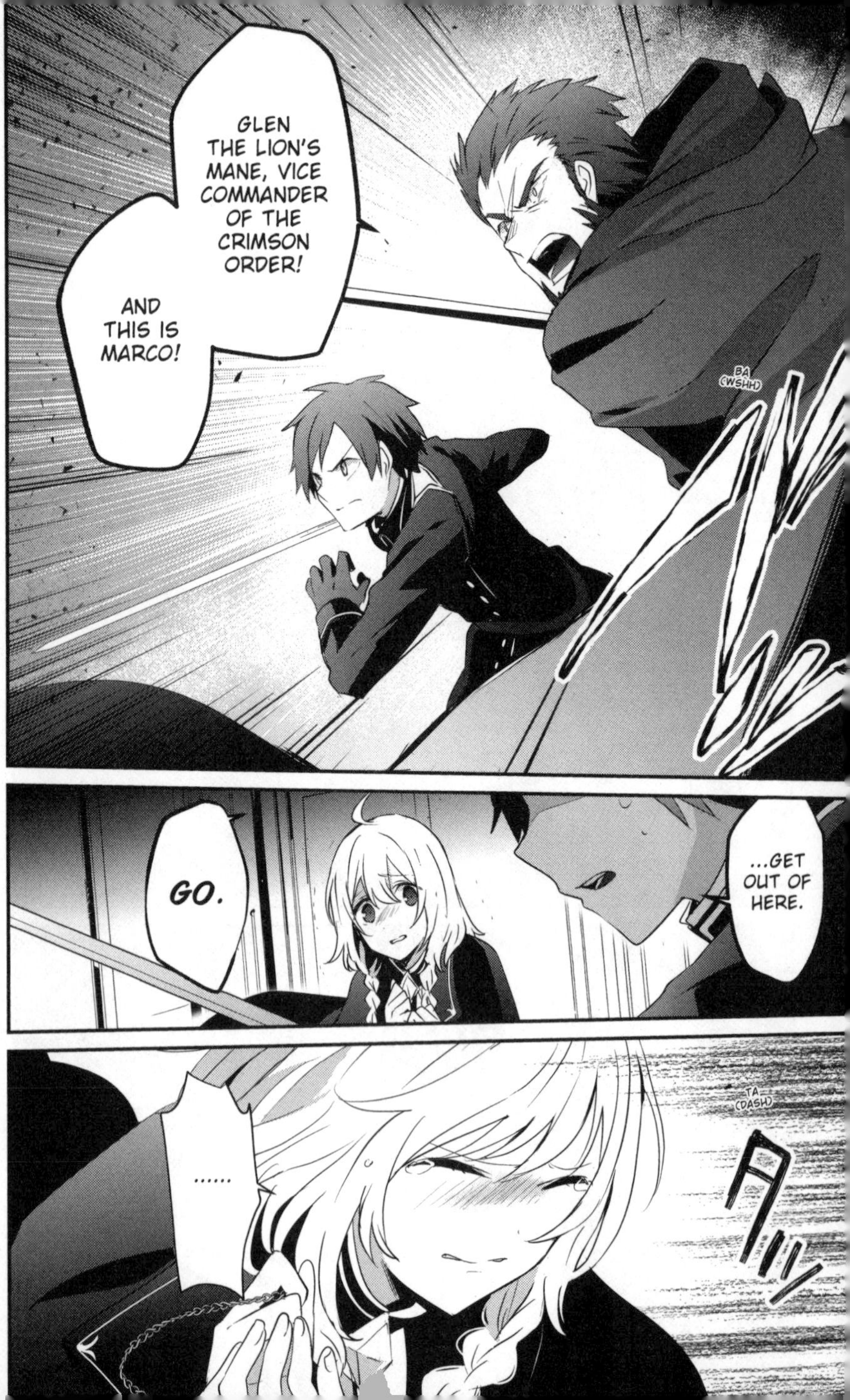
GLEN THE LION'S MANE, VICE COMMANDER OF THE CRIMSON ORDER!
AND THIS IS MARCO!
BA (WSHH)
...GET OUT OF HERE.
GO.
TA (DASH)
......

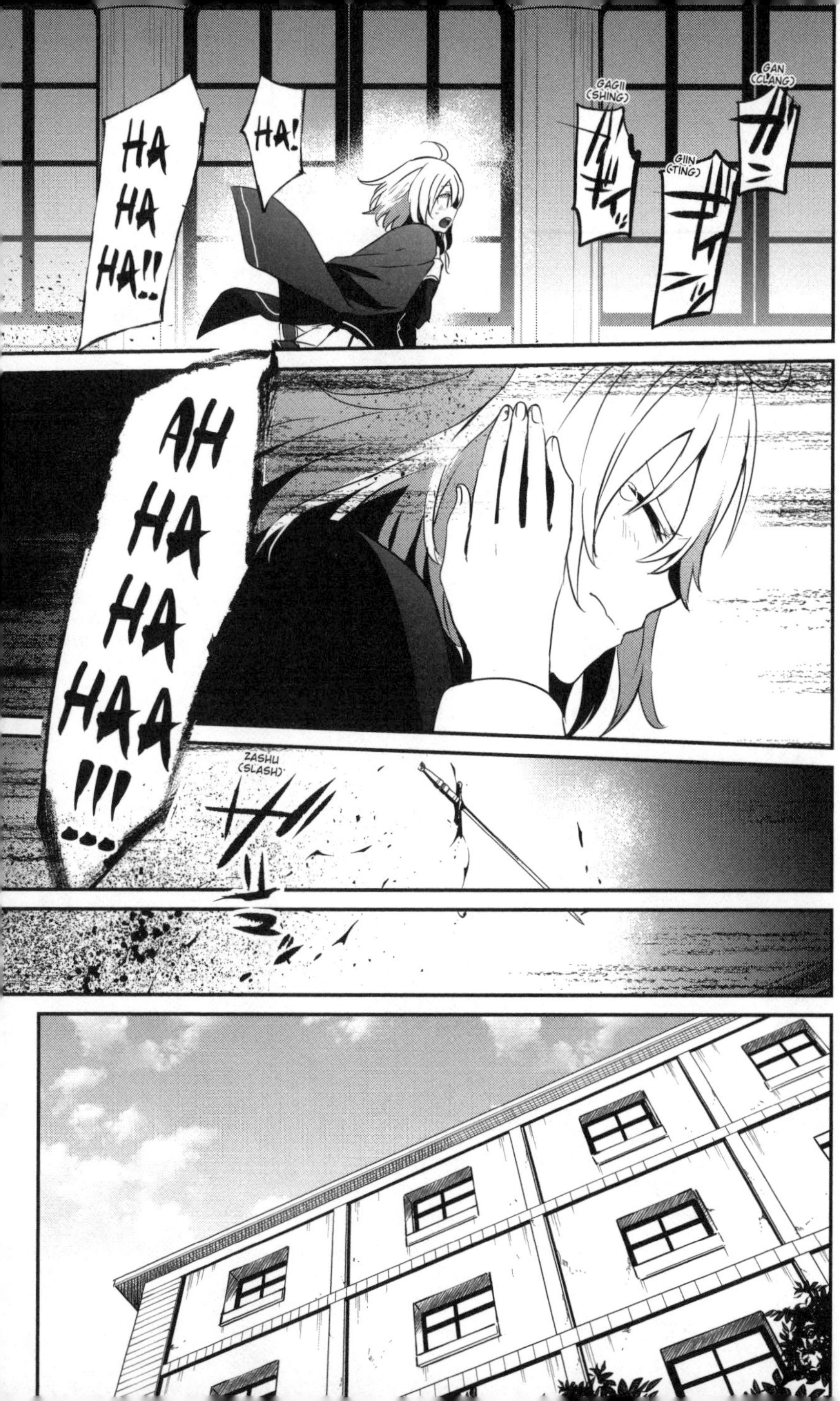
GAN (CLANG)
GIIN (TING)
GAGII (SHING)
HA!
HA HA HA!!
AH HA HA HA HAA!!!...
ZASHU (SLASH)

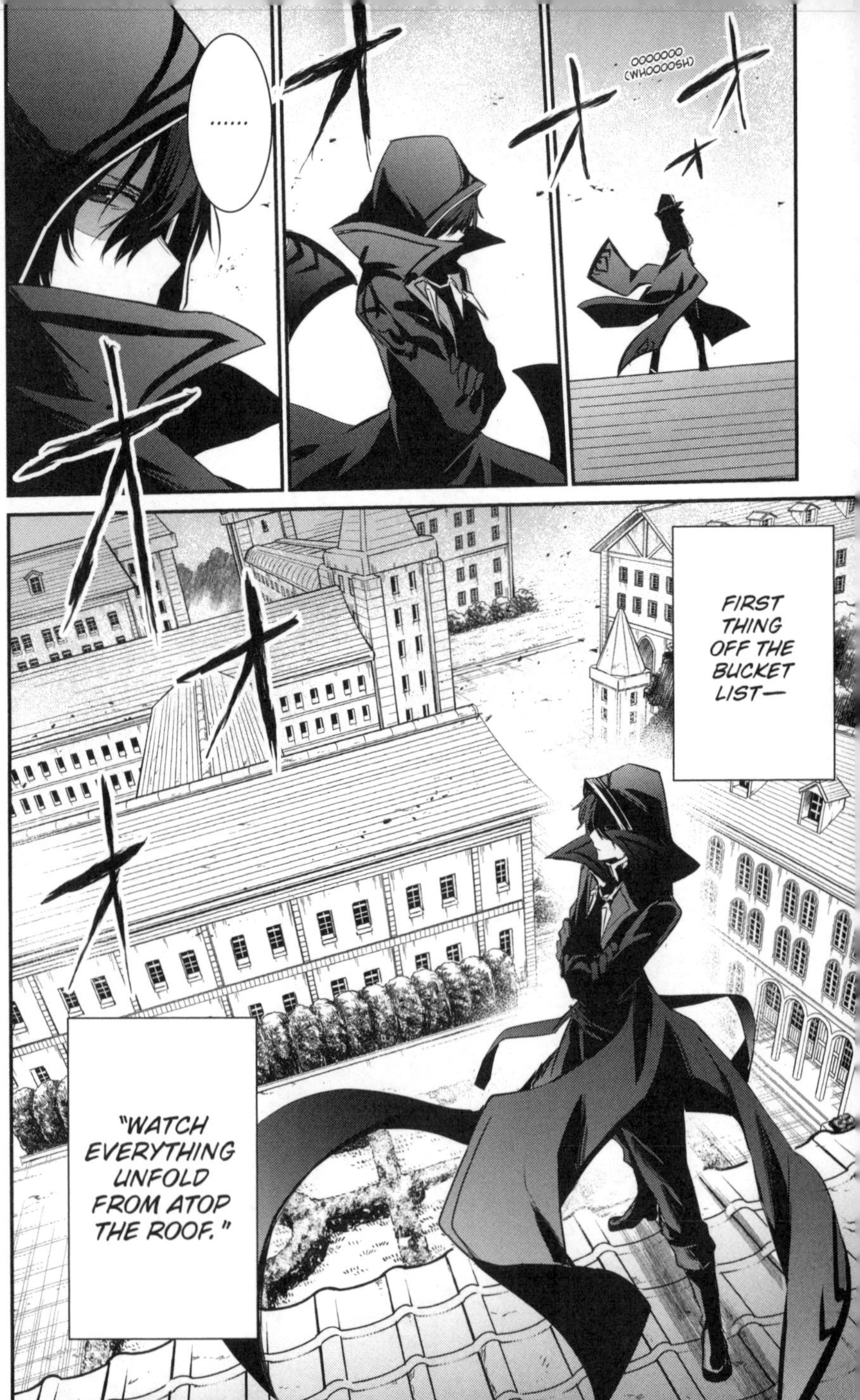
OOOOOOO (WHOOOOSH)
......
FIRST THING OFF THE BUCKET LIST—
"WATCH EVERYTHING UNFOLD FROM ATOP THE ROOF."

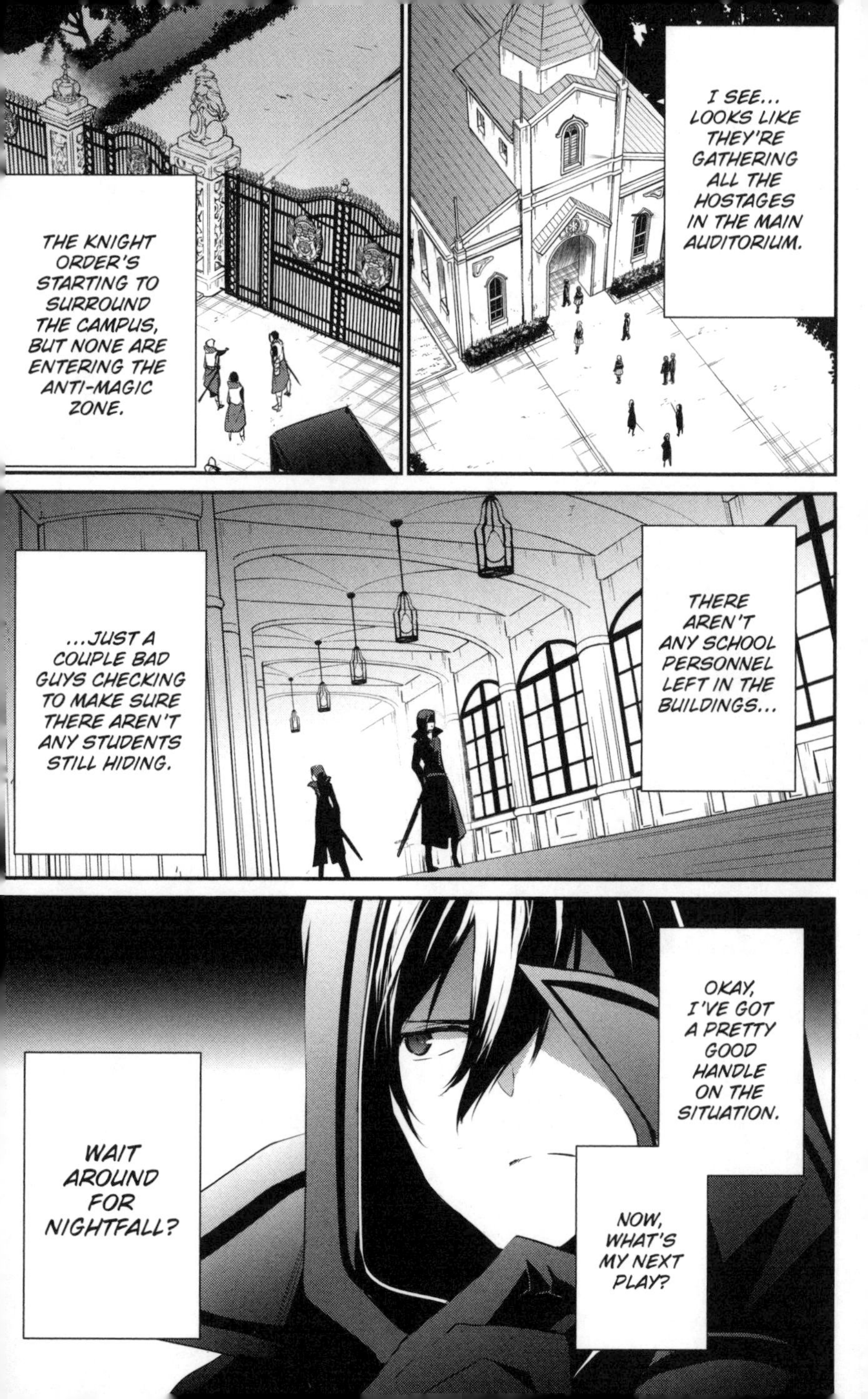
I SEE... LOOKS LIKE THEY'RE GATHERING ALL THE HOSTAGES IN THE MAIN AUDITORIUM.
THE KNIGHT ORDER'S STARTING TO SURROUND THE CAMPUS, BUT NONE ARE ENTERING THE ANTI-MAGIC ZONE.
THERE AREN'T ANY SCHOOL PERSONNEL LEFT IN THE BUILDINGS...
...JUST A COUPLE BAD GUYS CHECKING TO MAKE SURE THERE AREN'T ANY STUDENTS STILL HIDING.
OKAY, I'VE GOT A PRETTY GOOD HANDLE ON THE SITUATION.
NOW, WHAT'S MY NEXT PLAY?
WAIT AROUND FOR NIGHTFALL?

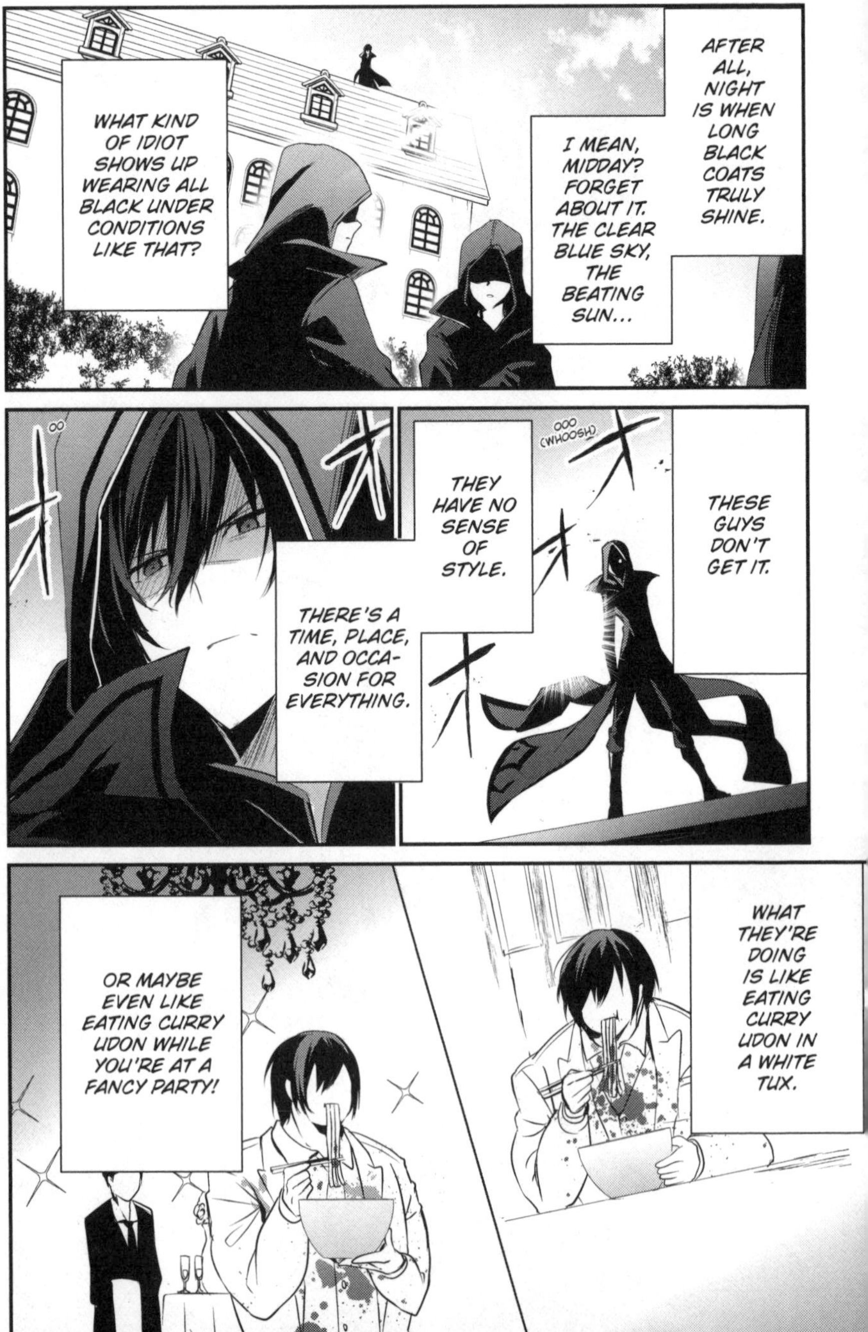
AFTER ALL, NIGHT IS WHEN LONG BLACK COATS TRULY SHINE.
I MEAN, MIDDAY? FORGET ABOUT IT. THE CLEAR BLUE SKY, THE BEATING SUN...
WHAT KIND OF IDIOT SHOWS UP WEARING ALL BLACK UNDER CONDITIONS LIKE THAT?
OOO (WHOOSH)
THESE GUYS DON'T GET IT.
THEY HAVE NO SENSE OF STYLE.
OO
THERE'S A TIME, PLACE, AND OCCA-SION FOR EVERYTHING.
WHAT THEY'RE DOING IS LIKE EATING CURRY UDON IN A WHITE TUX.
OR MAYBE EVEN LIKE EATING CURRY UDON WHILE YOU'RE AT A FANCY PARTY!

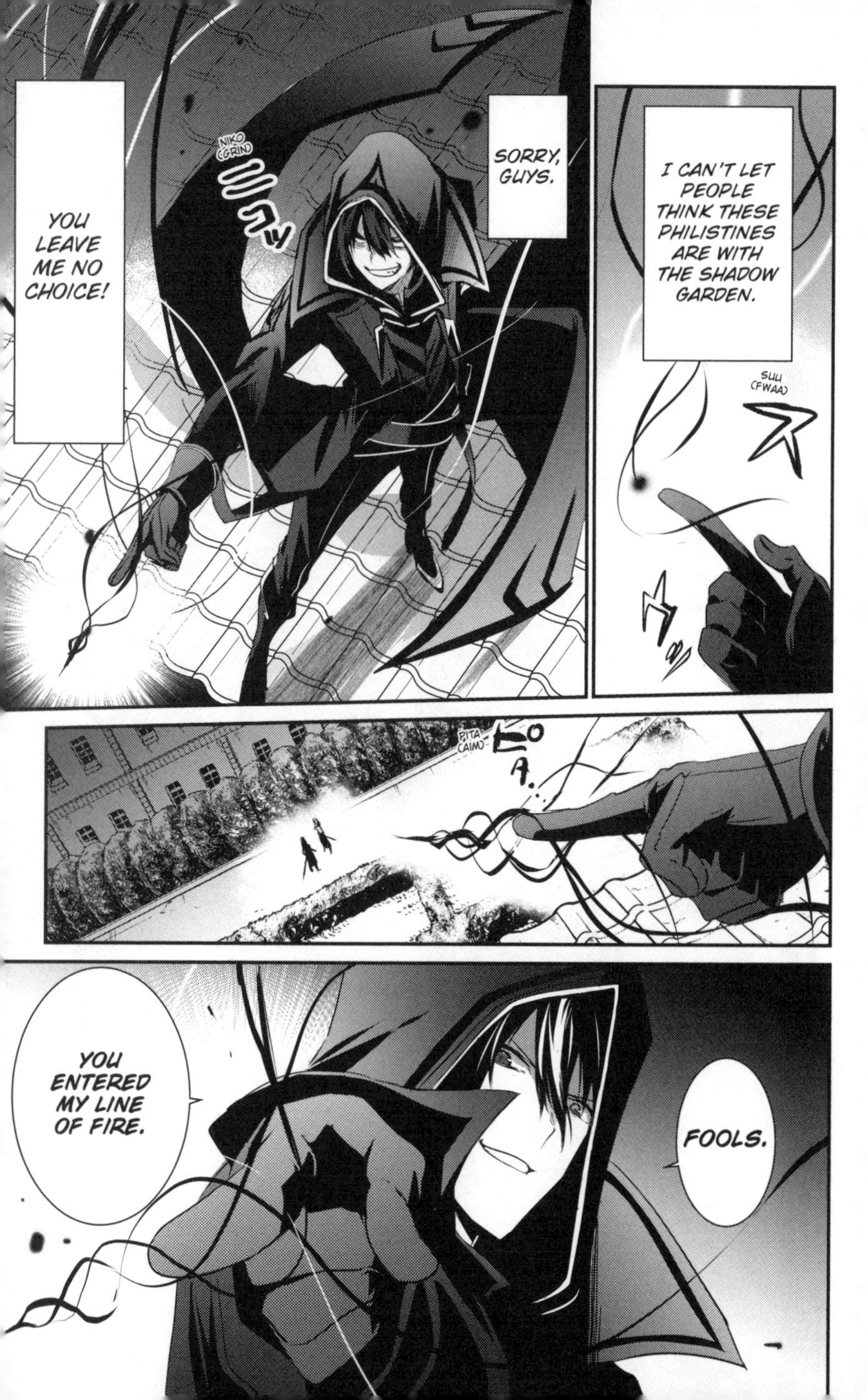
I CAN'T LET PEOPLE THINK THESE PHILISTINES ARE WITH THE SHADOW GARDEN.
SUU (FWAA)
SORRY, GUYS.
NIKO (GRIN)
YOU LEAVE ME NO CHOICE!
PITA (AIM)
FOOLS.
YOU ENTERED MY LINE OF FIRE.

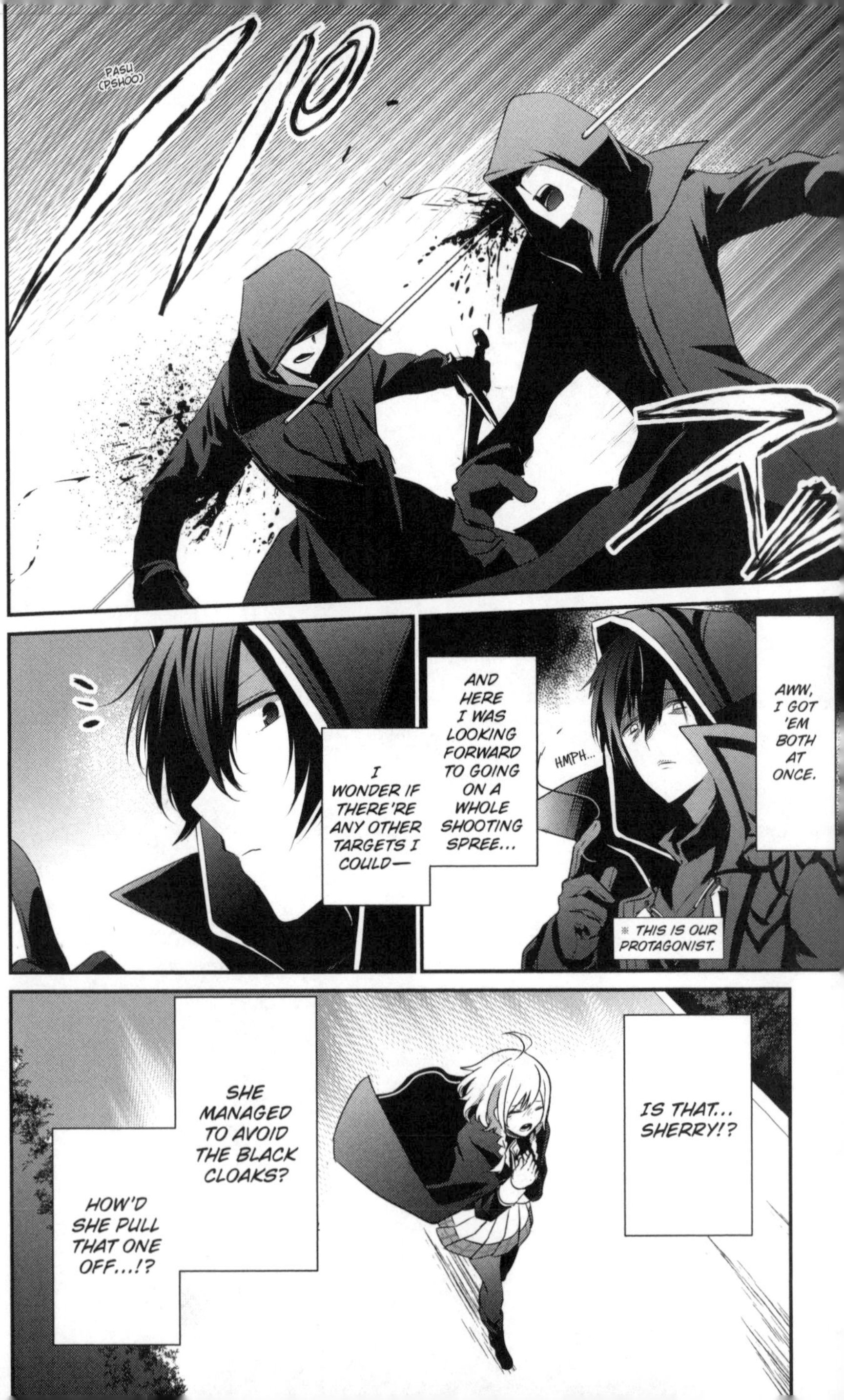
PASHU (PSHOO)
AWW, I GOT 'EM BOTH AT ONCE.
HMPH...
AND HERE I WAS LOOKING FORWARD TO GOING ON A WHOLE SHOOTING SPREE...
※ THIS IS OUR PROTAGONIST.
I WONDER IF THERE'RE ANY OTHER TARGETS I COULD—
IS THAT... SHERRY!?
SHE MANAGED TO AVOID THE BLACK CLOAKS?
HOW'D SHE PULL THAT ONE OFF...!?

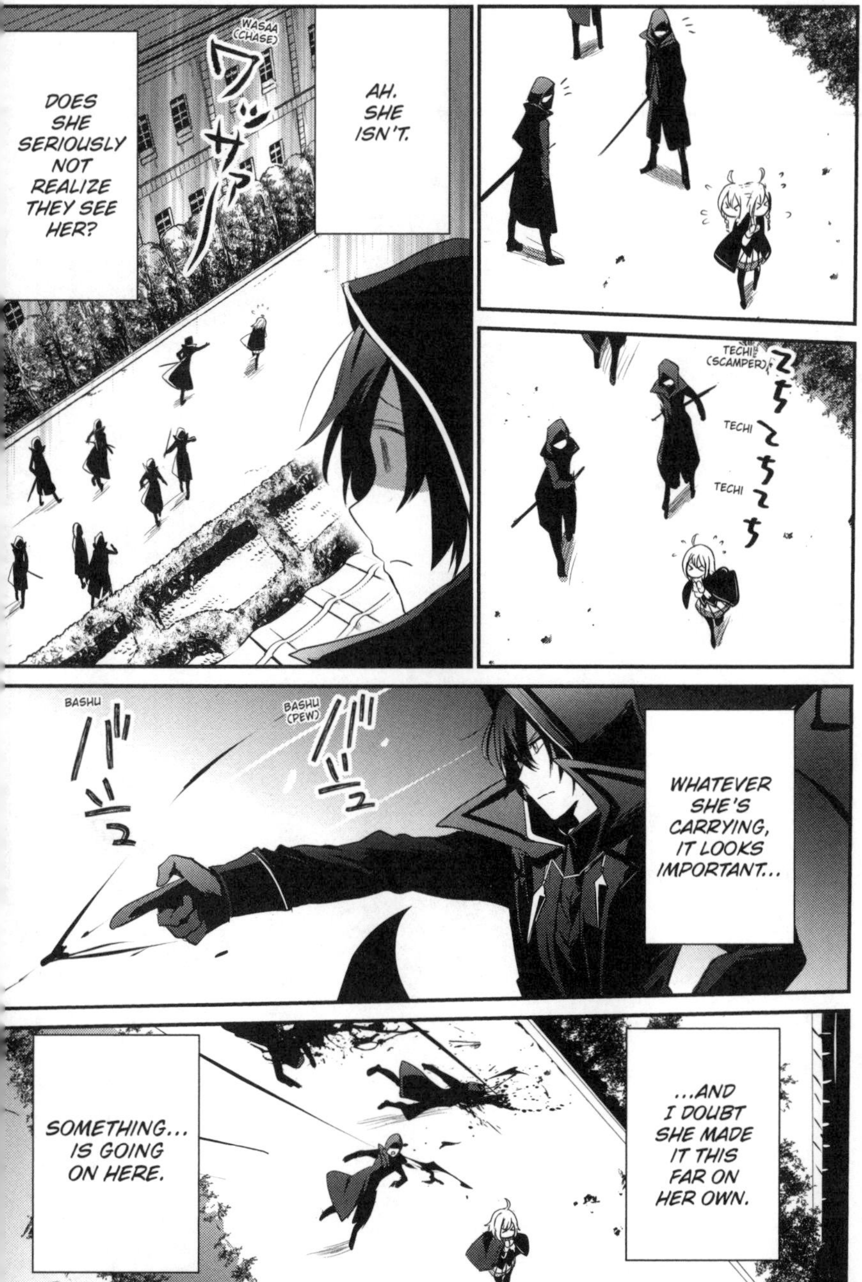
TECHI (SCAMPER)
TECHI
TECHI
AH. SHE ISN'T.
WASAA (CHASE)
DOES SHE SERIOUSLY NOT REALIZE THEY SEE HER?
WHATEVER SHE'S CARRYING, IT LOOKS IMPORTANT...
BASHU (PEW)
BASHU
...AND I DOUBT SHE MADE IT THIS FAR ON HER OWN.
SOMETHING... IS GOING ON HERE.

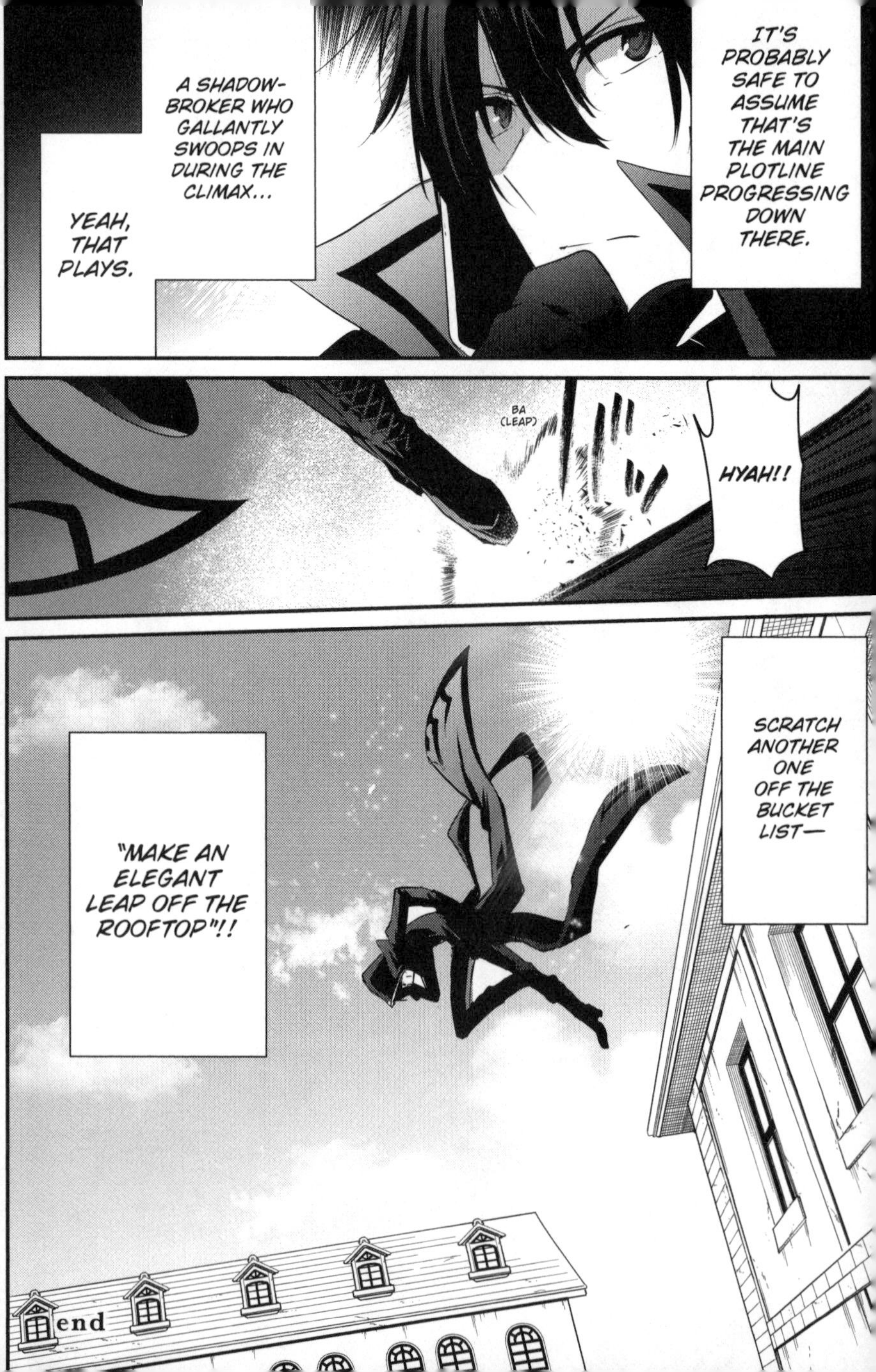
IT'S PROBABLY SAFE TO ASSUME THAT'S THE MAIN PLOTLINE PROGRESSING DOWN THERE.
A SHADOW-BROKER WHO GALLANTLY SWOOPS IN DURING THE CLIMAX...
YEAH, THAT PLAYS.
HYAH!!
BA (LEAP)
SCRATCH ANOTHER ONE OFF THE BUCKET LIST—
"MAKE AN ELEGANT LEAP OFF THE ROOFTOP"!!
end

THE Eminence IN Shadow

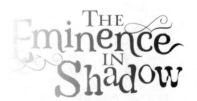

Episode.11

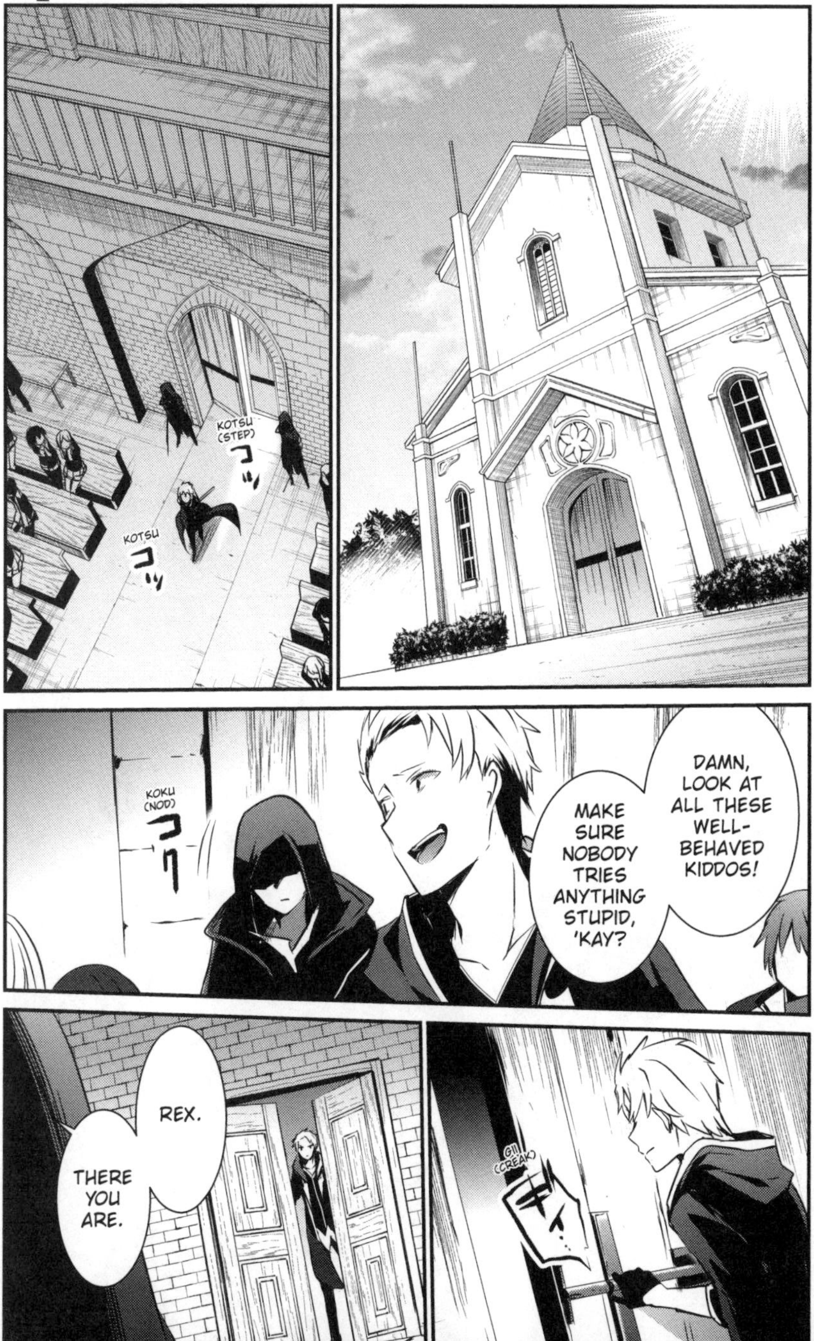
KOTSU (STEP)
KOTSU
DAMN, LOOK AT ALL THESE WELL-BEHAVED KIDDOS!
MAKE SURE NOBODY TRIES ANYTHING STUPID, 'KAY?
KOKU (NOD)
GII (CREAK)
REX.
THERE YOU ARE.

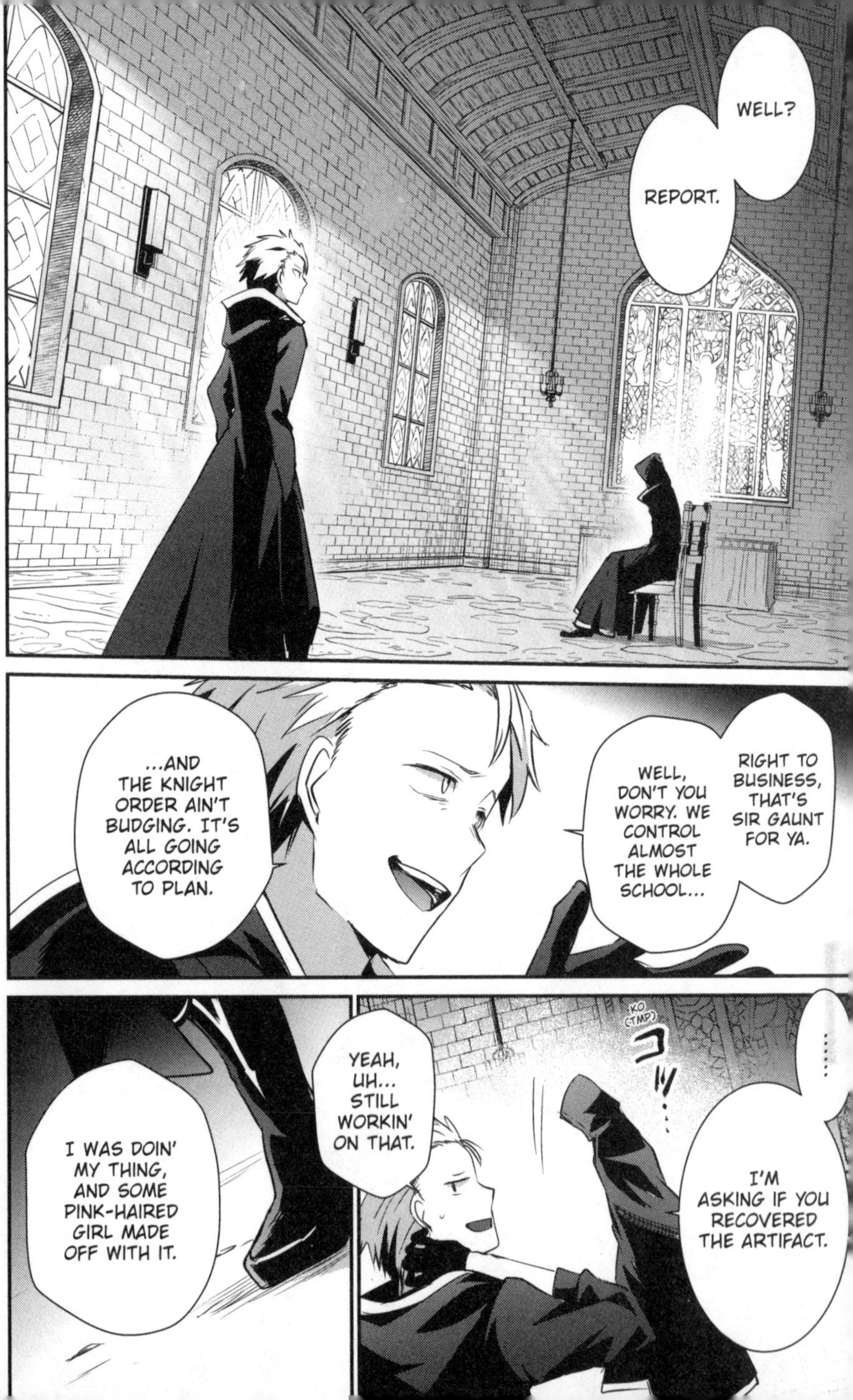
WELL?
REPORT.
RIGHT TO BUSINESS, THAT'S SIR GAUNT FOR YA.
WELL, DON'T YOU WORRY. WE CONTROL ALMOST THE WHOLE SCHOOL...
...AND THE KNIGHT ORDER AIN'T BUDGING. IT'S ALL GOING ACCORDING TO PLAN.
......
KO (TMP)
I'M ASKING IF YOU RECOVERED THE ARTIFACT.
YEAH, UH... STILL WORKIN' ON THAT.
I WAS DOIN' MY THING, AND SOME PINK-HAIRED GIRL MADE OFF WITH IT.

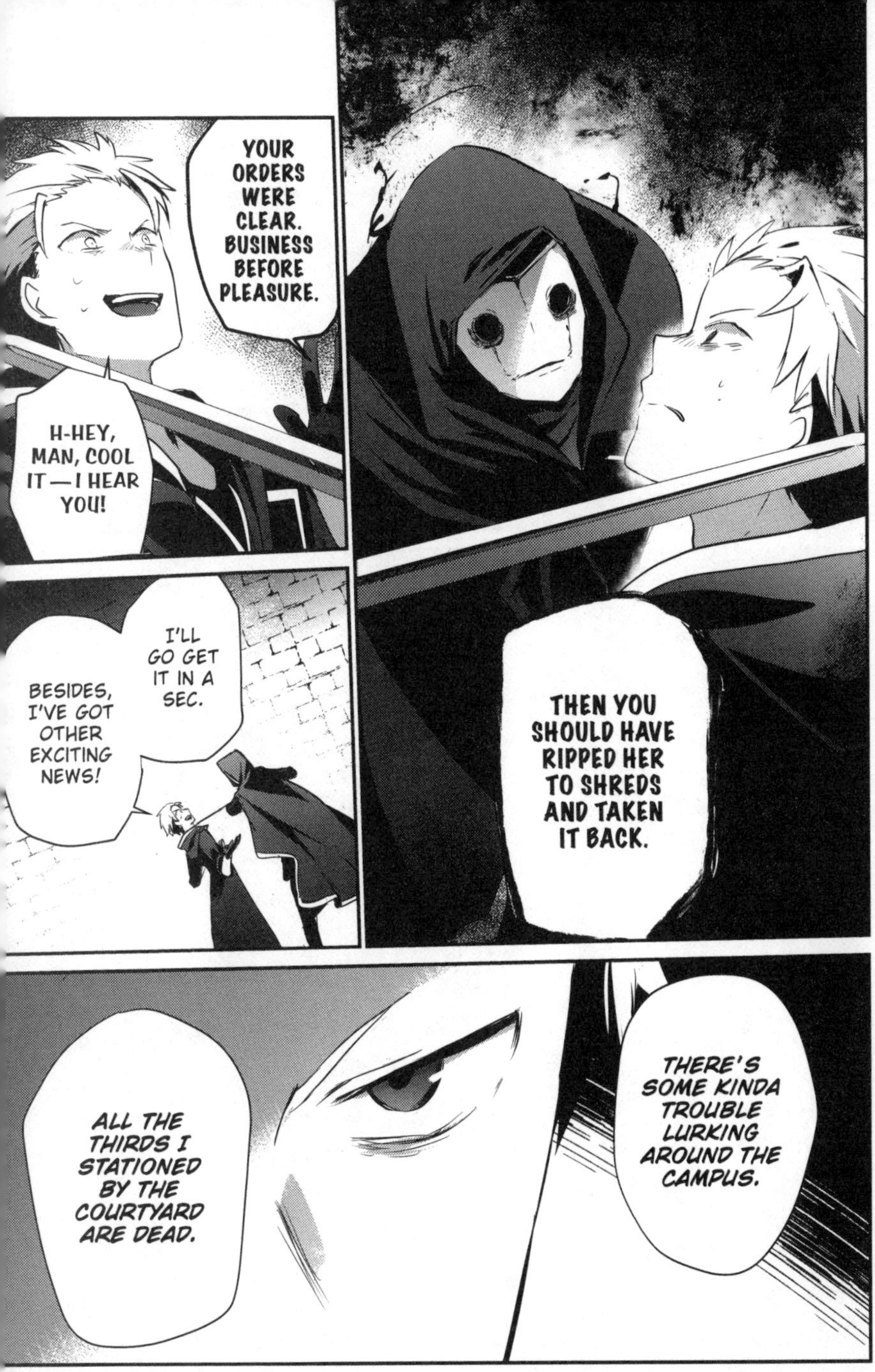
THEN YOU SHOULD HAVE RIPPED HER TO SHREDS AND TAKEN IT BACK.
YOUR ORDERS WERE CLEAR. BUSINESS BEFORE PLEASURE.
H-HEY, MAN, COOL IT—I HEAR YOU!
I'LL GO GET IT IN A SEC.
BESIDES, I'VE GOT OTHER EXCITING NEWS!
THERE'S SOME KINDA TROUBLE LURKING AROUND THE CAMPUS.
ALL THE THIRDS I STATIONED BY THE COURTYARD ARE DEAD.

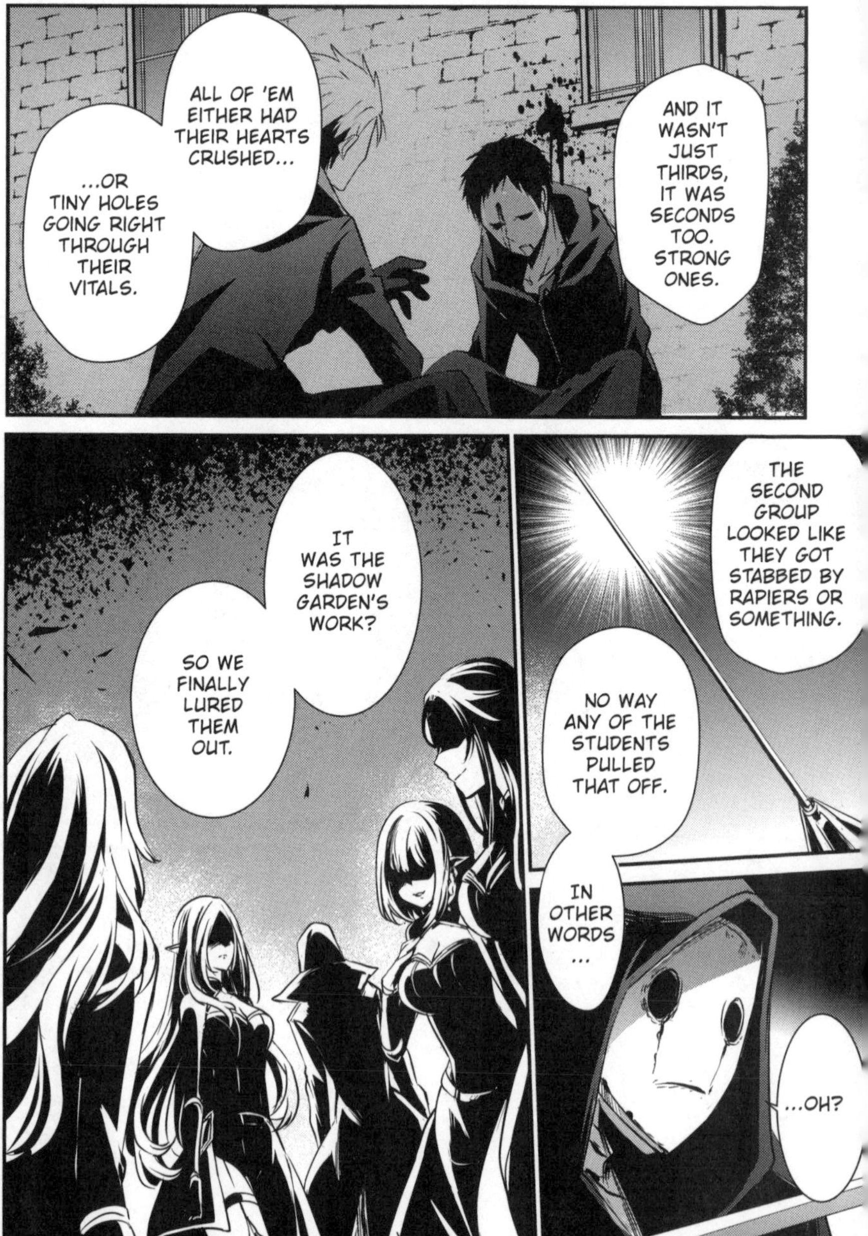
AND IT WASN'T JUST THIRDS, IT WAS SECONDS TOO. STRONG ONES.
ALL OF 'EM EITHER HAD THEIR HEARTS CRUSHED...
...OR TINY HOLES GOING RIGHT THROUGH THEIR VITALS.
THE SECOND GROUP LOOKED LIKE THEY GOT STABBED BY RAPIERS OR SOMETHING.
NO WAY ANY OF THE STUDENTS PULLED THAT OFF.
IN OTHER WORDS...
...OH?
IT WAS THE SHADOW GARDEN'S WORK?
SO WE FINALLY LURED THEM OUT.

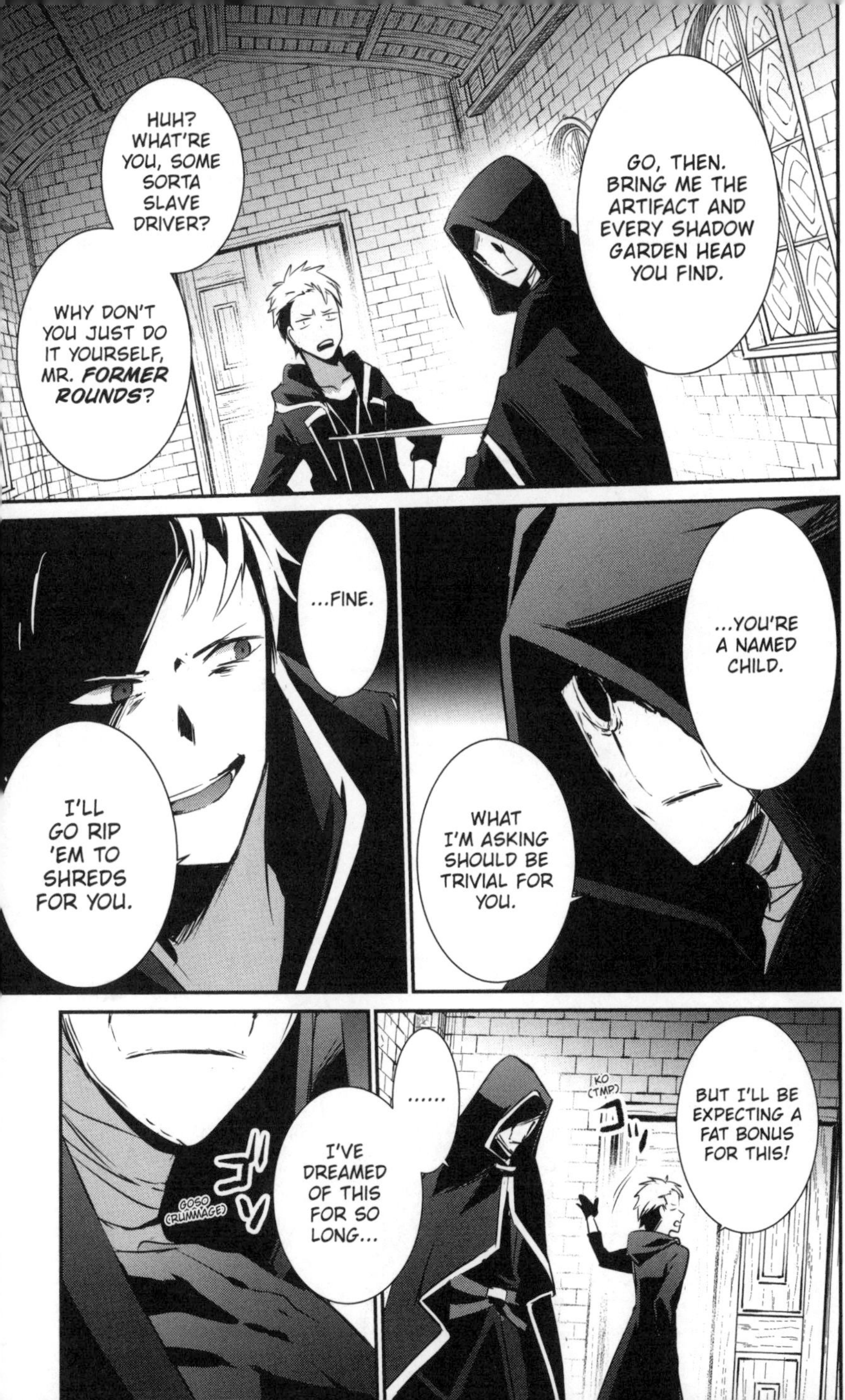
GO, THEN. BRING ME THE ARTIFACT AND EVERY SHADOW GARDEN HEAD YOU FIND.
HUH? WHAT'RE YOU, SOME SORTA SLAVE DRIVER?
WHY DON'T YOU JUST DO IT YOURSELF, MR. ***FORMER ROUNDS***?
...YOU'RE A NAMED CHILD.
WHAT I'M ASKING SHOULD BE TRIVIAL FOR YOU.
...FINE.
I'LL GO RIP 'EM TO SHREDS FOR YOU.
BUT I'LL BE EXPECTING A FAT BONUS FOR THIS!
KO (TMP)
......
I'VE DREAMED OF THIS FOR SO LONG...
GOSO (RUMMAGE)

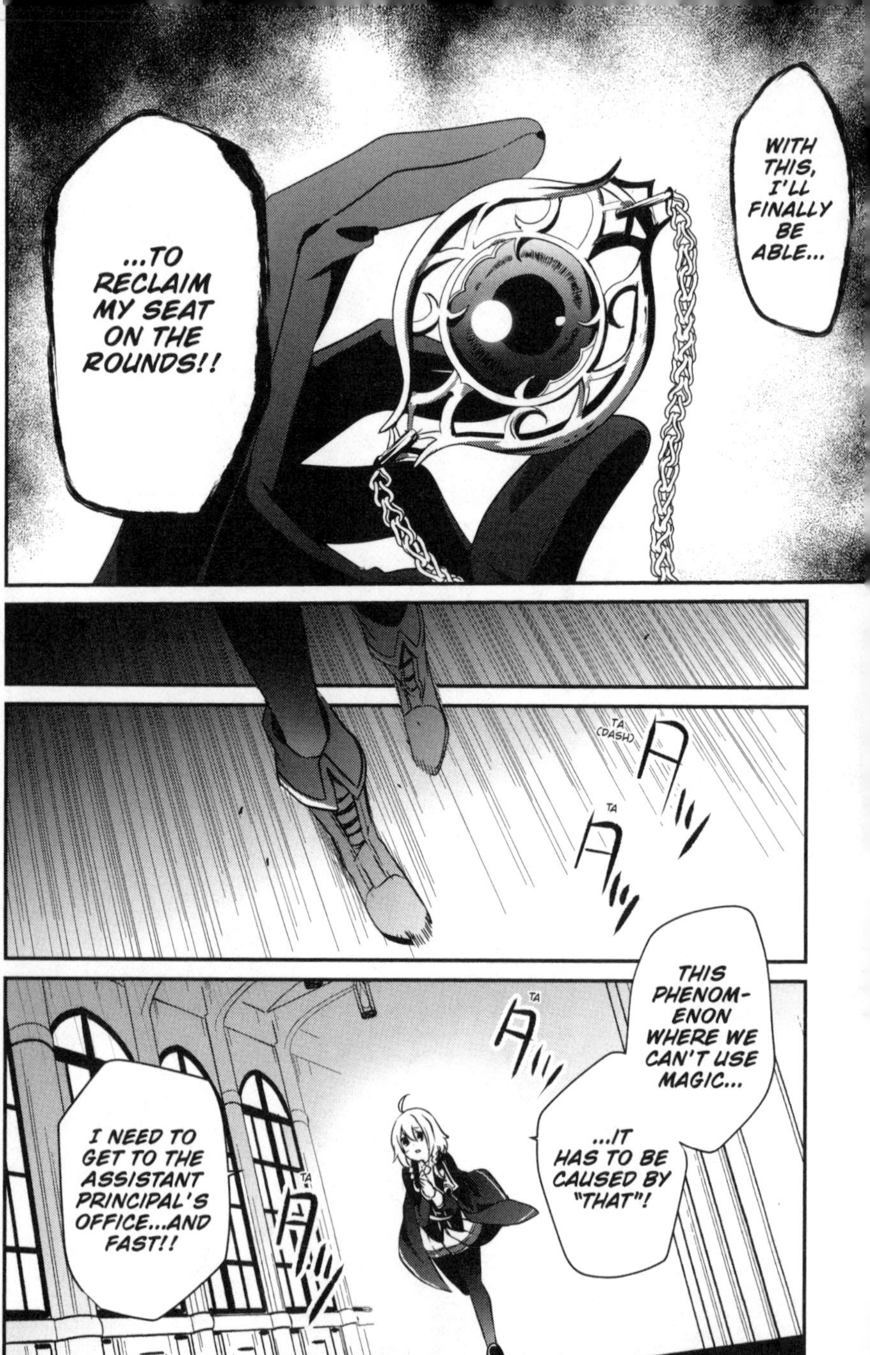
WITH THIS, I'LL FINALLY BE ABLE...
...TO RECLAIM MY SEAT ON THE ROUNDS!!
TA (DASH)
TA
TA
THIS PHENOM-ENON WHERE WE CAN'T USE MAGIC...
...IT HAS TO BE CAUSED BY "THAT"!
TA
I NEED TO GET TO THE ASSISTANT PRINCIPAL'S OFFICE...AND FAST!!

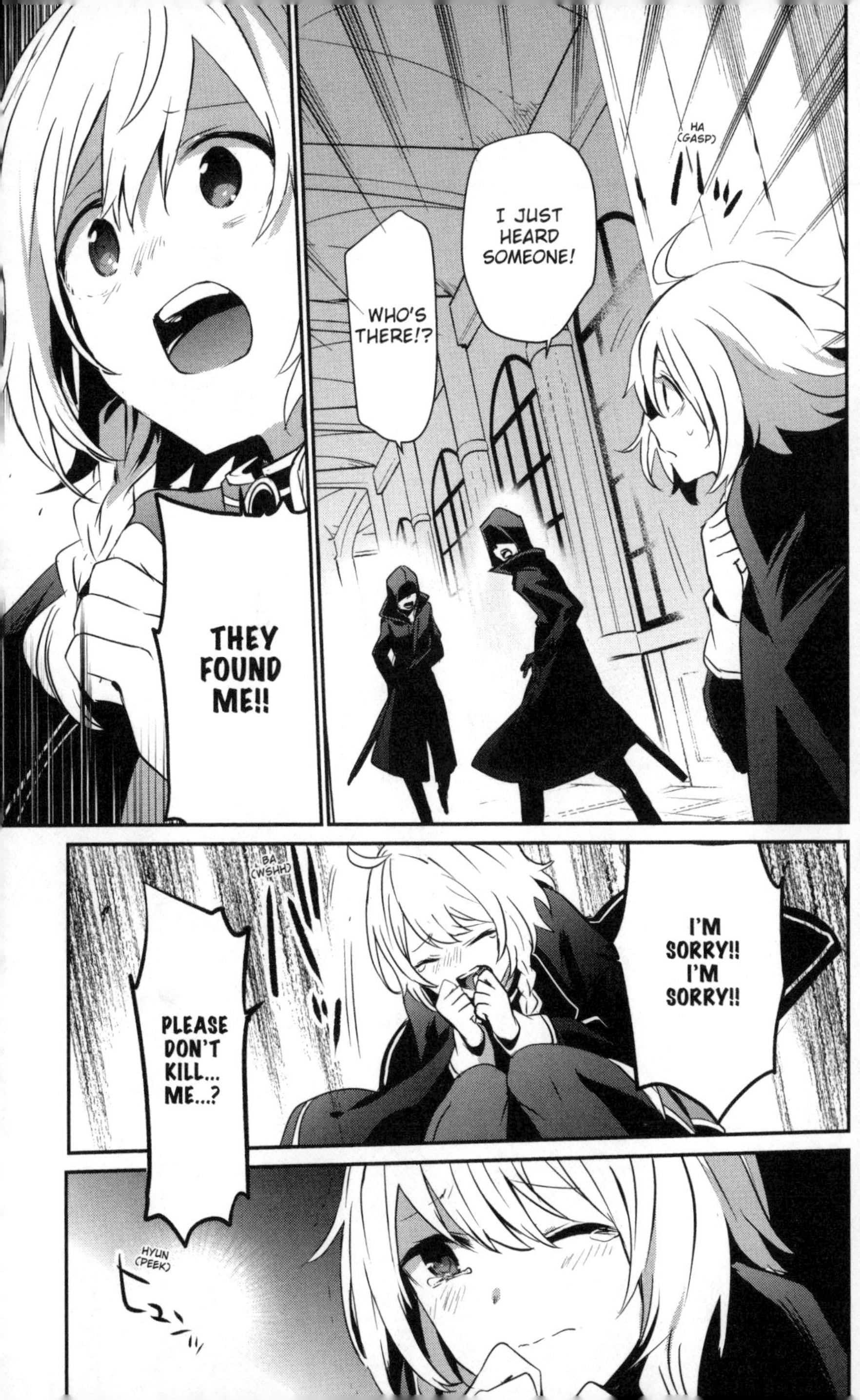
HA (GASP)
I JUST HEARD SOMEONE!
WHO'S THERE!?
THEY FOUND ME!!
I'M SORRY!! I'M SORRY!!
BA (WSHH)
PLEASE DON'T KILL... ME...?
HYUN (PEEK)

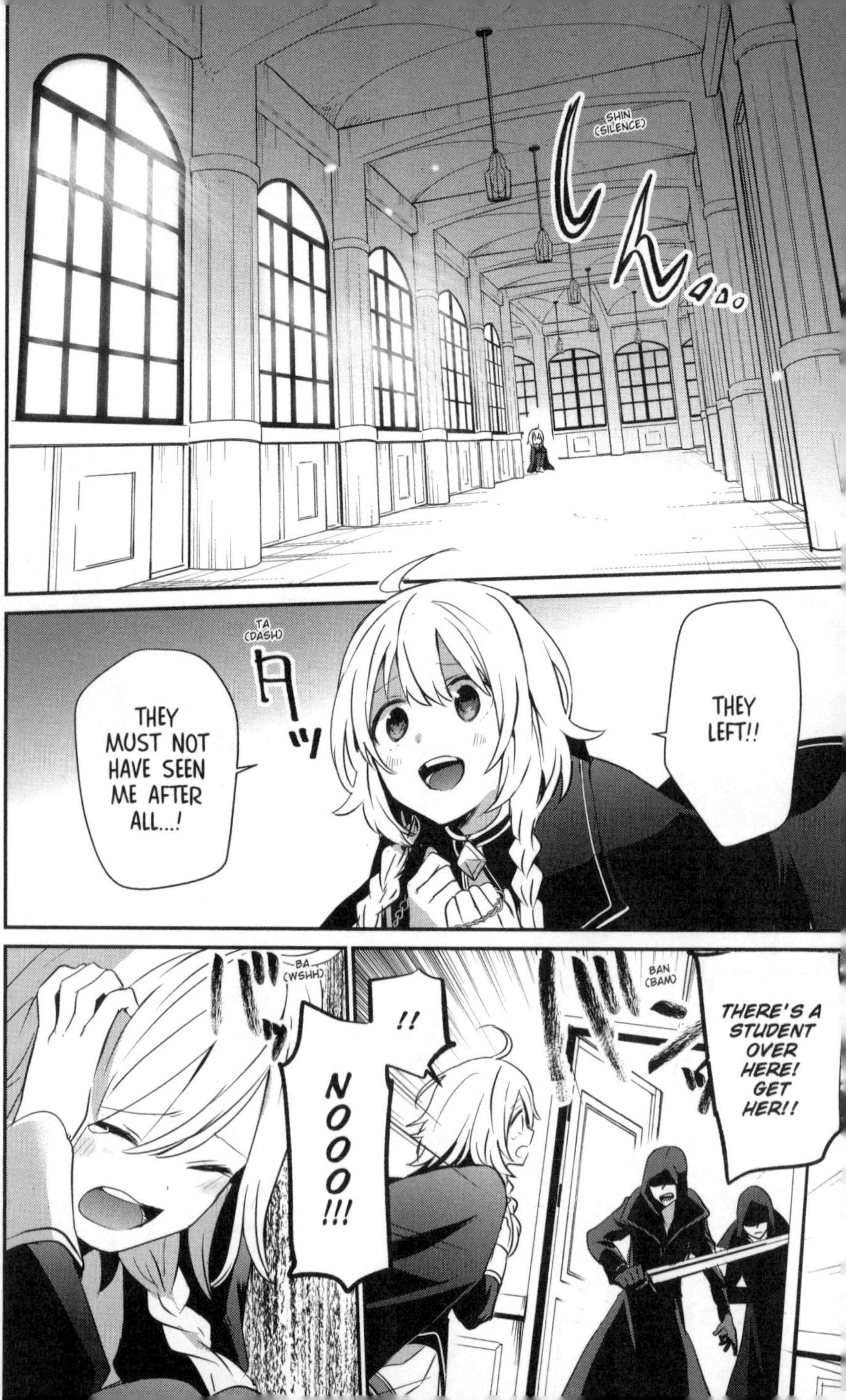
SHIN (SILENCE)
TA (DASH)
THEY LEFT!!
THEY MUST NOT HAVE SEEN ME AFTER ALL...!
BAN (BAM)
THERE'S A STUDENT OVER HERE! GET HER!!
!!
BA (WSHH)
NOOOO!!!

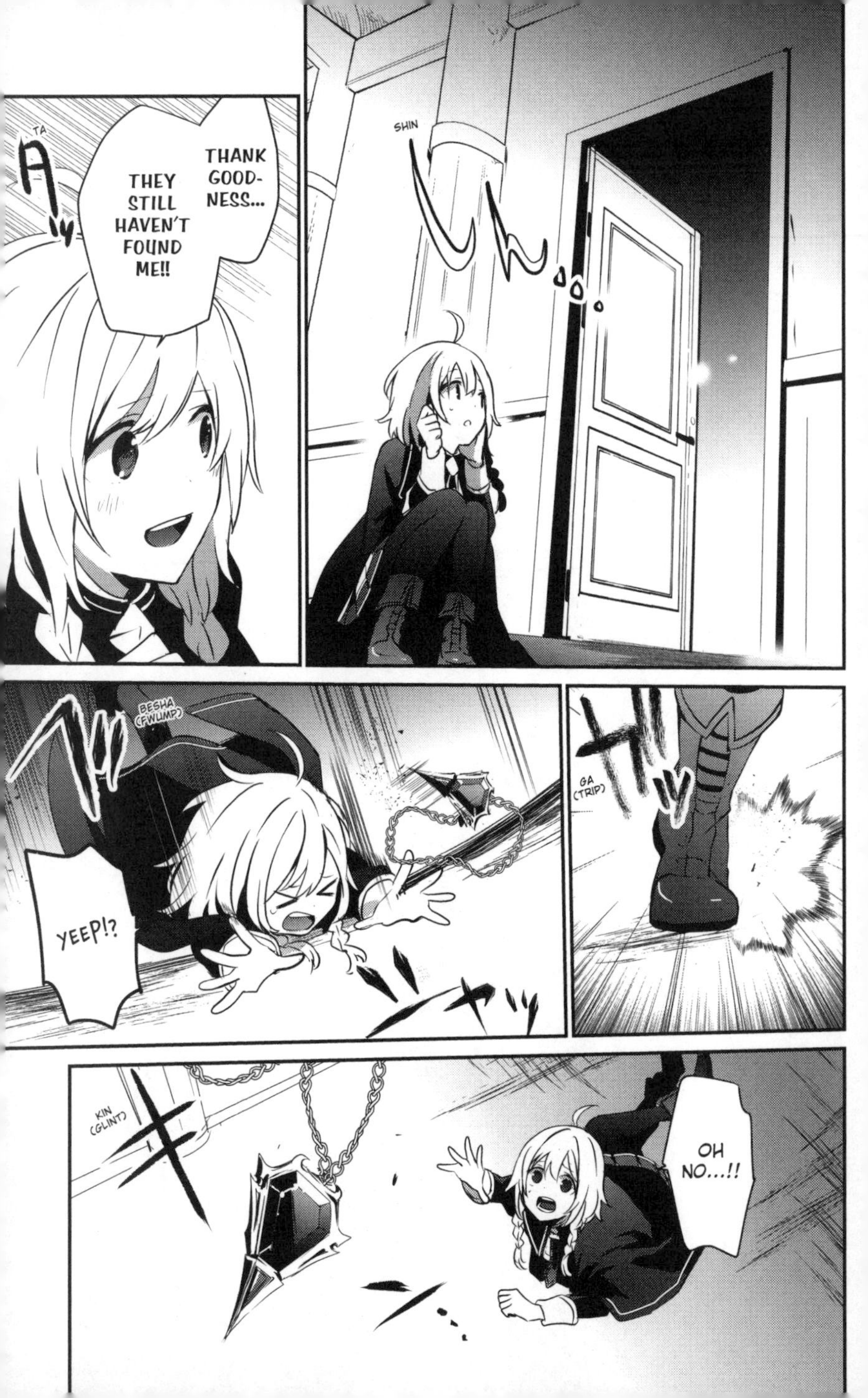
SHIN
THANK GOODNESS... THEY STILL HAVEN'T FOUND ME!!
TA
GA (TRIP)
BESHA (FWUMP)
YEEP!?
OH NO...!!
KIN (GLINT)

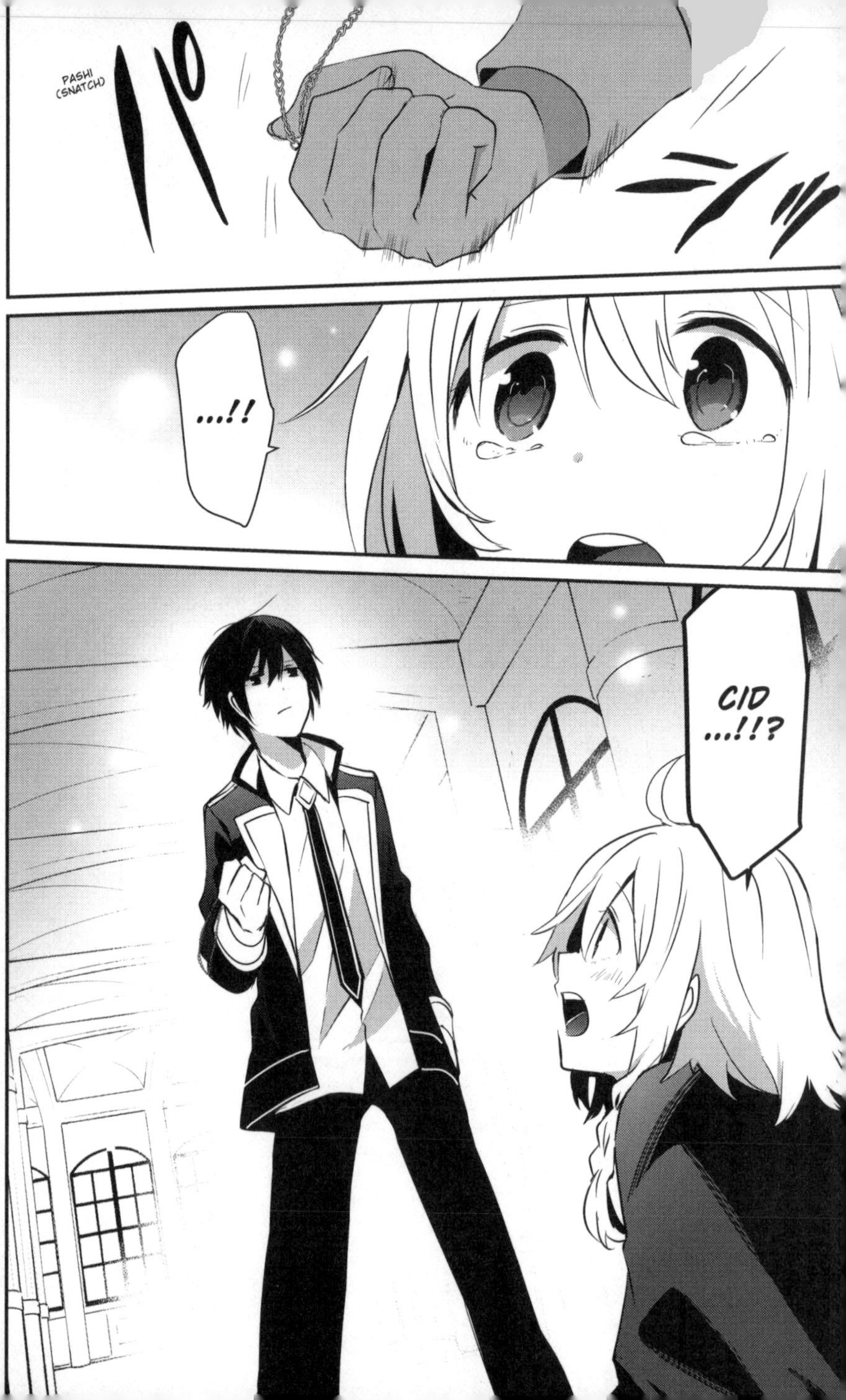
PASHI (SNATCH)
...!!
CID ...!!?

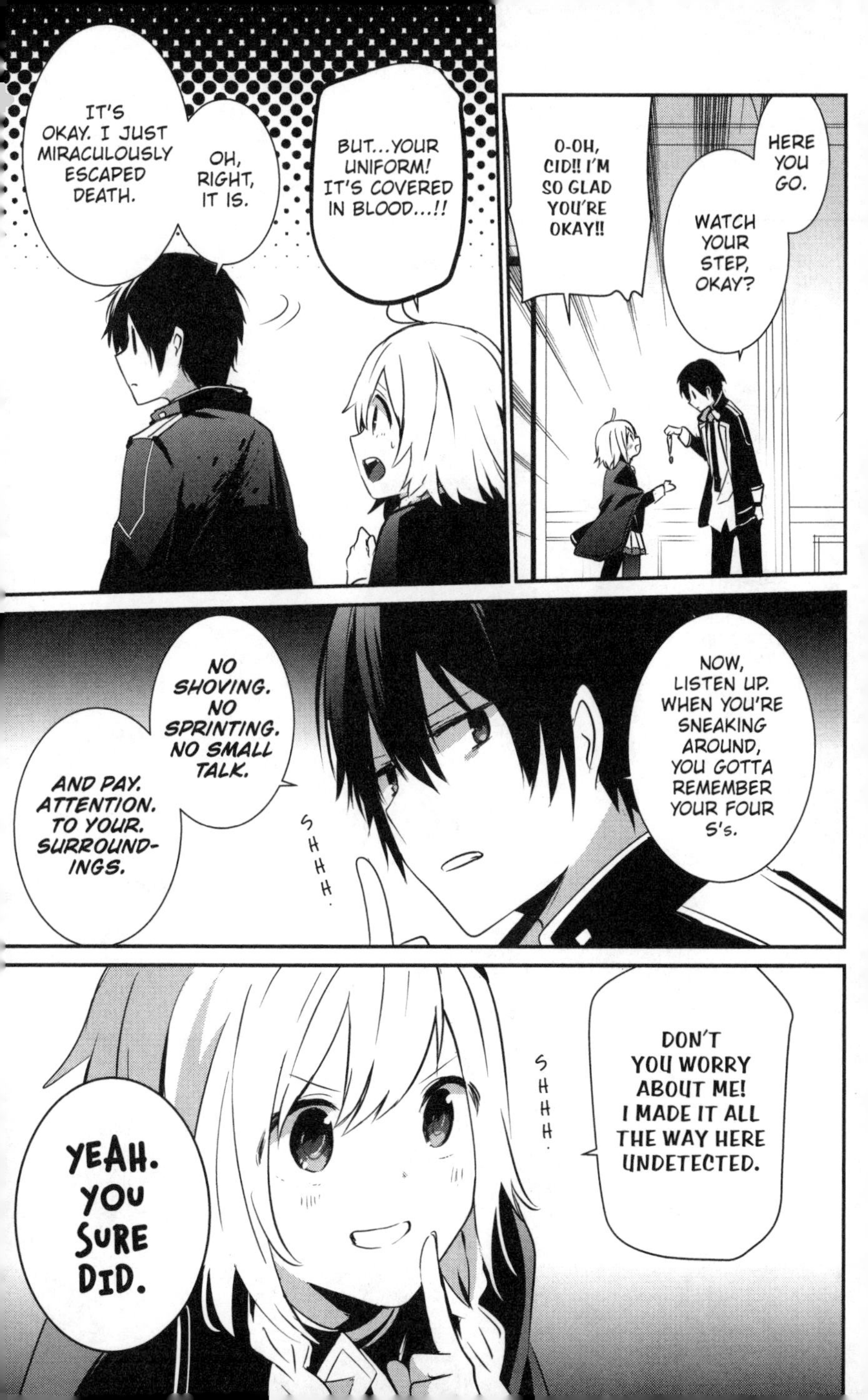
HERE YOU GO.
WATCH YOUR STEP, OKAY?
O-OH, CID!! I'M SO GLAD YOU'RE OKAY!!
BUT...YOUR UNIFORM! IT'S COVERED IN BLOOD...!!
OH, RIGHT, IT IS.
IT'S OKAY. I JUST MIRACULOUSLY ESCAPED DEATH.
NOW, LISTEN UP. WHEN YOU'RE SNEAKING AROUND, YOU GOTTA REMEMBER YOUR FOUR S's.
SHHH.
NO SHOVING. NO SPRINTING. NO SMALL TALK.
AND PAY. ATTENTION. TO YOUR. SURROUNDINGS.
DON'T YOU WORRY ABOUT ME! I MADE IT ALL THE WAY HERE UNDETECTED.
SHHH.
YEAH. YOU SURE DID.

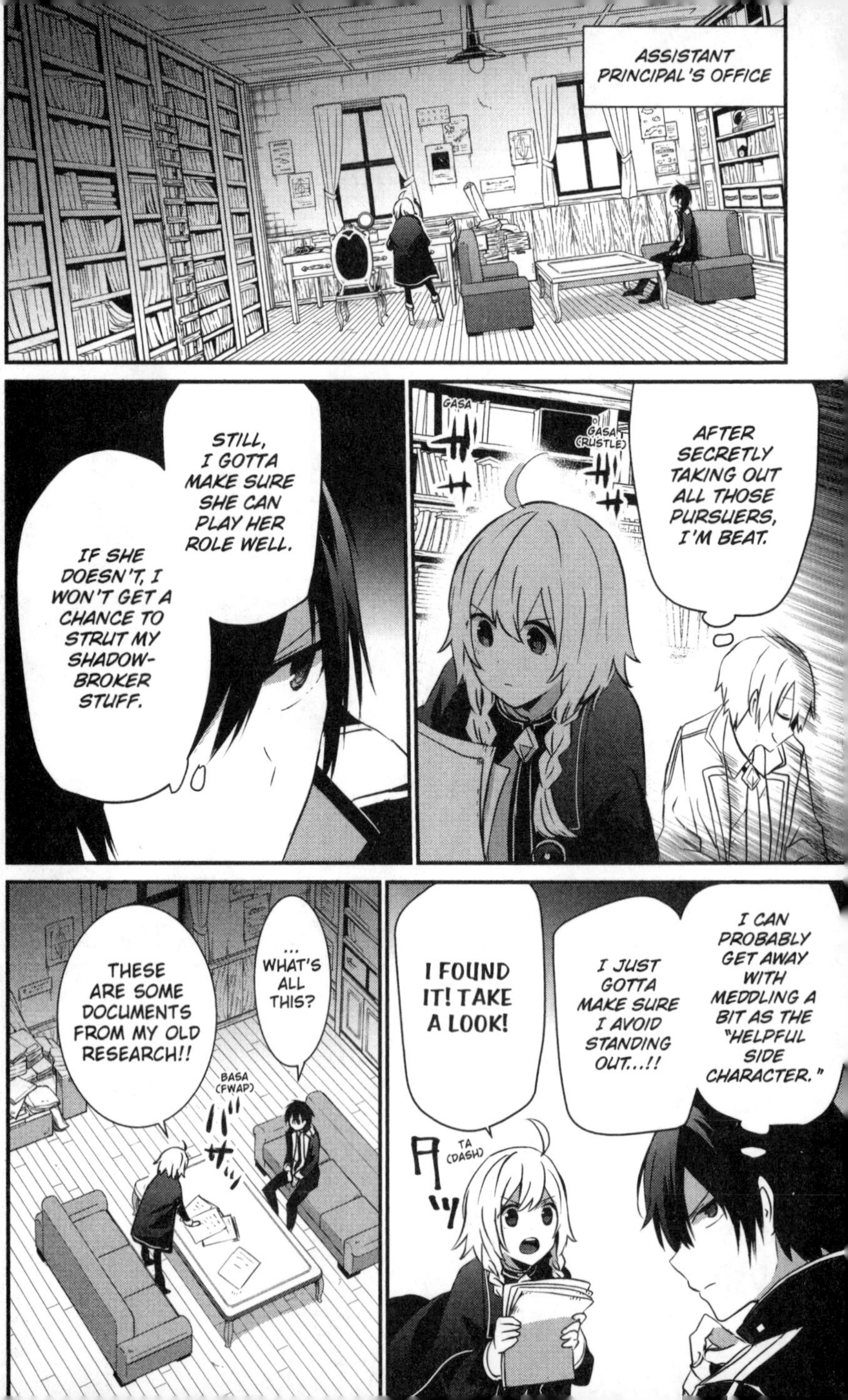
ASSISTANT PRINCIPAL'S OFFICE
GASA
GASA (RUSTLE)
AFTER SECRETLY TAKING OUT ALL THOSE PURSUERS, I'M BEAT.
STILL, I GOTTA MAKE SURE SHE CAN PLAY HER ROLE WELL.
IF SHE DOESN'T, I WON'T GET A CHANCE TO STRUT MY SHADOW-BROKER STUFF.
I CAN PROBABLY GET AWAY WITH MEDDLING A BIT AS THE "HELPFUL SIDE CHARACTER."
I JUST GOTTA MAKE SURE I AVOID STANDING OUT...!!
I FOUND IT! TAKE A LOOK!
TA (DASH)
... WHAT'S ALL THIS?
THESE ARE SOME DOCUMENTS FROM MY OLD RESEARCH!!
BASA (FWAP)

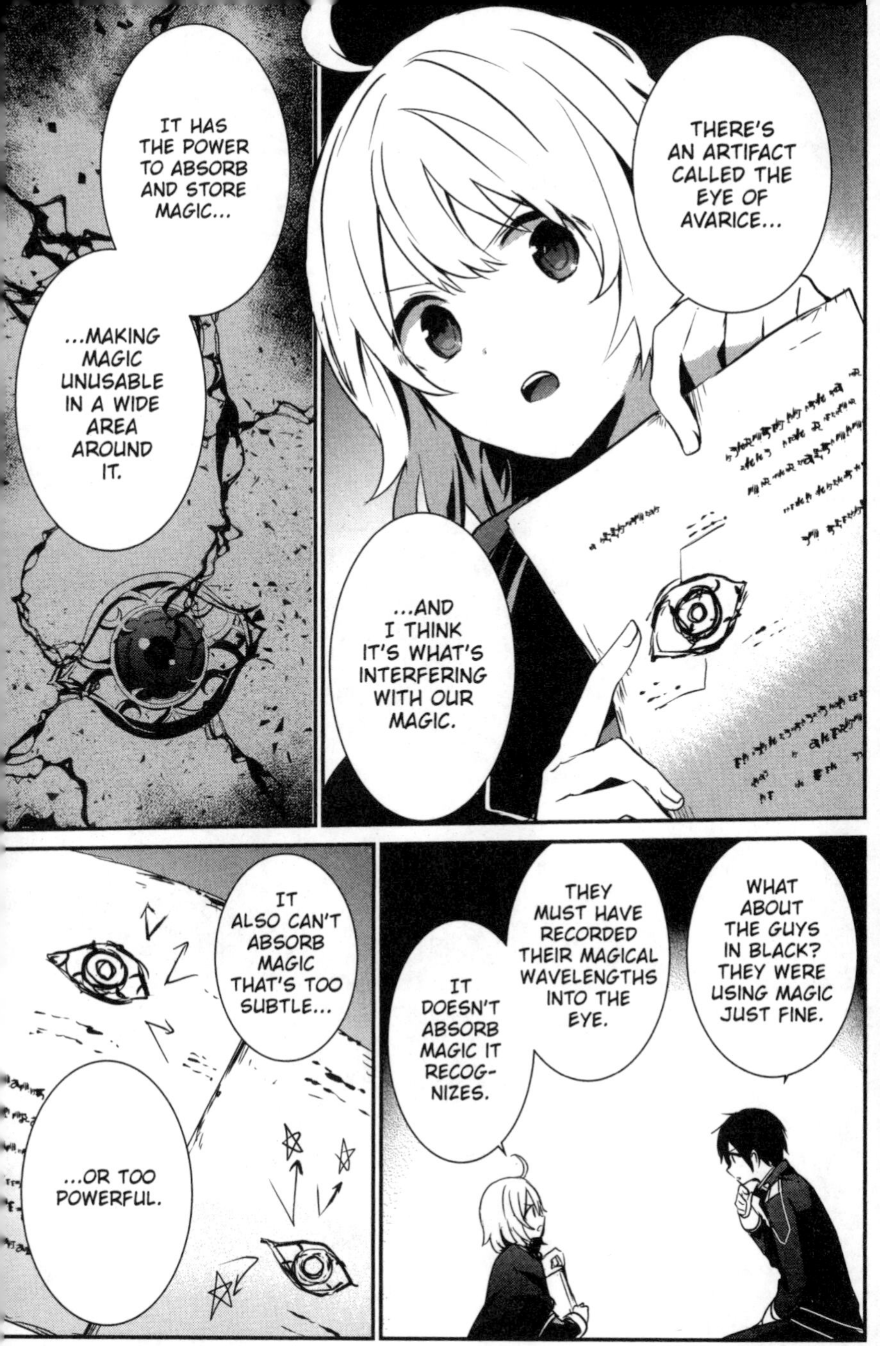
THERE'S AN ARTIFACT CALLED THE EYE OF AVARICE...
...AND I THINK IT'S WHAT'S INTERFERING WITH OUR MAGIC.
IT HAS THE POWER TO ABSORB AND STORE MAGIC...
...MAKING MAGIC UNUSABLE IN A WIDE AREA AROUND IT.
WHAT ABOUT THE GUYS IN BLACK? THEY WERE USING MAGIC JUST FINE.
THEY MUST HAVE RECORDED THEIR MAGICAL WAVELENGTHS INTO THE EYE.
IT DOESN'T ABSORB MAGIC IT RECOG-NIZES.
IT ALSO CAN'T ABSORB MAGIC THAT'S TOO SUBTLE...
...OR TOO POWERFUL.

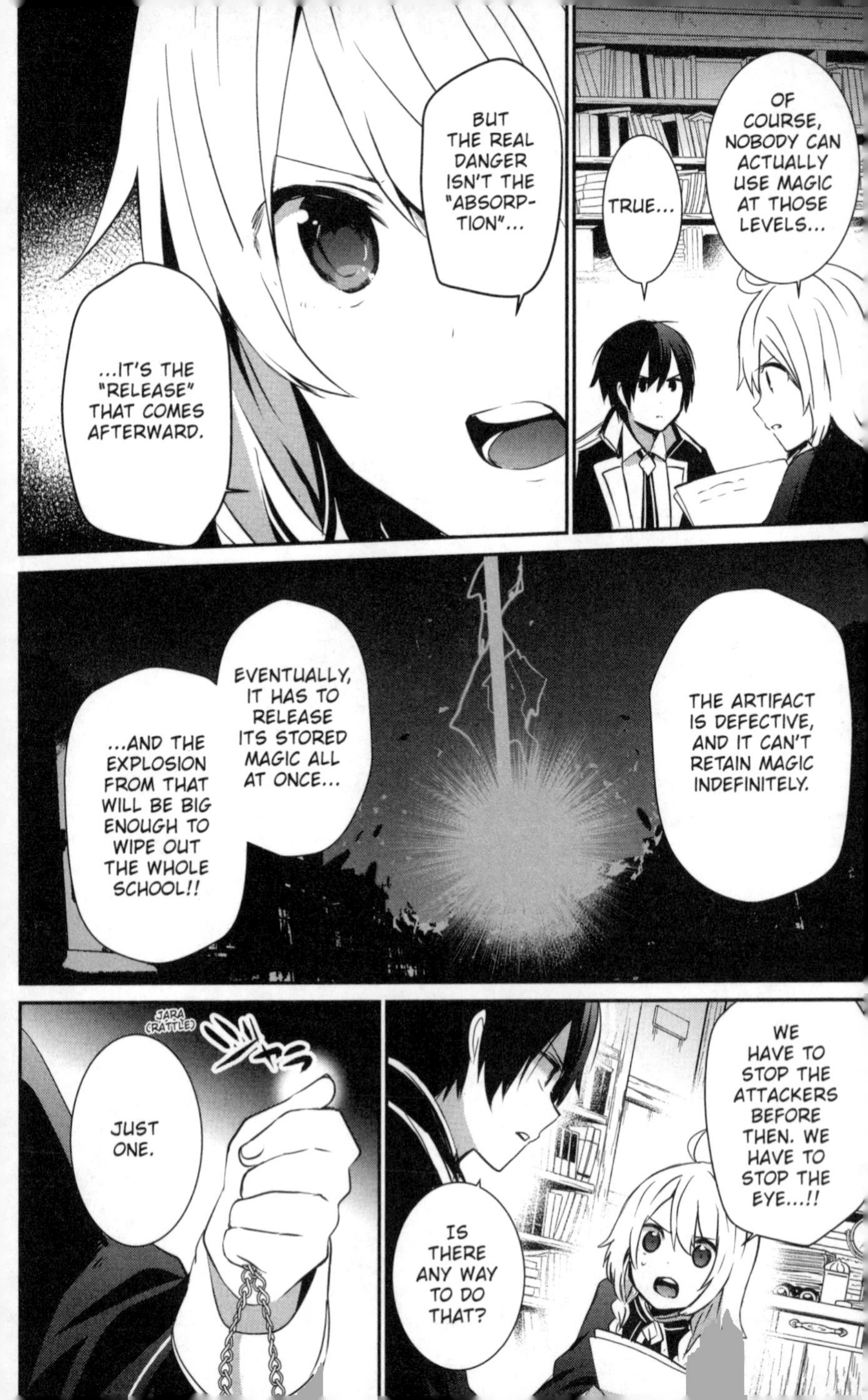
OF COURSE, NOBODY CAN ACTUALLY USE MAGIC AT THOSE LEVELS...
TRUE...
BUT THE REAL DANGER ISN'T THE "ABSORPTION"...
...IT'S THE "RELEASE" THAT COMES AFTERWARD.
THE ARTIFACT IS DEFECTIVE, AND IT CAN'T RETAIN MAGIC INDEFINITELY.
EVENTUALLY, IT HAS TO RELEASE ITS STORED MAGIC ALL AT ONCE...
...AND THE EXPLOSION FROM THAT WILL BE BIG ENOUGH TO WIPE OUT THE WHOLE SCHOOL!!
WE HAVE TO STOP THE ATTACKERS BEFORE THEN. WE HAVE TO STOP THE EYE...!!
IS THERE ANY WAY TO DO THAT?
JARA (RATTLE)
JUST ONE.

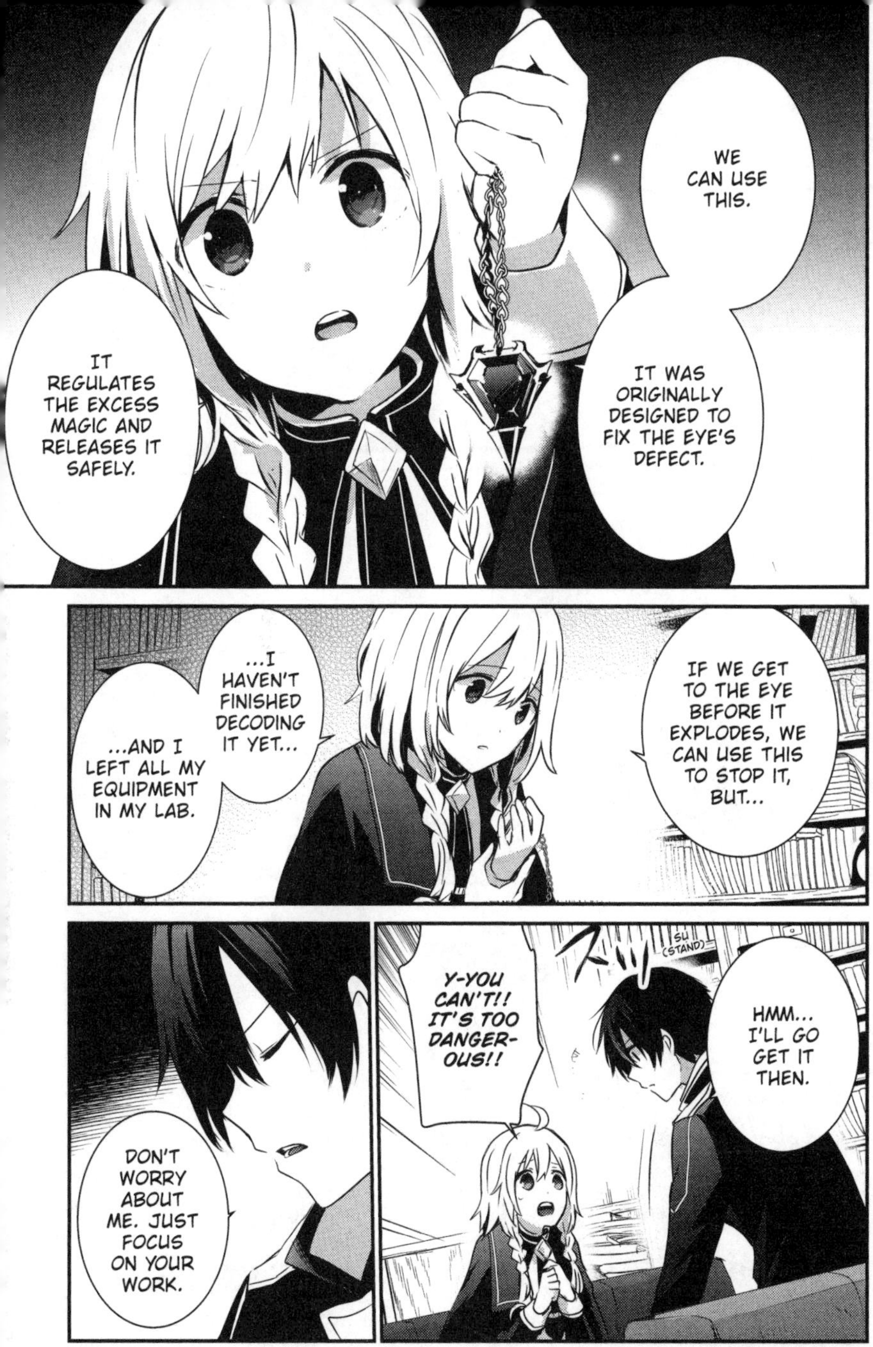
WE CAN USE THIS.
IT WAS ORIGINALLY DESIGNED TO FIX THE EYE'S DEFECT.
IT REGULATES THE EXCESS MAGIC AND RELEASES IT SAFELY.
IF WE GET TO THE EYE BEFORE IT EXPLODES, WE CAN USE THIS TO STOP IT, BUT...
...I HAVEN'T FINISHED DECODING IT YET...
...AND I LEFT ALL MY EQUIPMENT IN MY LAB.
SU (STAND)
HMM... I'LL GO GET IT THEN.
Y-YOU CAN'T!! IT'S TOO DANGER-OUS!!
DON'T WORRY ABOUT ME. JUST FOCUS ON YOUR WORK.

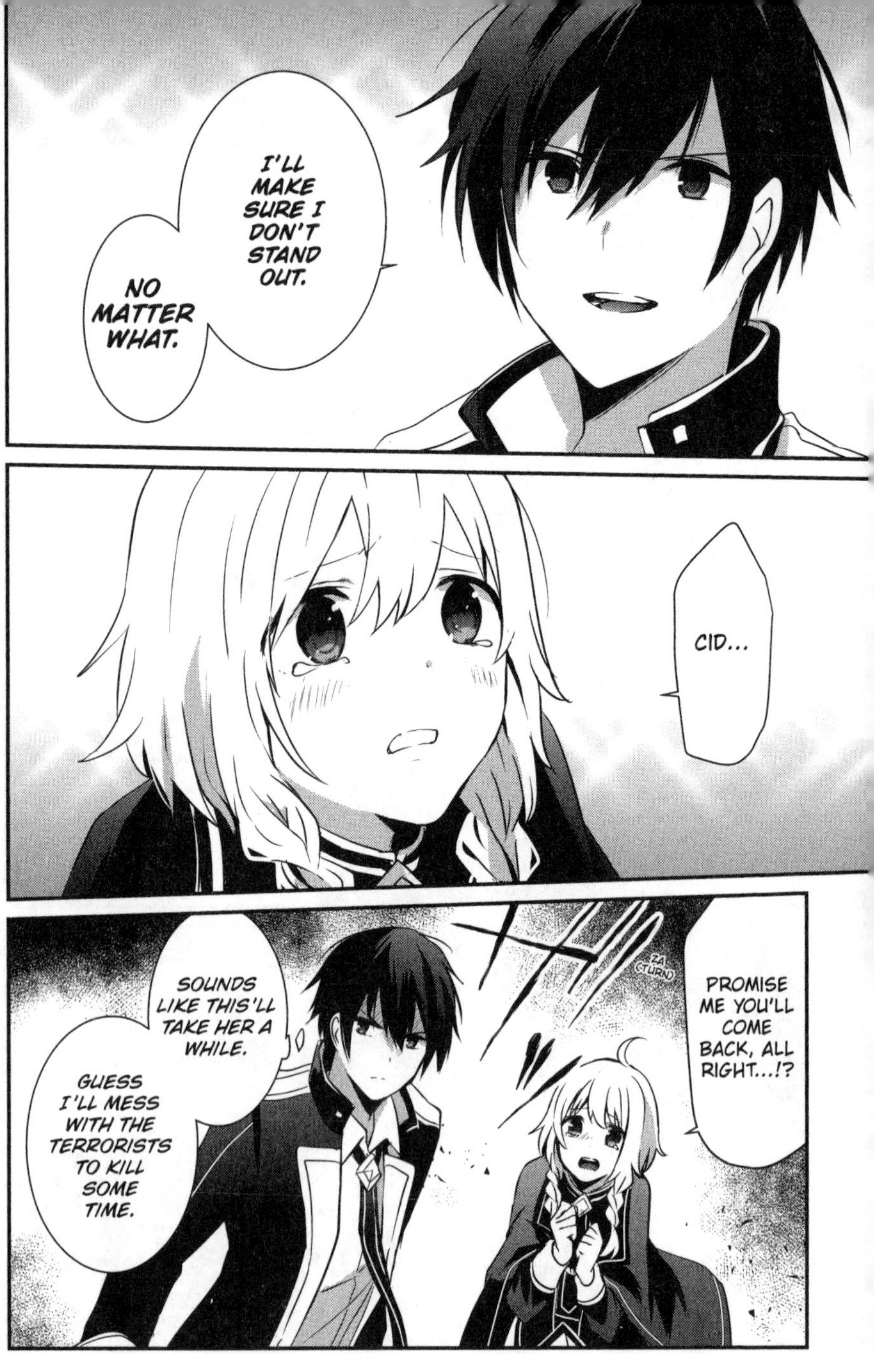
I'LL MAKE SURE I DON'T STAND OUT.
NO MATTER WHAT.
CID...
PROMISE ME YOU'LL COME BACK, ALL RIGHT...!?
ZA (TURN)
SOUNDS LIKE THIS'LL TAKE HER A WHILE.
GUESS I'LL MESS WITH THE TERRORISTS TO KILL SOME TIME.

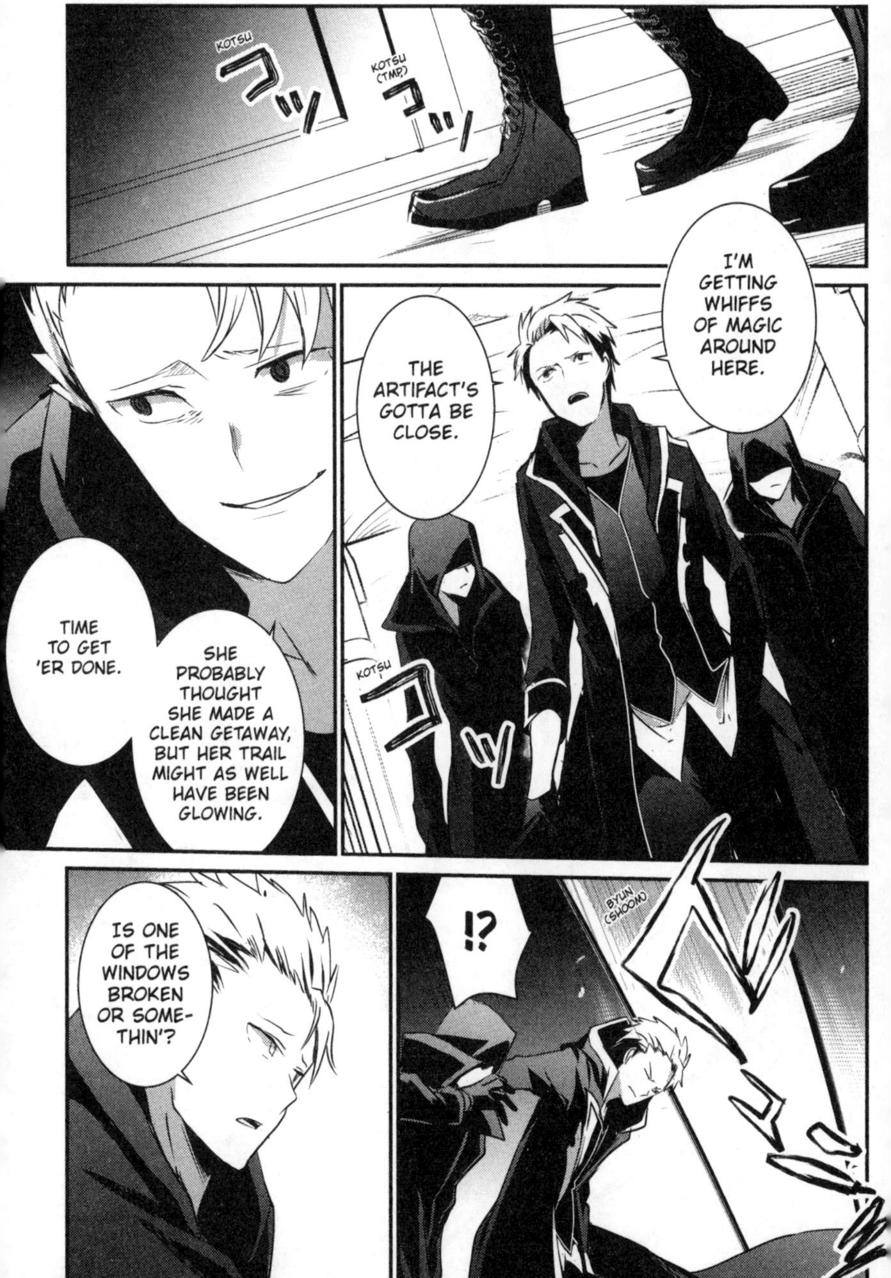
KOTSU (TMP)
KOTSU
I'M GETTING WHIFFS OF MAGIC AROUND HERE.
THE ARTIFACT'S GOTTA BE CLOSE.
KOTSU
SHE PROBABLY THOUGHT SHE MADE A CLEAN GETAWAY, BUT HER TRAIL MIGHT AS WELL HAVE BEEN GLOWING.
TIME TO GET 'ER DONE.
BYUN (SHOOM)
!?
IS ONE OF THE WINDOWS BROKEN OR SOME-THIN'?

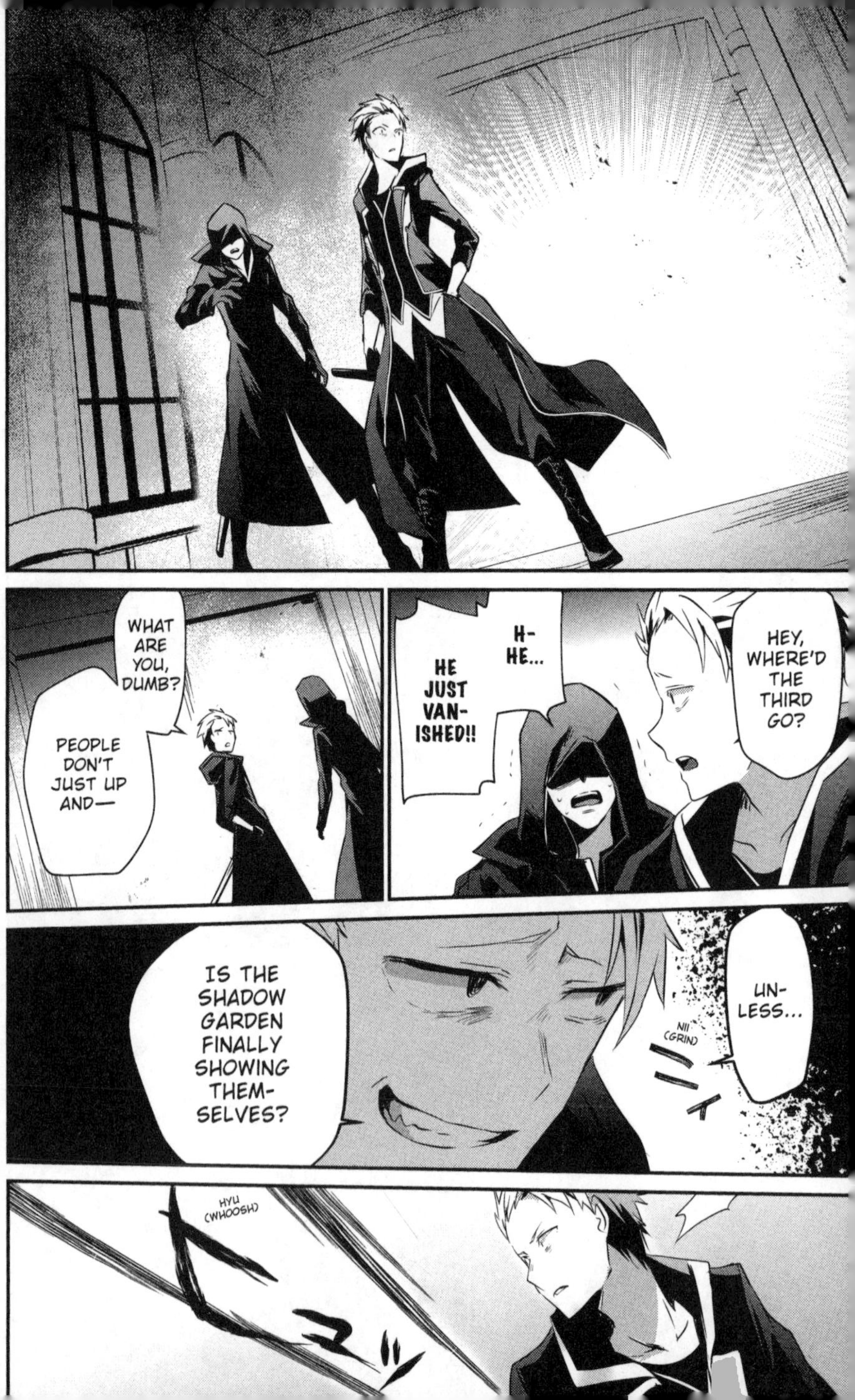
HEY, WHERE'D THE THIRD GO?
H-HE...
HE JUST VAN-ISHED!!
WHAT ARE YOU, DUMB?
PEOPLE DON'T JUST UP AND—
UN-LESS...
NII (GRIN)
IS THE SHADOW GARDEN FINALLY SHOWING THEM-SELVES?
HYU (WHOOSH)

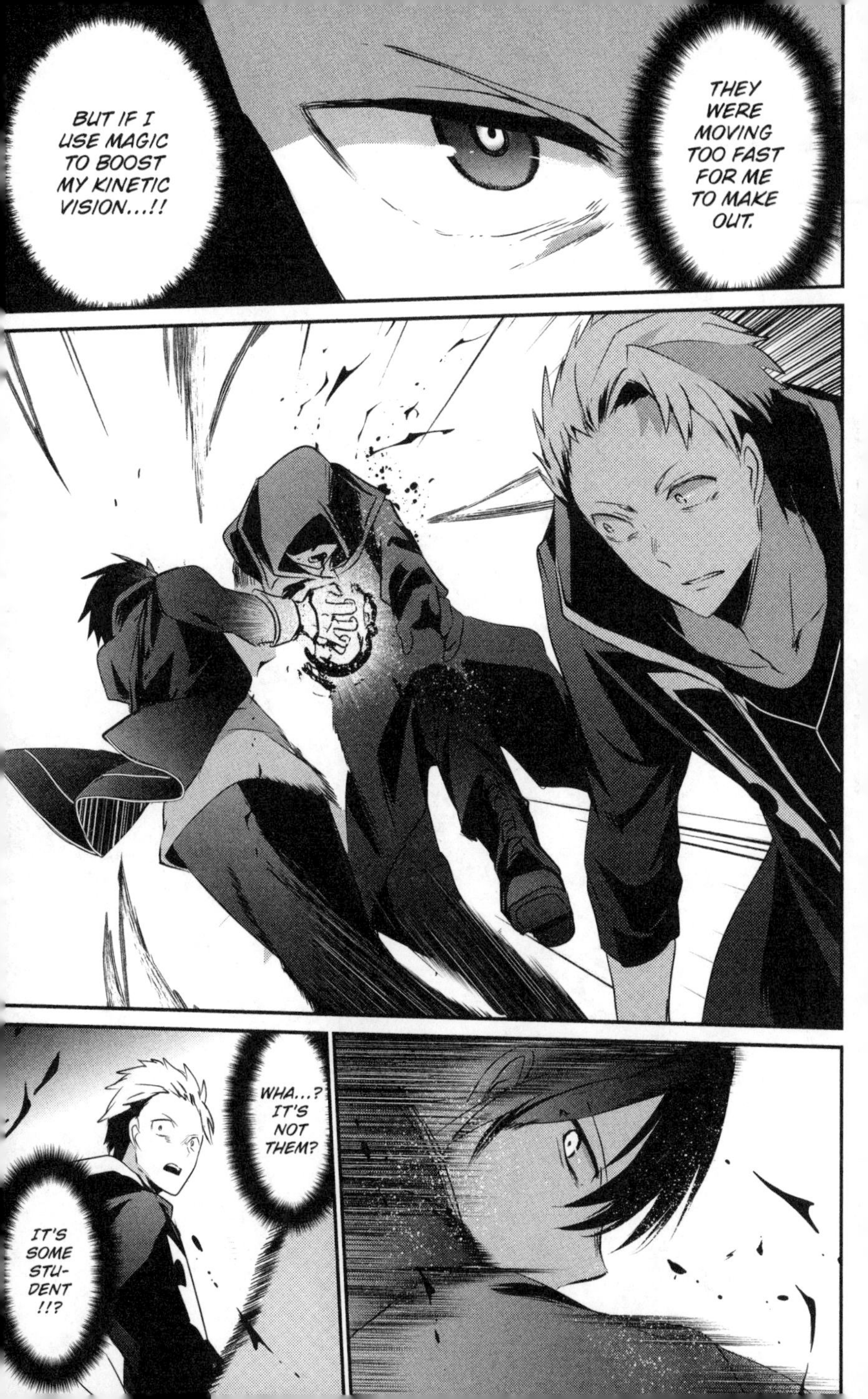
THEY WERE MOVING TOO FAST FOR ME TO MAKE OUT.
BUT IF I USE MAGIC TO BOOST MY KINETIC VISION...!!
WHA...? IT'S NOT THEM?
IT'S SOME STU-DENT!!?

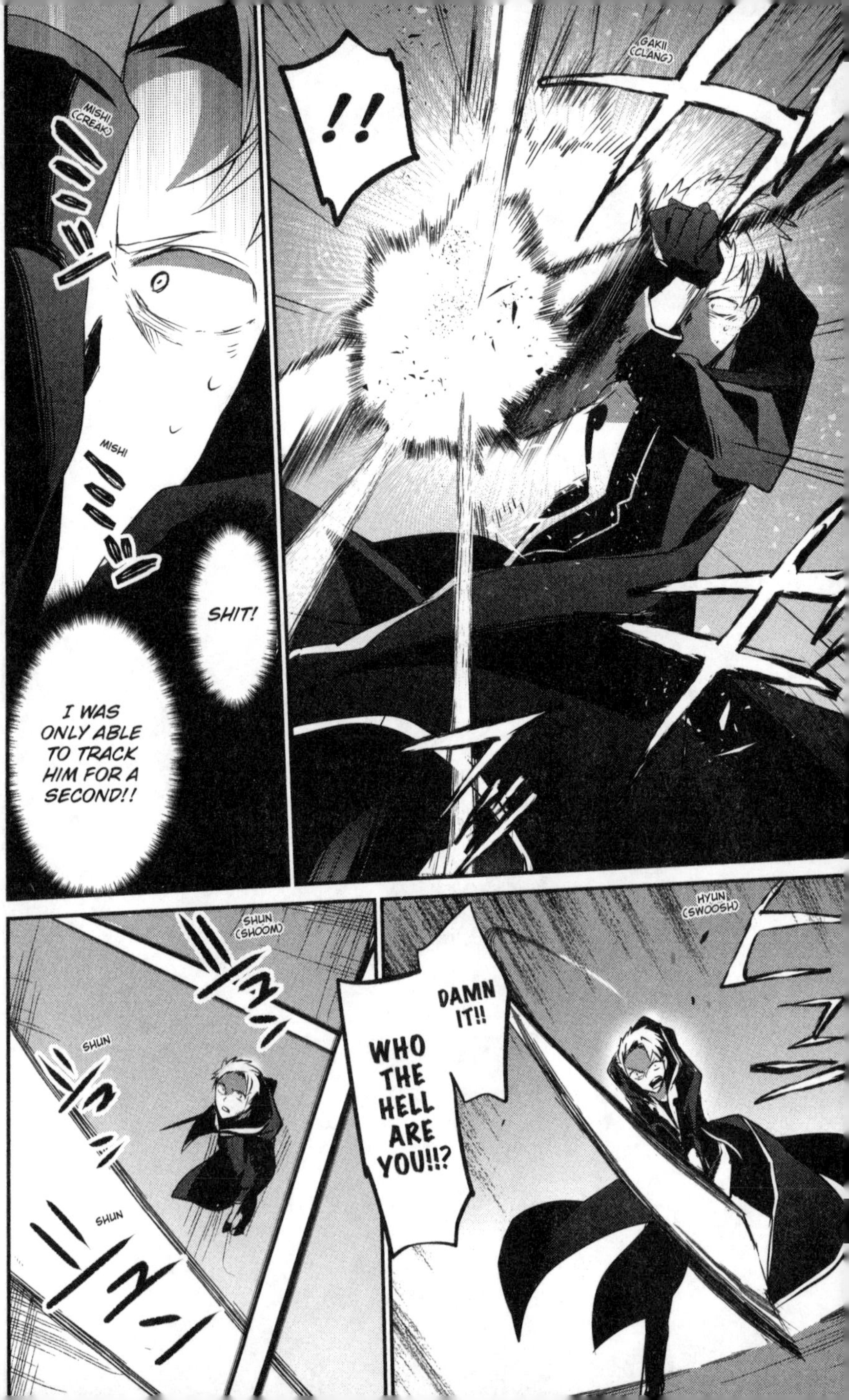
GAKII (CLANG)
!!
MISHI (CREAK)
MISHI
SHIT!
I WAS ONLY ABLE TO TRACK HIM FOR A SECOND!!
HYUN (SWOOSH)
DAMN IT!!
WHO THE HELL ARE YOU!!?
SHUN (SHOOM)
SHUN
SHUN

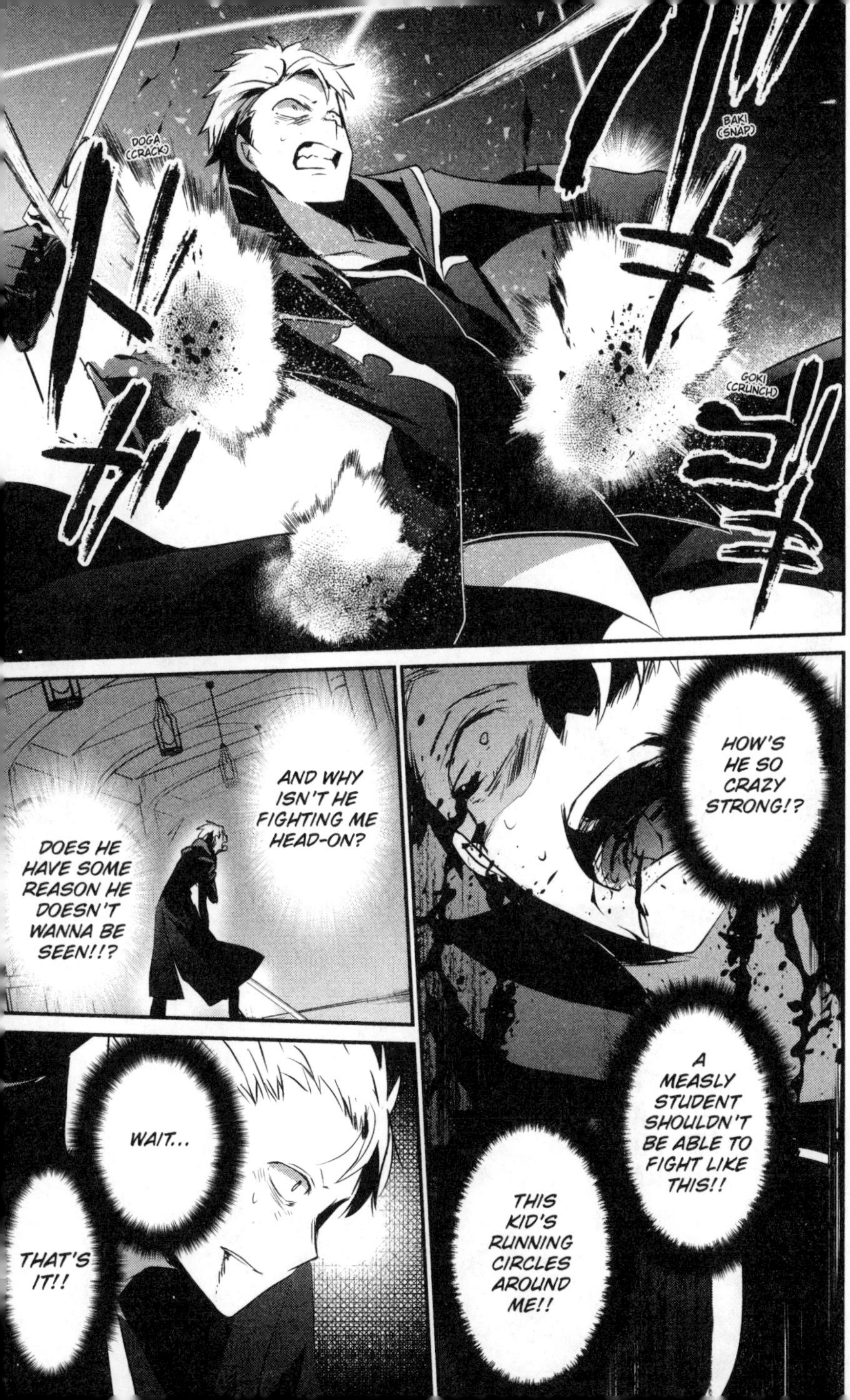
BAKI (SNAP)
GOKI (CRUNCH)
DOGA (CRACK)
HOW'S HE SO CRAZY STRONG!?
A MEASLY STUDENT SHOULDN'T BE ABLE TO FIGHT LIKE THIS!!
THIS KID'S RUNNING CIRCLES AROUND ME!!
AND WHY ISN'T HE FIGHTING ME HEAD-ON?
DOES HE HAVE SOME REASON HE DOESN'T WANNA BE SEEN!!?
WAIT...
THAT'S IT!!

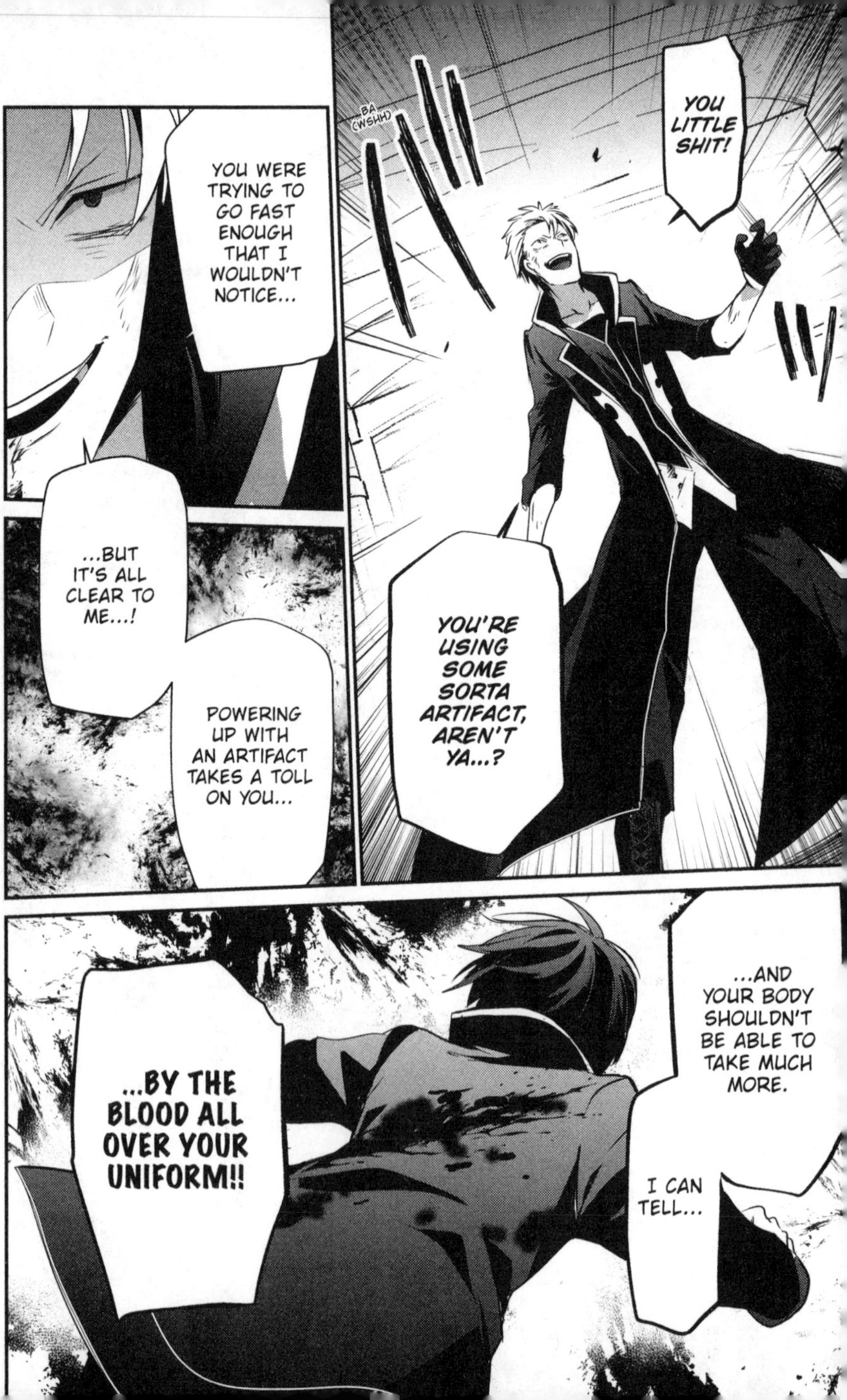
YOU LITTLE SHIT!
BA (WSHH)
YOU'RE USING SOME SORTA ARTIFACT, AREN'T YA...?
YOU WERE TRYING TO GO FAST ENOUGH THAT I WOULDN'T NOTICE...
...BUT IT'S ALL CLEAR TO ME...!
POWERING UP WITH AN ARTIFACT TAKES A TOLL ON YOU...
...AND YOUR BODY SHOULDN'T BE ABLE TO TAKE MUCH MORE.
I CAN TELL...
...BY THE BLOOD ALL OVER YOUR UNIFORM!!

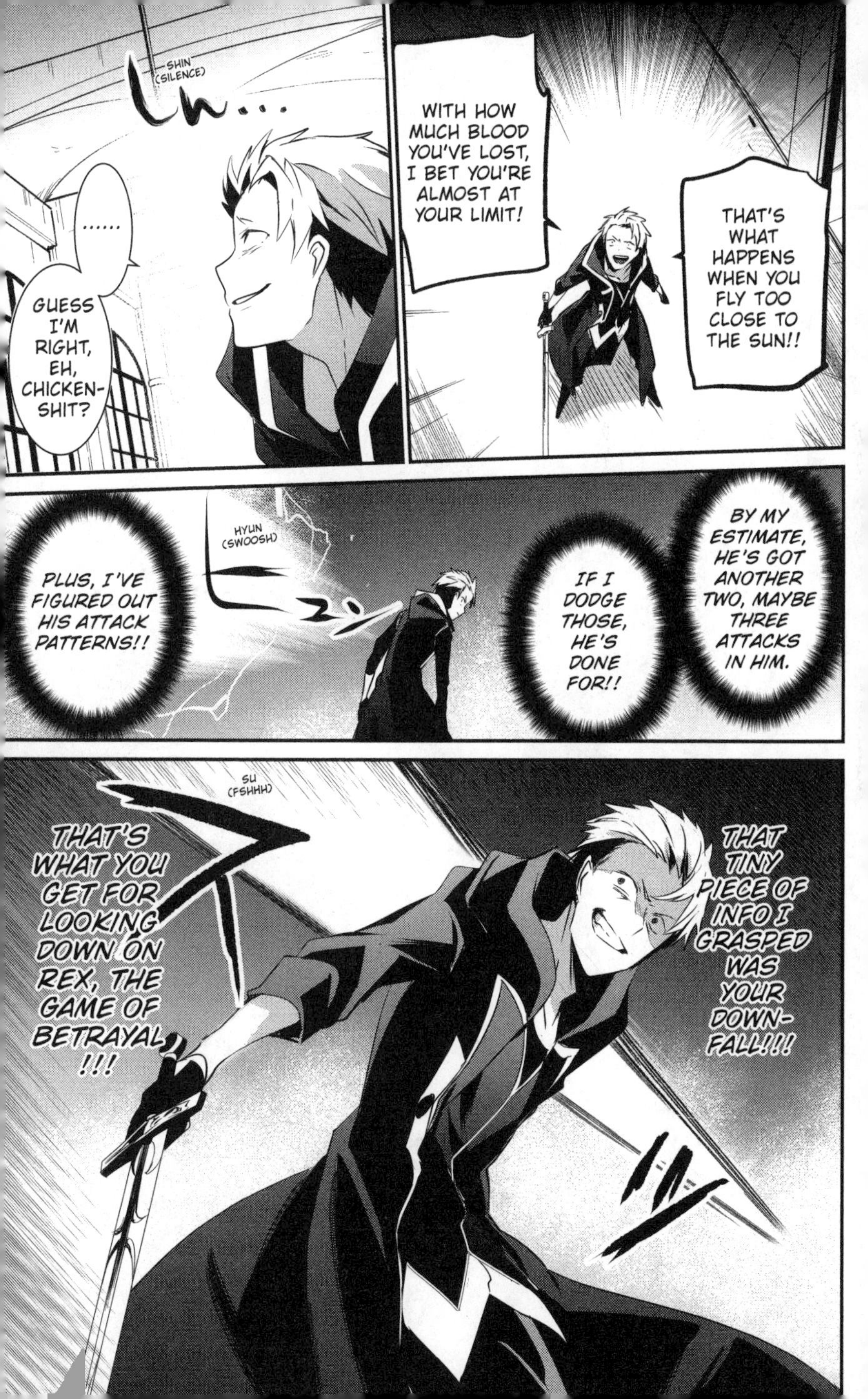
THAT'S WHAT HAPPENS WHEN YOU FLY TOO CLOSE TO THE SUN!!
WITH HOW MUCH BLOOD YOU'VE LOST, I BET YOU'RE ALMOST AT YOUR LIMIT!
SHIN (SILENCE)
......
GUESS I'M RIGHT, EH, CHICKEN-SHIT?
BY MY ESTIMATE, HE'S GOT ANOTHER TWO, MAYBE THREE ATTACKS IN HIM.
IF I DODGE THOSE, HE'S DONE FOR!!
HYUN (SWOOSH)
PLUS, I'VE FIGURED OUT HIS ATTACK PATTERNS!!
SU (FSHHH)
THAT TINY PIECE OF INFO I GRASPED WAS YOUR DOWN-FALL!!!
THAT'S WHAT YOU GET FOR LOOKING DOWN ON REX, THE GAME OF BETRAYAL!!!

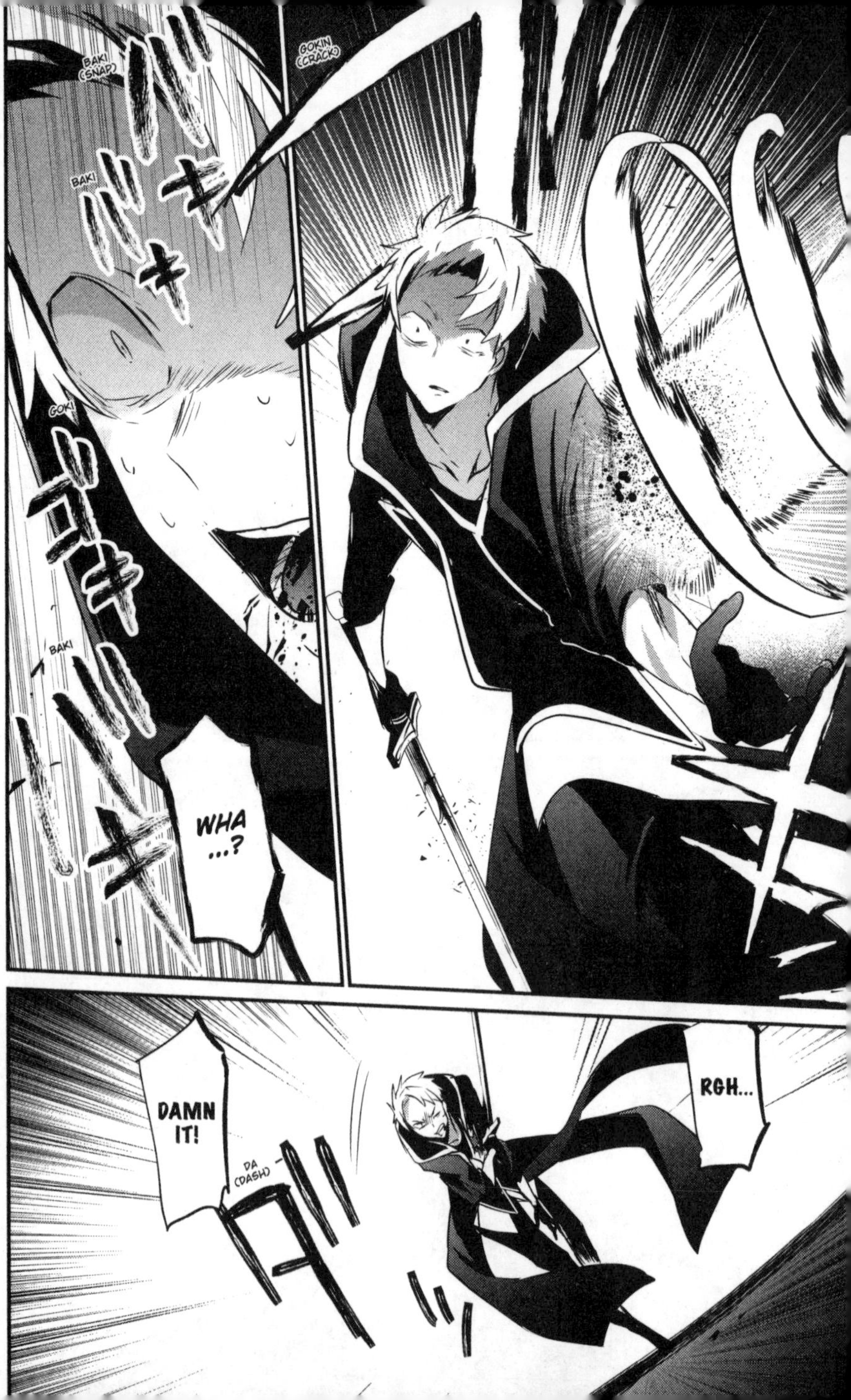
GOKIN (CRACK)
BAKI (SNAP)
BAKI
GOKI
BAKI
WHA ...?
RGH...
DAMN IT!
DA (DASH)

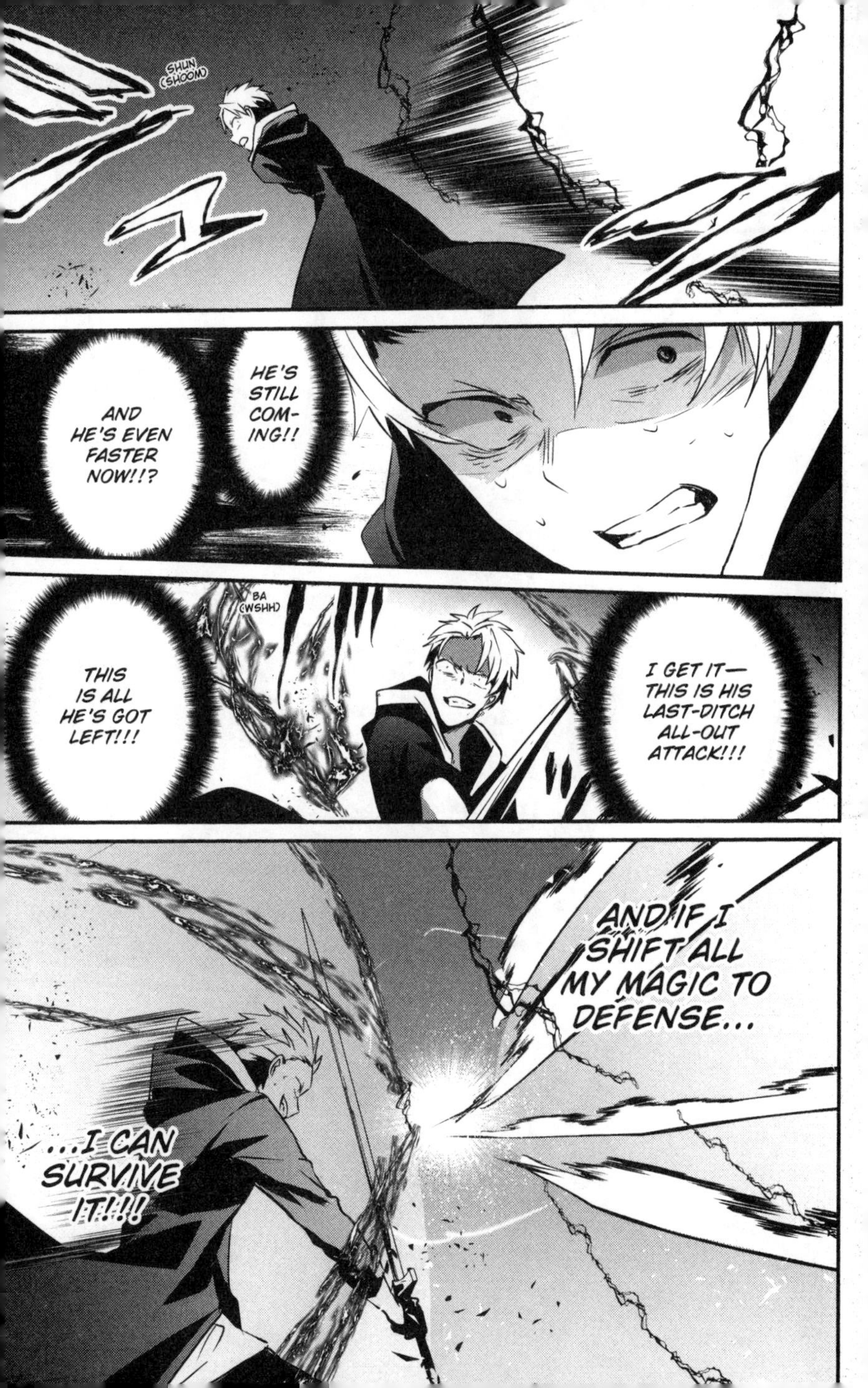
SHUN (SHOOM)
HE'S STILL COMING!!
AND HE'S EVEN FASTER NOW!!?
I GET IT—THIS IS HIS LAST-DITCH ALL-OUT ATTACK!!!
BA (WSHH)
THIS IS ALL HE'S GOT LEFT!!!
AND IF I SHIFT ALL MY MAGIC TO DEFENSE...
...I CAN SURVIVE IT!!!

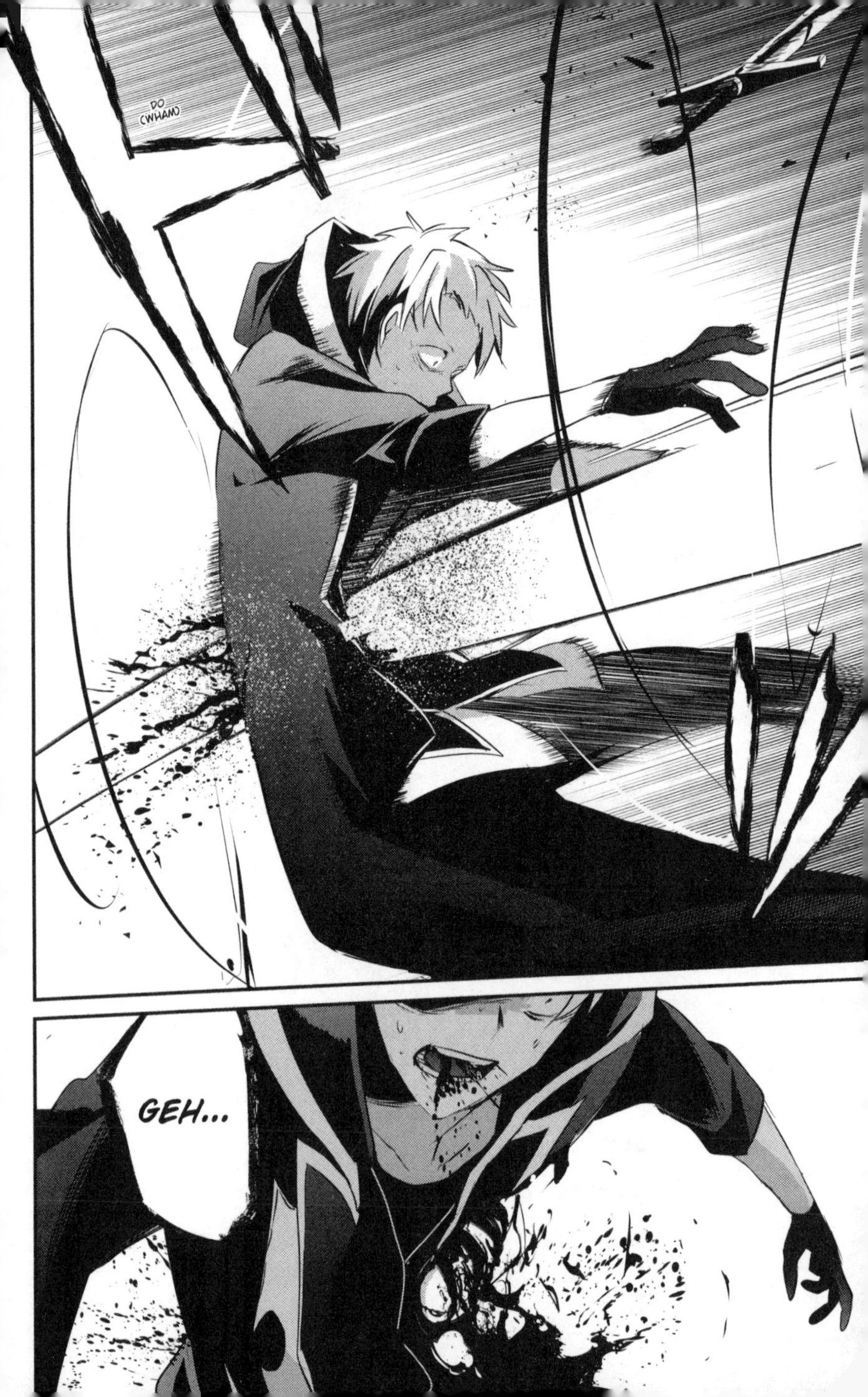
DO
(WHAM)
GEH...

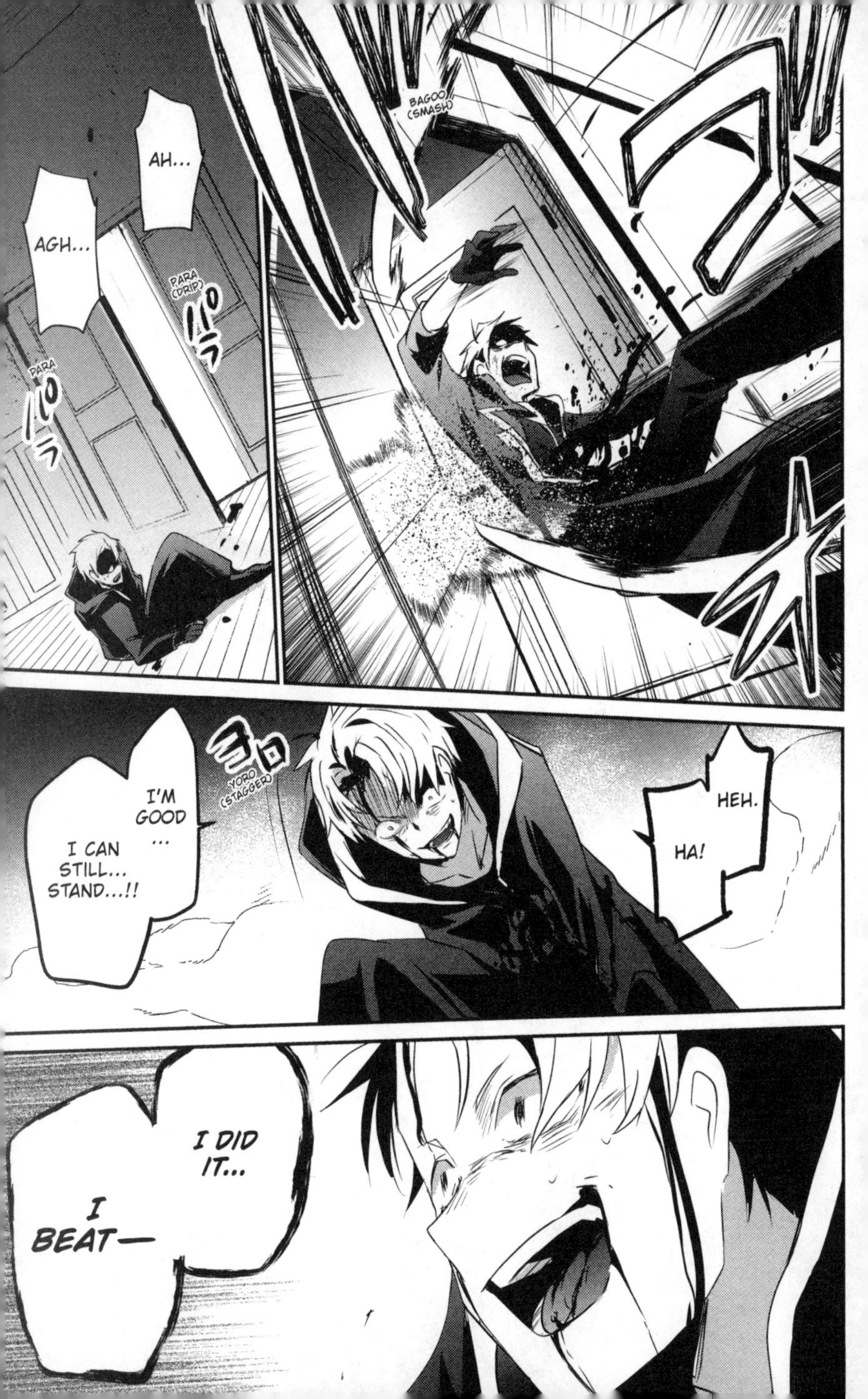
BAGOO (SMASH)
AH...
AGH...
PARA (DRIP)
パラ
PARA
パラ
HEH.
HA!
ヨロ
YORO (STAGGER)
I'M GOOD...
I CAN STILL... STAND...!!
I DID IT...
I BEAT—

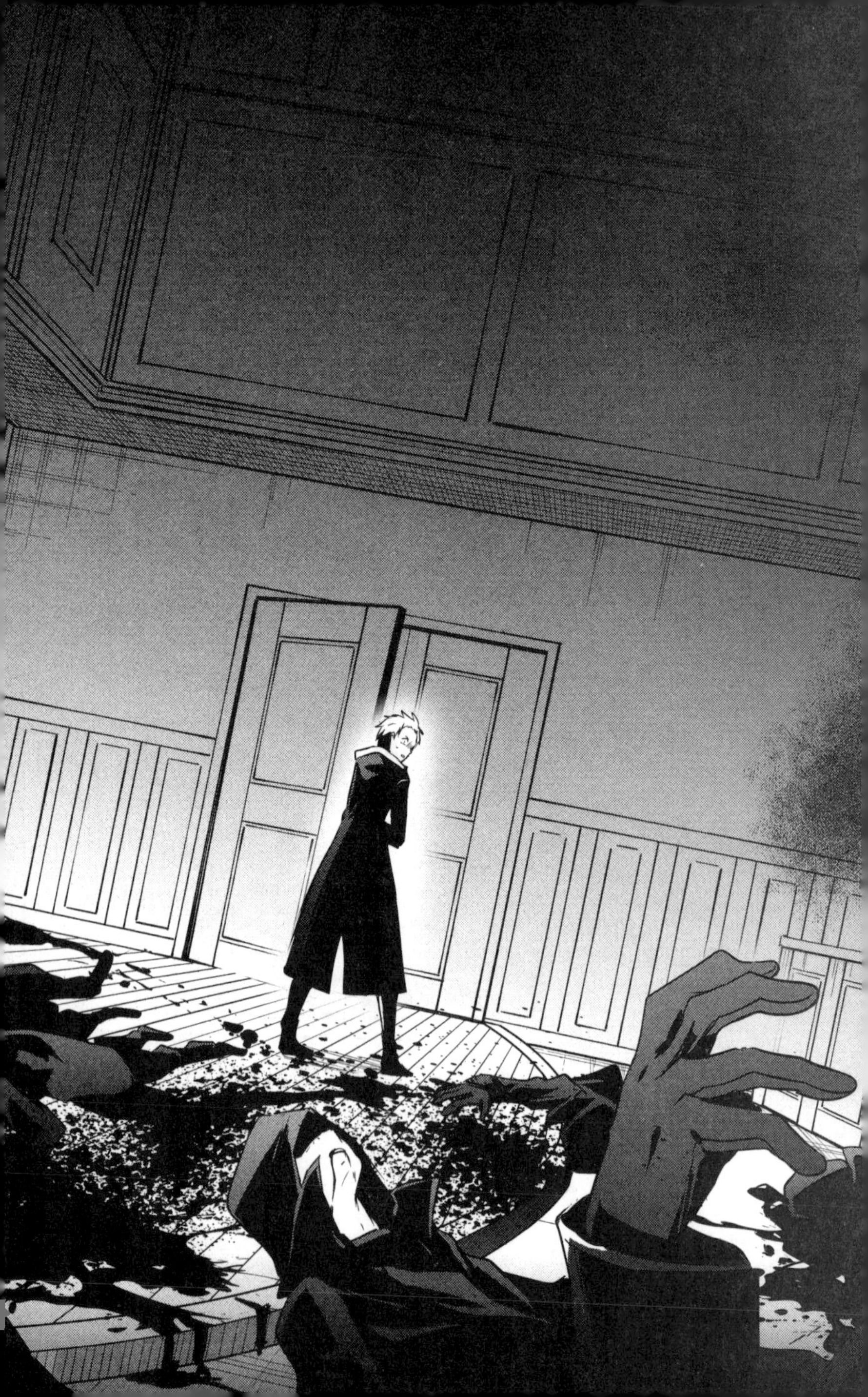

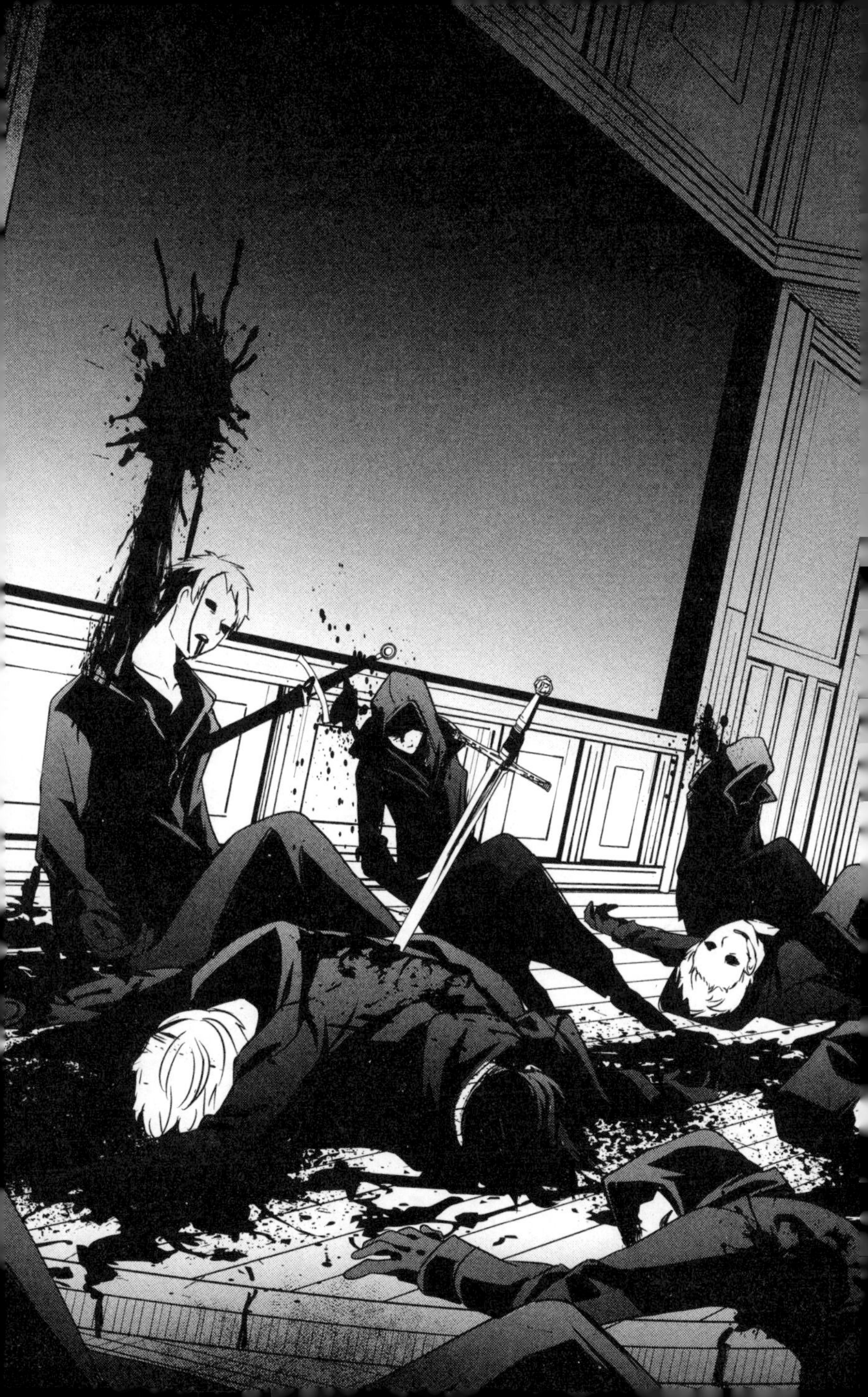

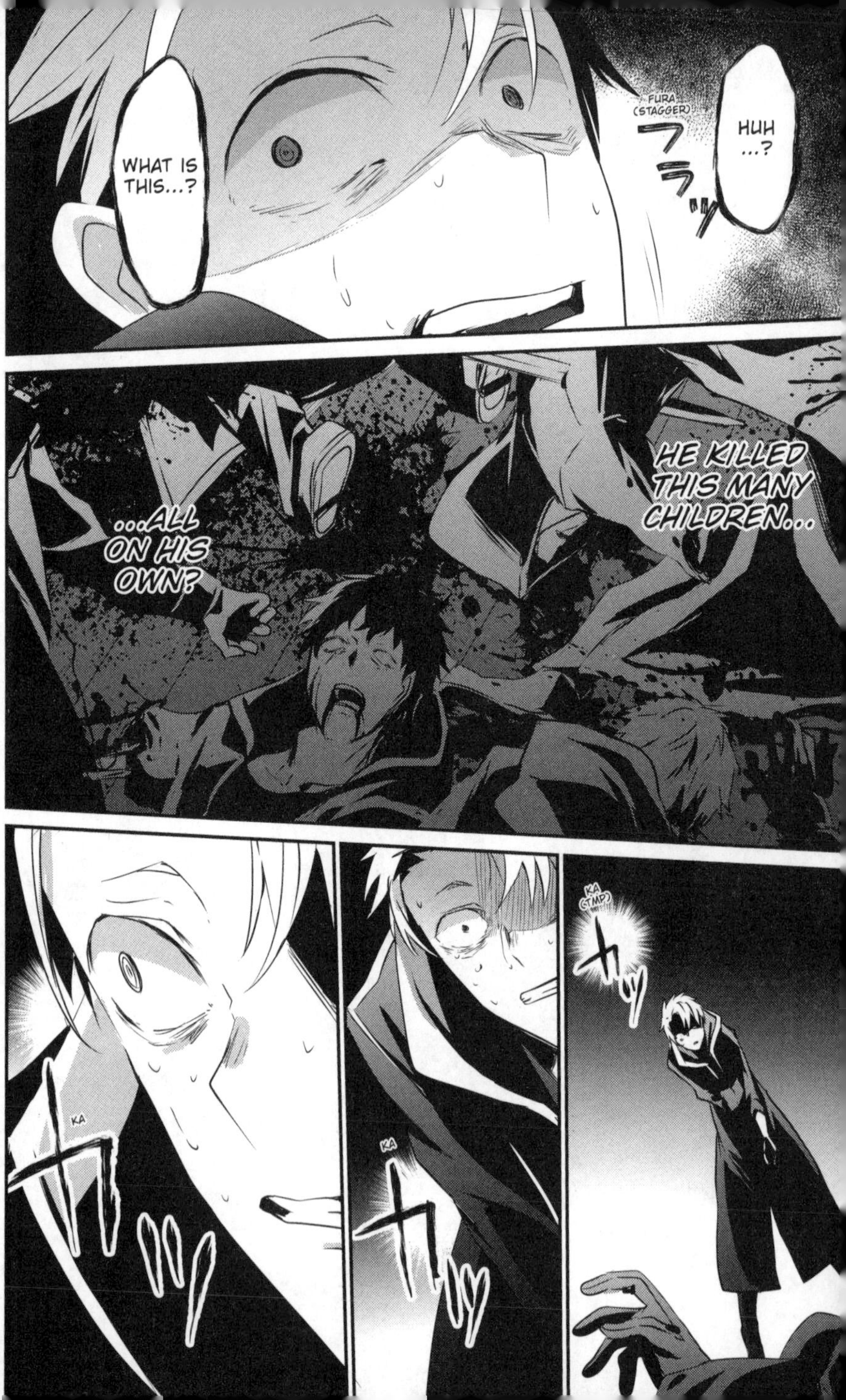
FURA (STAGGER)
HUH ...?
WHAT IS THIS...?
HE KILLED THIS MANY CHILDREN...
...ALL ON HIS OWN?
KA (STMP)
KA
KA

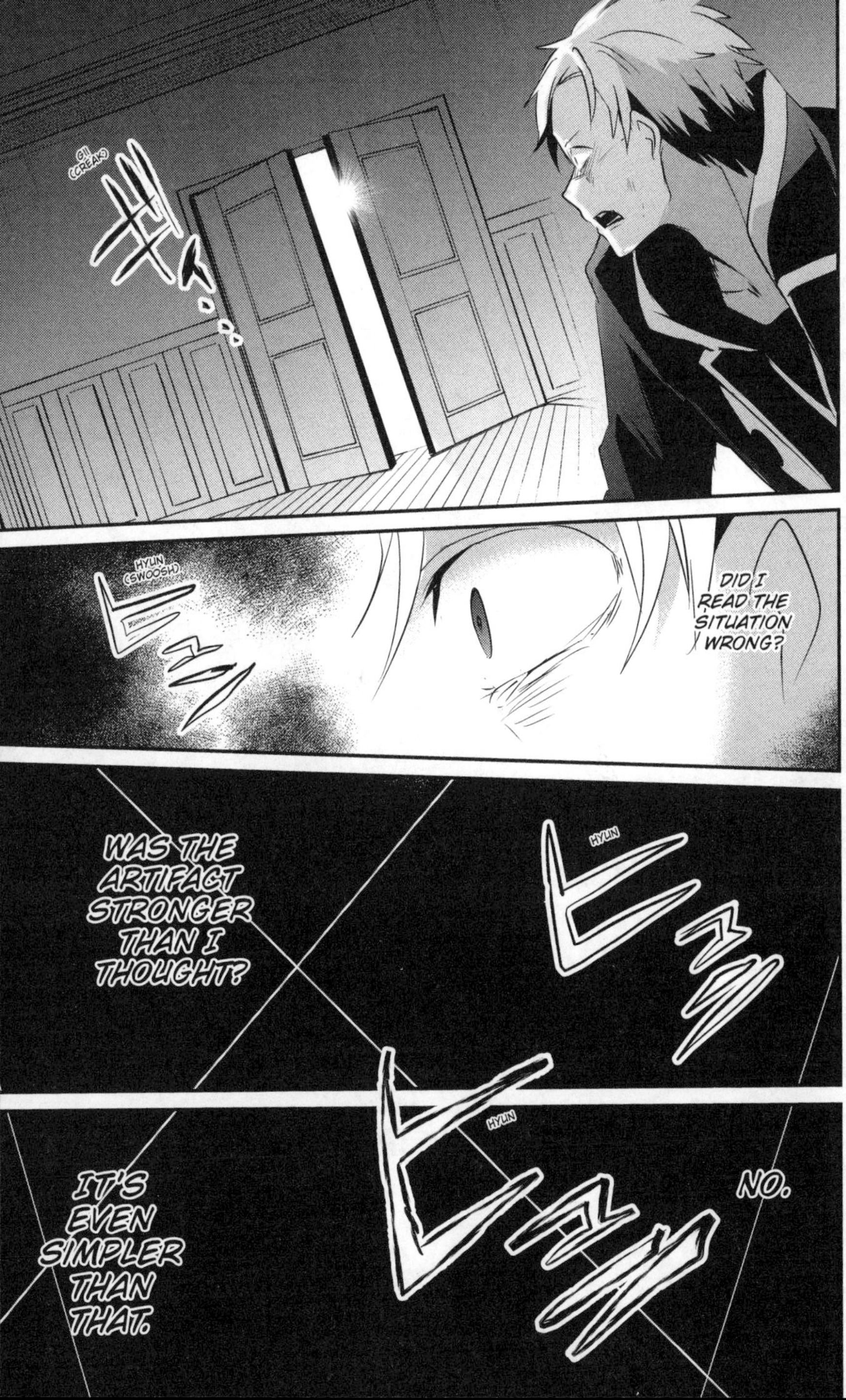
GII (CREAK)
DID I READ THE SITUATION WRONG?
HYUN (SWOOSH)
HYUN
WAS THE ARTIFACT STRONGER THAN I THOUGHT?
NO.
HYUN
IT'S EVEN SIMPLER THAN THAT.

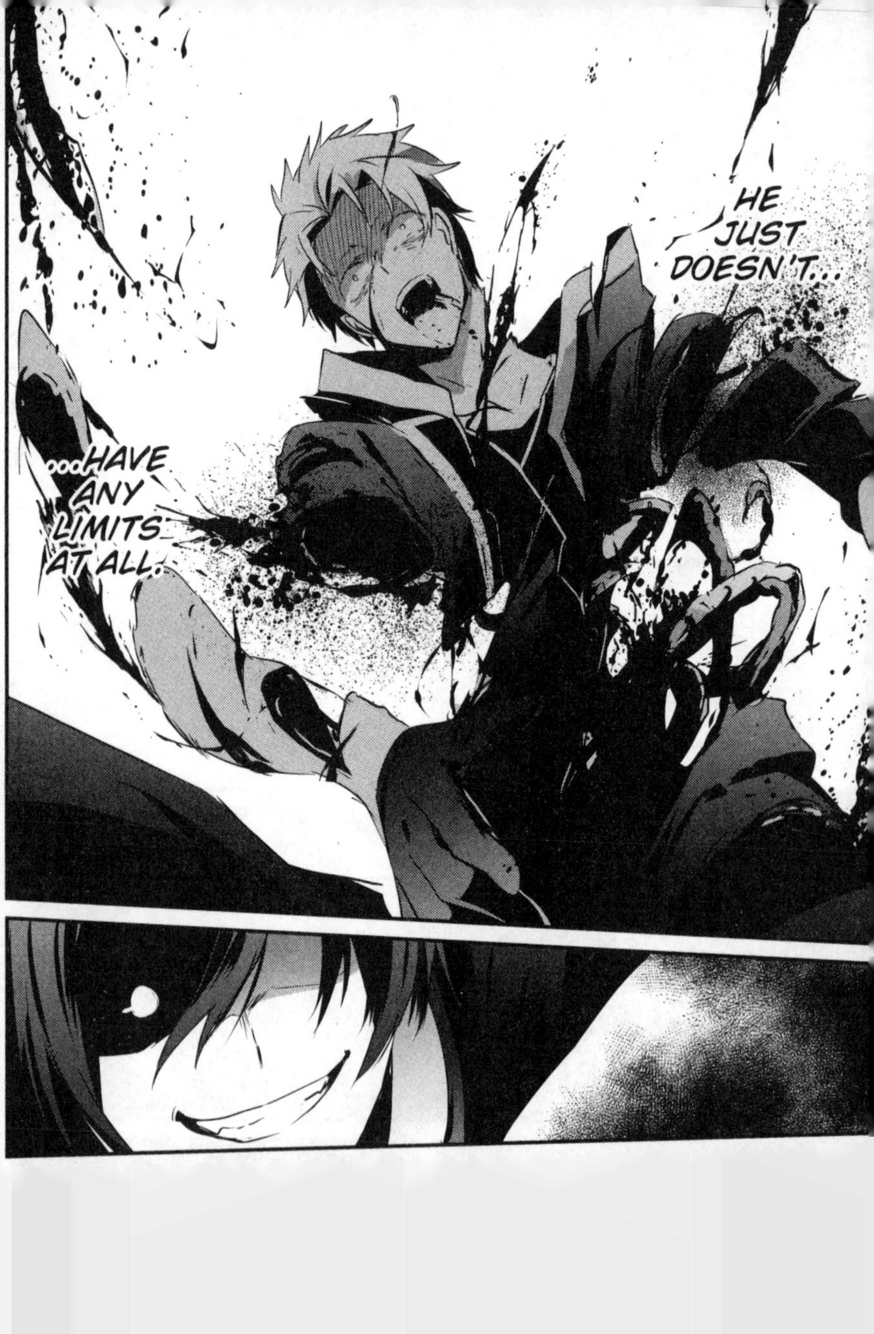
HE JUST DOESN'T...
...HAVE ANY LIMITS AT ALL.

THE Eminence IN Shadow

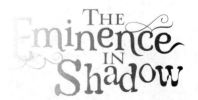

Episode.12

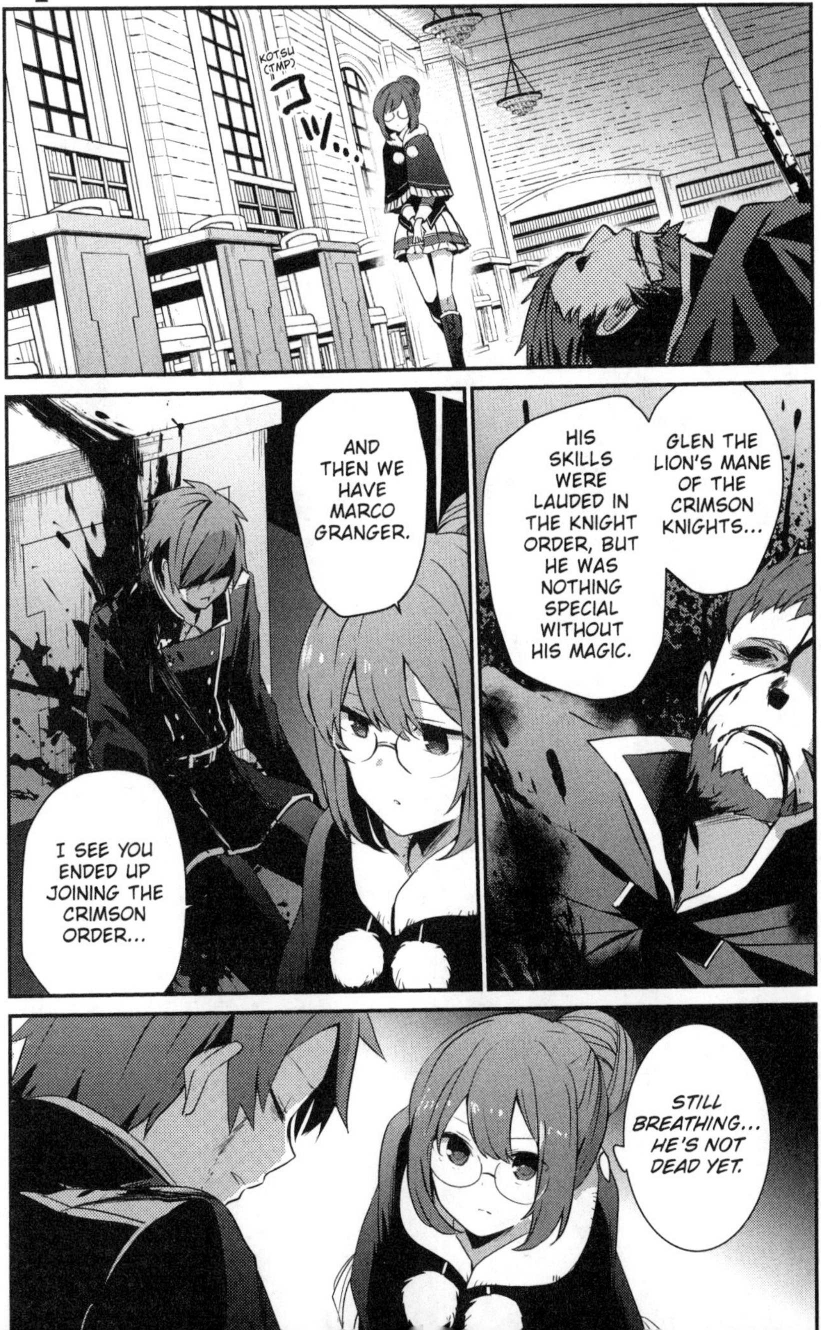
KOTSU (TMP)
コツ…
GLEN THE LION'S MANE OF THE CRIMSON KNIGHTS...
HIS SKILLS WERE LAUDED IN THE KNIGHT ORDER, BUT HE WAS NOTHING SPECIAL WITHOUT HIS MAGIC.
AND THEN WE HAVE MARCO GRANGER.
I SEE YOU ENDED UP JOINING THE CRIMSON ORDER...
STILL BREATHING... HE'S NOT DEAD YET.

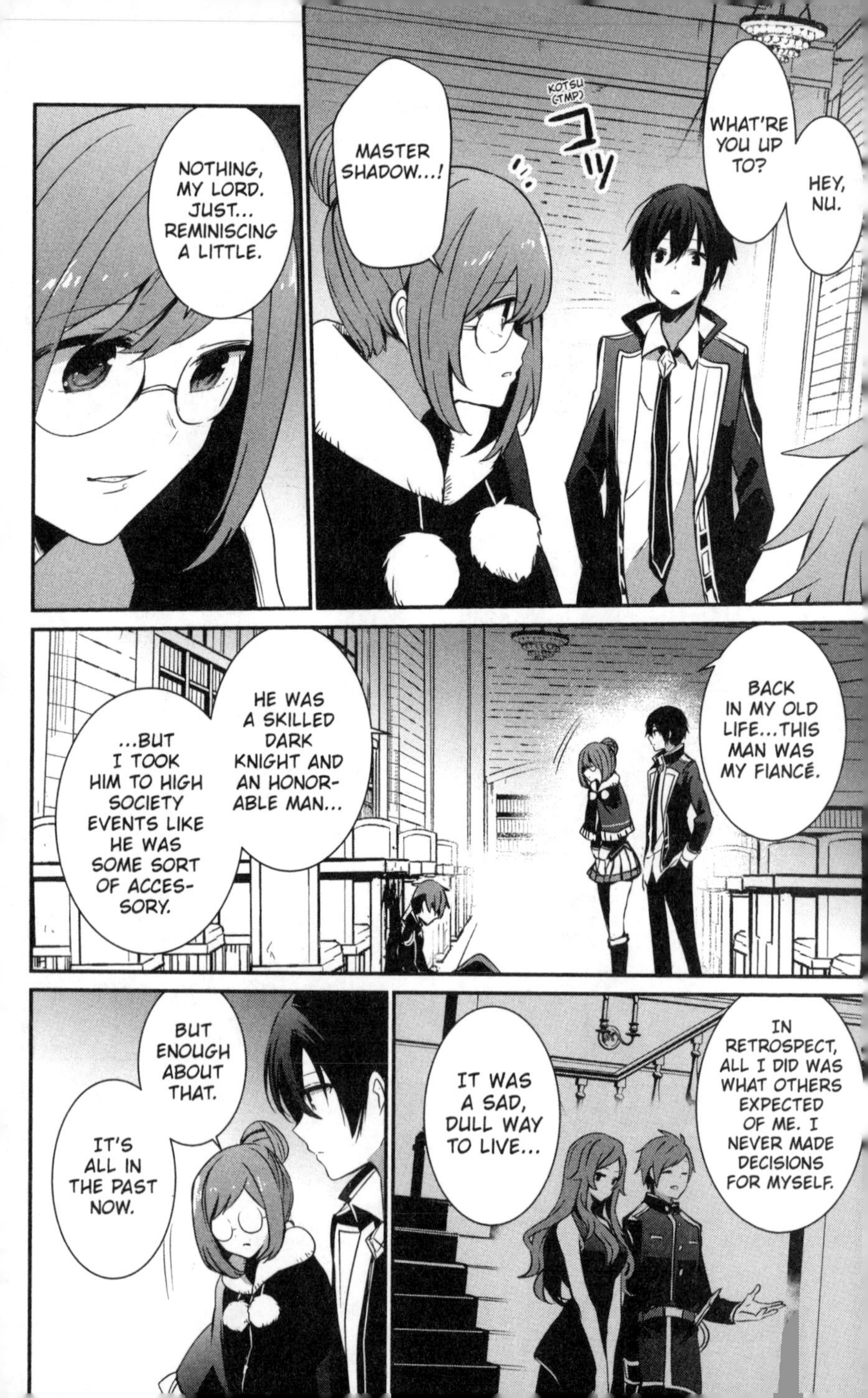
HEY, NU.
WHAT'RE YOU UP TO?
KOTSU (TMP)
MASTER SHADOW...!
NOTHING, MY LORD. JUST... REMINISCING A LITTLE.
BACK IN MY OLD LIFE...THIS MAN WAS MY FIANCÉ.
HE WAS A SKILLED DARK KNIGHT AND AN HONORABLE MAN...
...BUT I TOOK HIM TO HIGH SOCIETY EVENTS LIKE HE WAS SOME SORT OF ACCESSORY.
IN RETROSPECT, ALL I DID WAS WHAT OTHERS EXPECTED OF ME. I NEVER MADE DECISIONS FOR MYSELF.
IT WAS A SAD, DULL WAY TO LIVE...
BUT ENOUGH ABOUT THAT.
IT'S ALL IN THE PAST NOW.

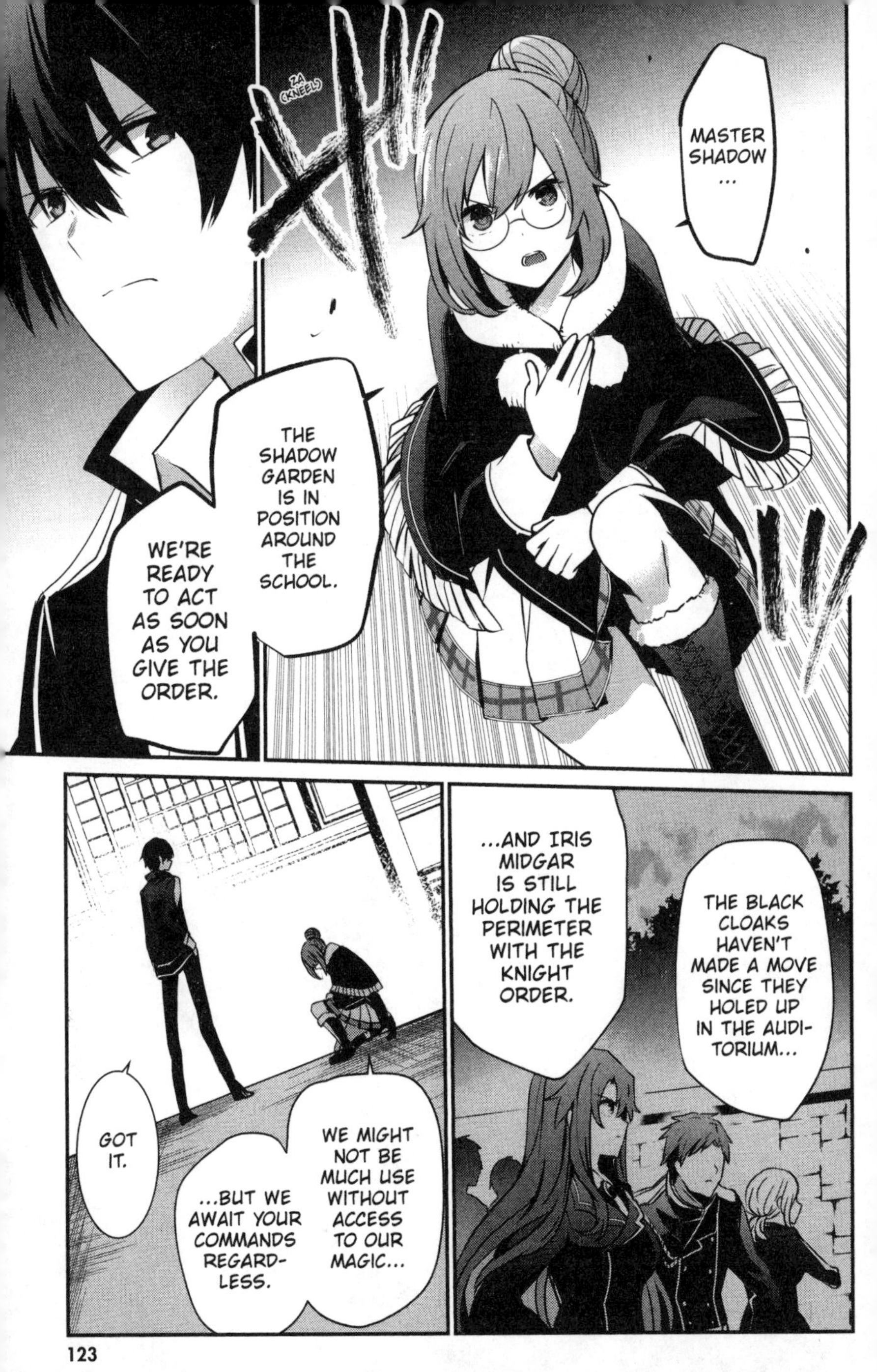
ZA (KNEEL)
MASTER SHADOW...
THE SHADOW GARDEN IS IN POSITION AROUND THE SCHOOL.
WE'RE READY TO ACT AS SOON AS YOU GIVE THE ORDER.
THE BLACK CLOAKS HAVEN'T MADE A MOVE SINCE THEY HOLED UP IN THE AUDI-TORIUM...
...AND IRIS MIDGAR IS STILL HOLDING THE PERIMETER WITH THE KNIGHT ORDER.
WE MIGHT NOT BE MUCH USE WITHOUT ACCESS TO OUR MAGIC...
...BUT WE AWAIT YOUR COMMANDS REGARD-LESS.
GOT IT.

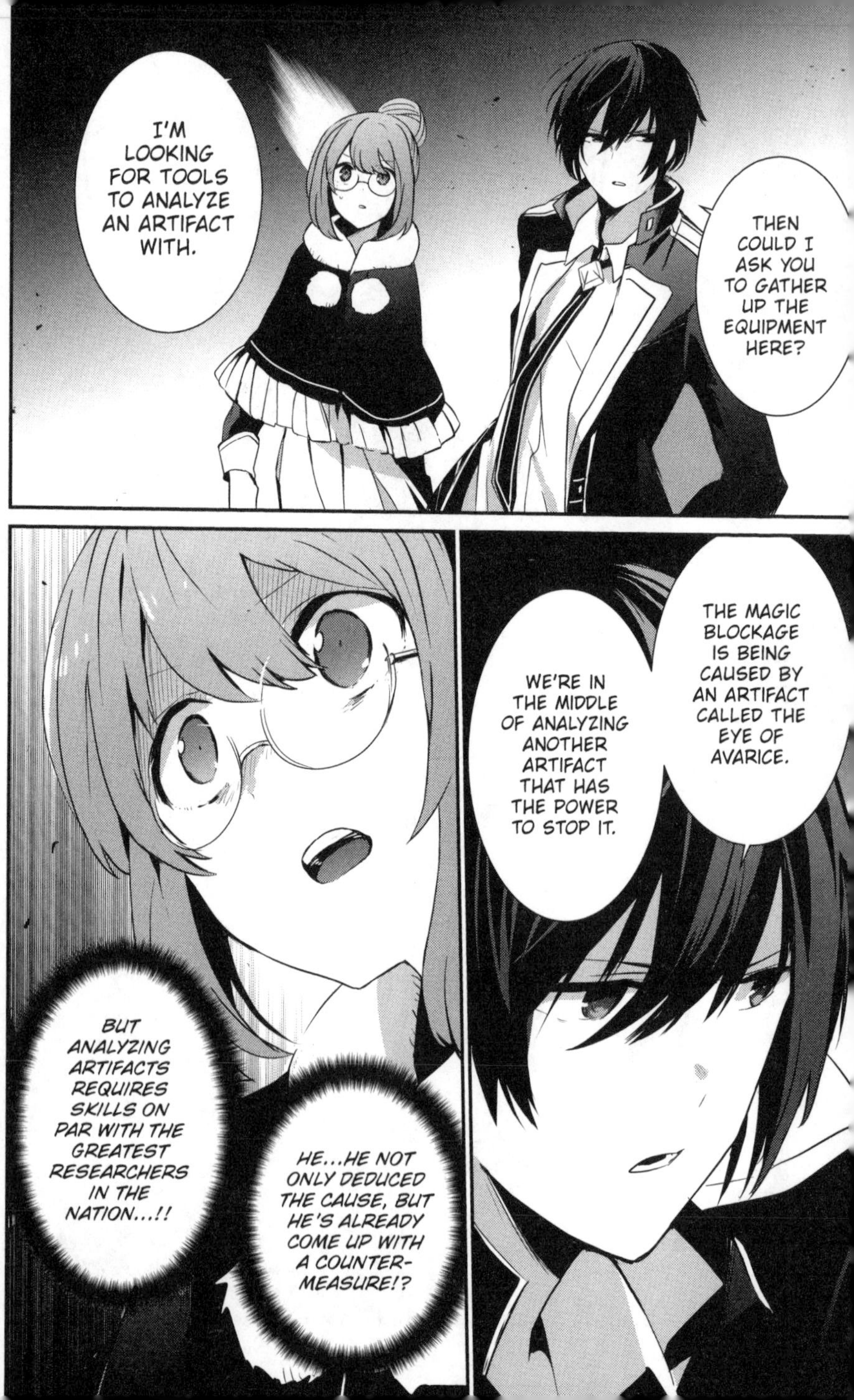
I'M LOOKING FOR TOOLS TO ANALYZE AN ARTIFACT WITH.
THEN COULD I ASK YOU TO GATHER UP THE EQUIPMENT HERE?
THE MAGIC BLOCKAGE IS BEING CAUSED BY AN ARTIFACT CALLED THE EYE OF AVARICE.
WE'RE IN THE MIDDLE OF ANALYZING ANOTHER ARTIFACT THAT HAS THE POWER TO STOP IT.
HE...HE NOT ONLY DEDUCED THE CAUSE, BUT HE'S ALREADY COME UP WITH A COUNTER-MEASURE!?
BUT ANALYZING ARTIFACTS REQUIRES SKILLS ON PAR WITH THE GREATEST RESEARCHERS IN THE NATION...!!

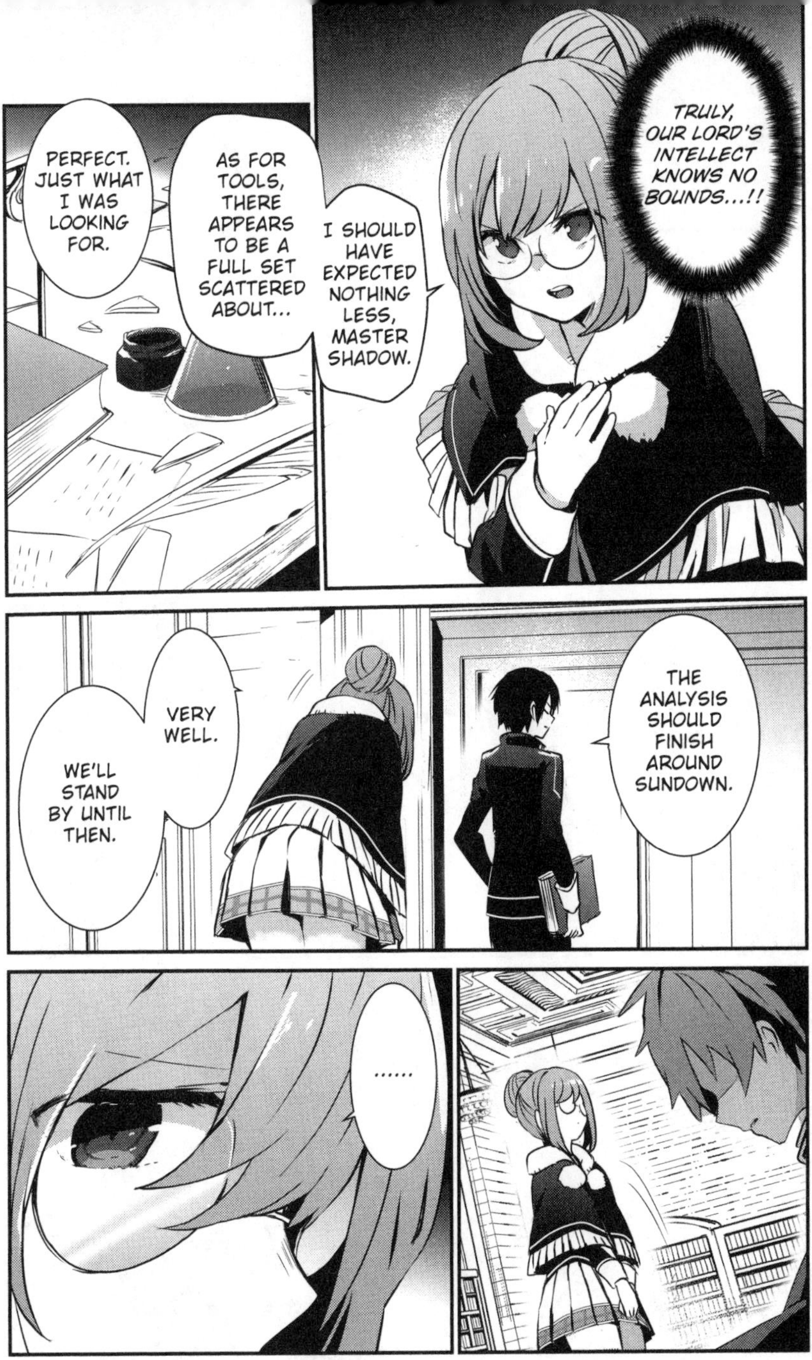
TRULY, OUR LORD'S INTELLECT KNOWS NO BOUNDS...!!
I SHOULD HAVE EXPECTED NOTHING LESS, MASTER SHADOW.
AS FOR TOOLS, THERE APPEARS TO BE A FULL SET SCATTERED ABOUT...
PERFECT. JUST WHAT I WAS LOOKING FOR.
THE ANALYSIS SHOULD FINISH AROUND SUNDOWN.
VERY WELL.
WE'LL STAND BY UNTIL THEN.
......

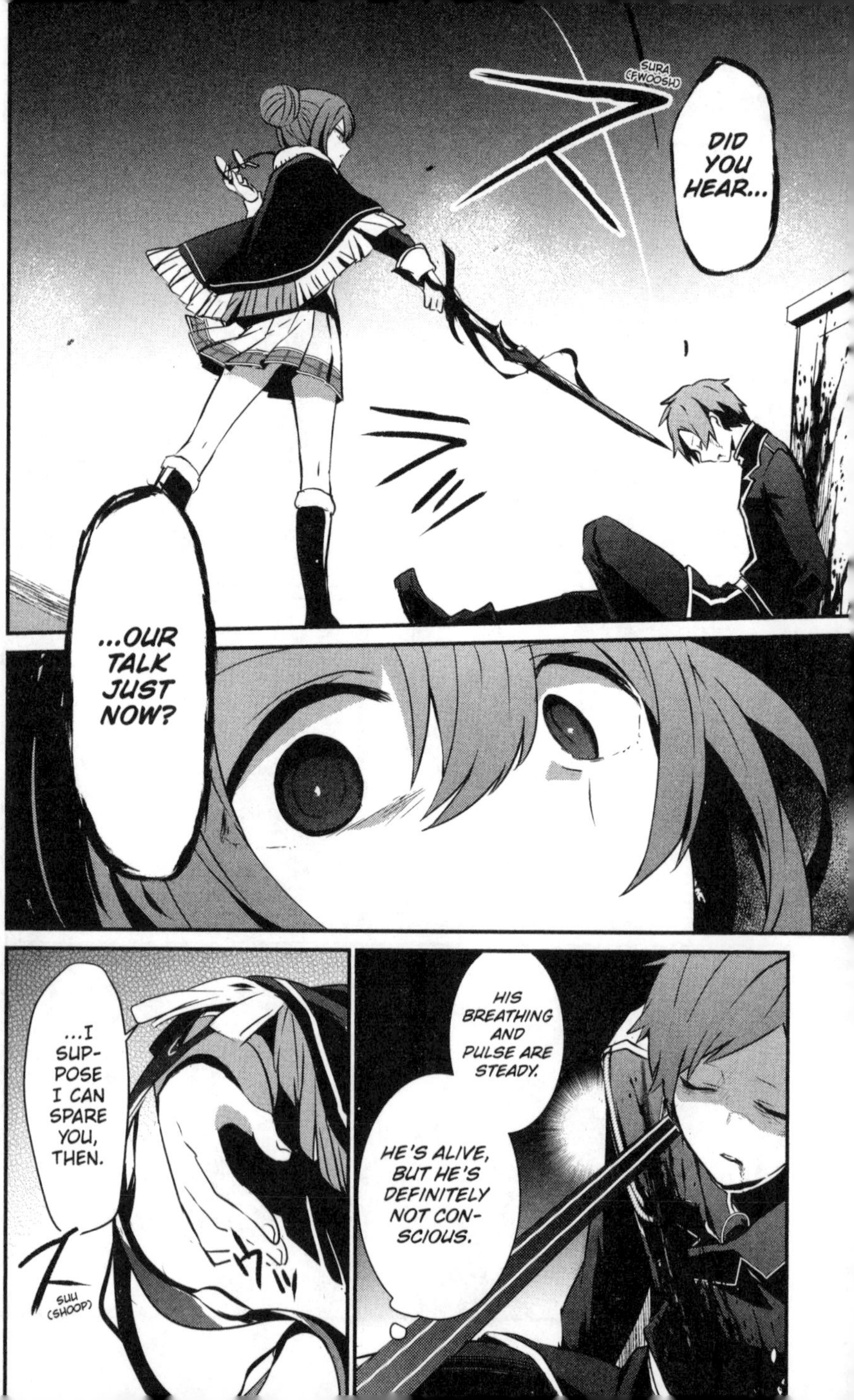
SURA (FWOOSH)
DID YOU HEAR...
...OUR TALK JUST NOW?
HIS BREATHING AND PULSE ARE STEADY.
HE'S ALIVE, BUT HE'S DEFINITELY NOT CONSCIOUS.
...I SUPPOSE I CAN SPARE YOU, THEN.
SUU (SHOOP)

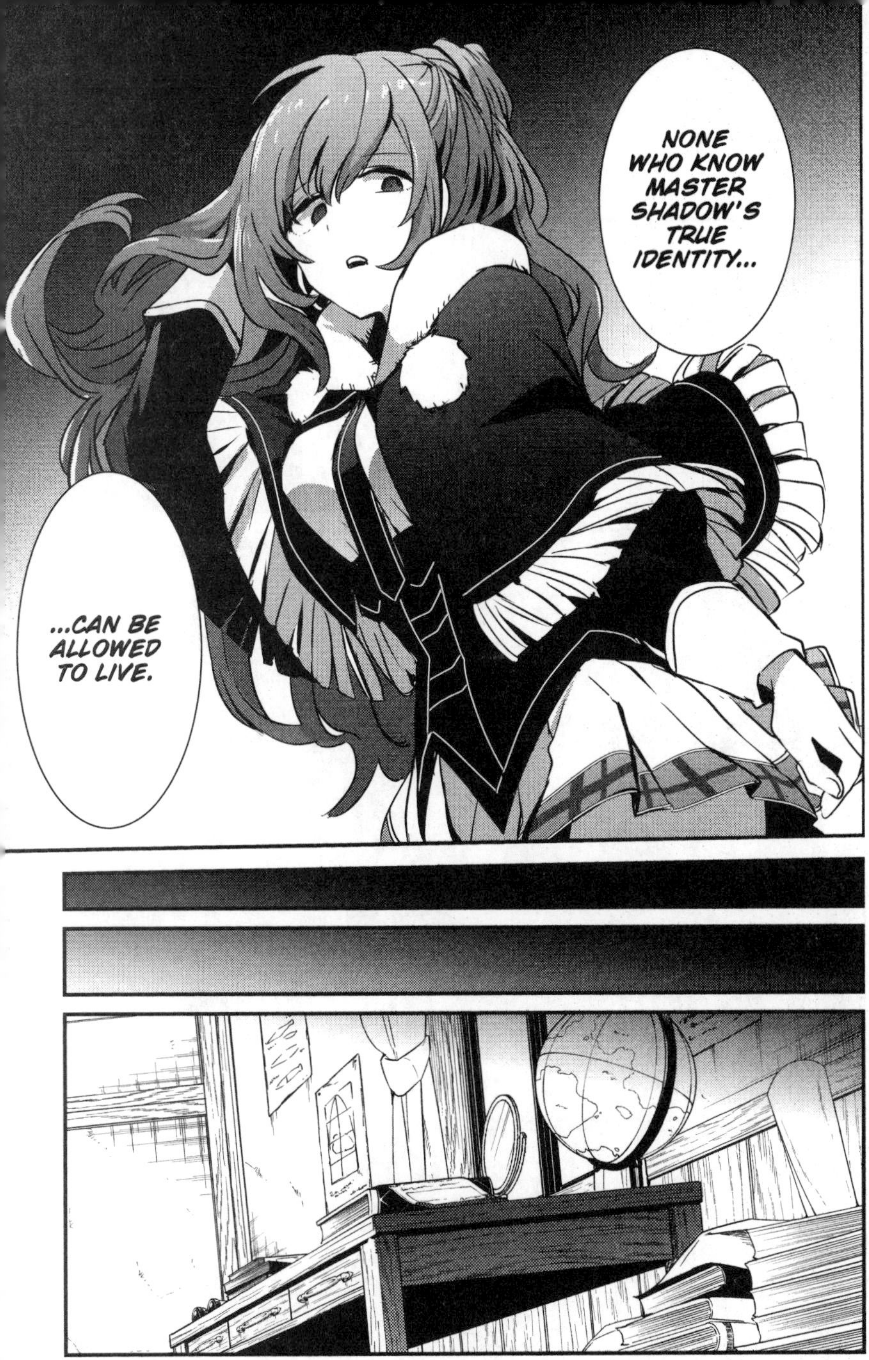
NONE WHO KNOW MASTER SHADOW'S TRUE IDENTITY...
...CAN BE ALLOWED TO LIVE.

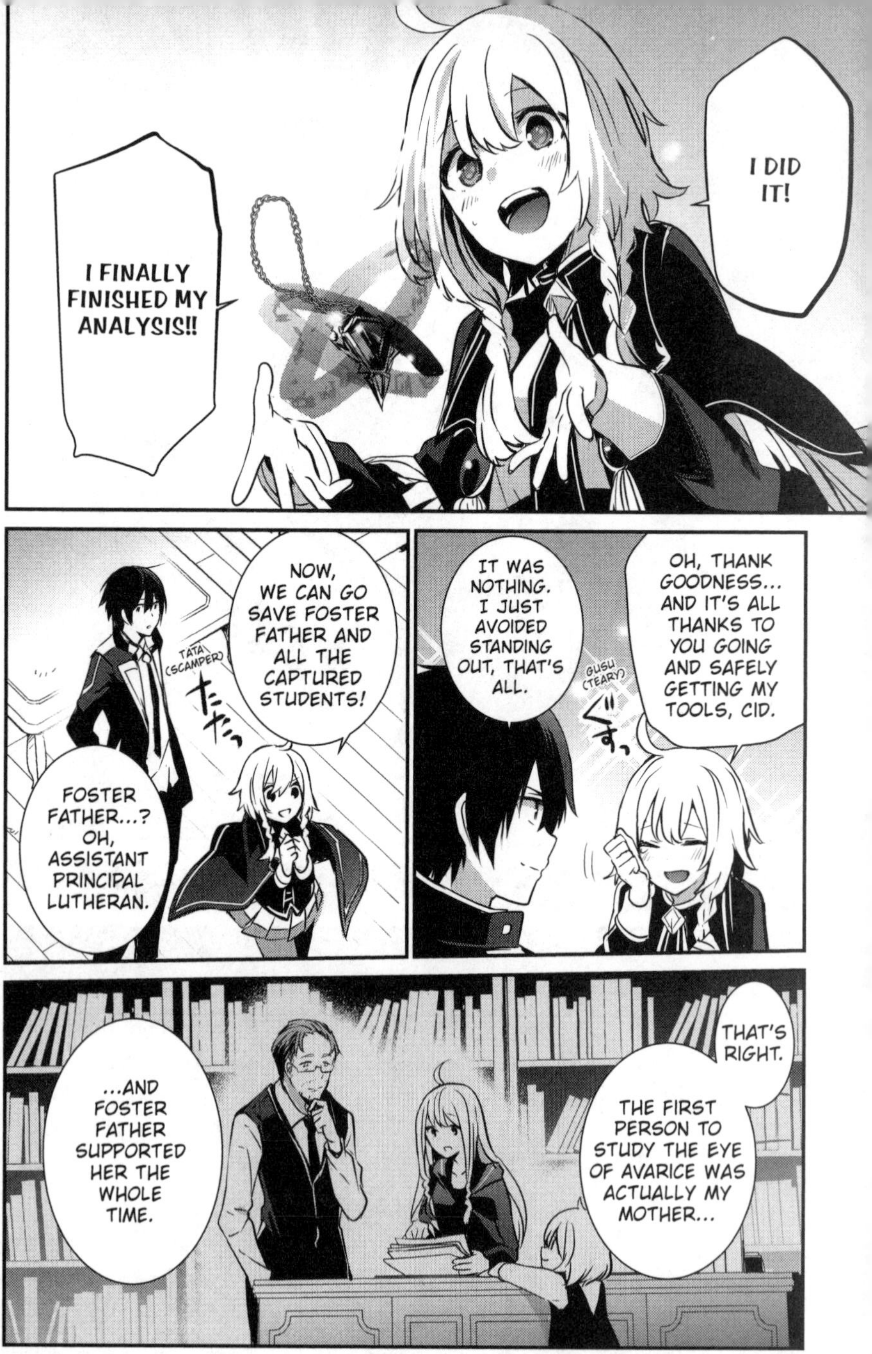
I DID IT!
I FINALLY FINISHED MY ANALYSIS!!
OH, THANK GOODNESS... AND IT'S ALL THANKS TO YOU GOING AND SAFELY GETTING MY TOOLS, CID.
GUSU (TEARY)
IT WAS NOTHING. I JUST AVOIDED STANDING OUT, THAT'S ALL.
NOW, WE CAN GO SAVE FOSTER FATHER AND ALL THE CAPTURED STUDENTS!
TATA (SCAMPER)
FOSTER FATHER...? OH, ASSISTANT PRINCIPAL LUTHERAN.
THAT'S RIGHT.
THE FIRST PERSON TO STUDY THE EYE OF AVARICE WAS ACTUALLY MY MOTHER...
...AND FOSTER FATHER SUPPORTED HER THE WHOLE TIME.

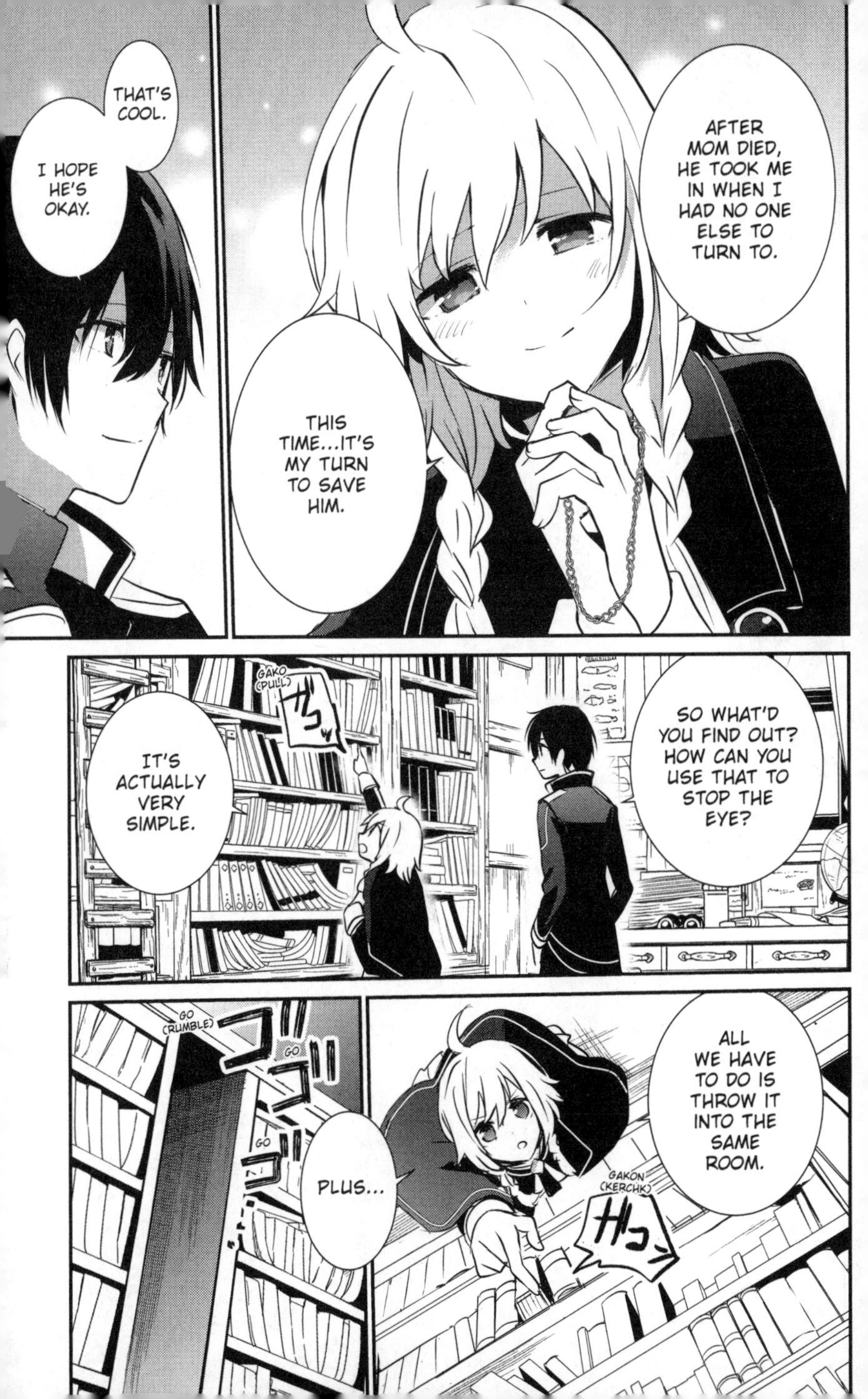
AFTER MOM DIED, HE TOOK ME IN WHEN I HAD NO ONE ELSE TO TURN TO.
THIS TIME...IT'S MY TURN TO SAVE HIM.
THAT'S COOL.
I HOPE HE'S OKAY.
SO WHAT'D YOU FIND OUT? HOW CAN YOU USE THAT TO STOP THE EYE?
GAKO (PULL)
IT'S ACTUALLY VERY SIMPLE.
ALL WE HAVE TO DO IS THROW IT INTO THE SAME ROOM.
GAKON (KERCHK)
PLUS...
GO (RUMBLE)
GO
GO

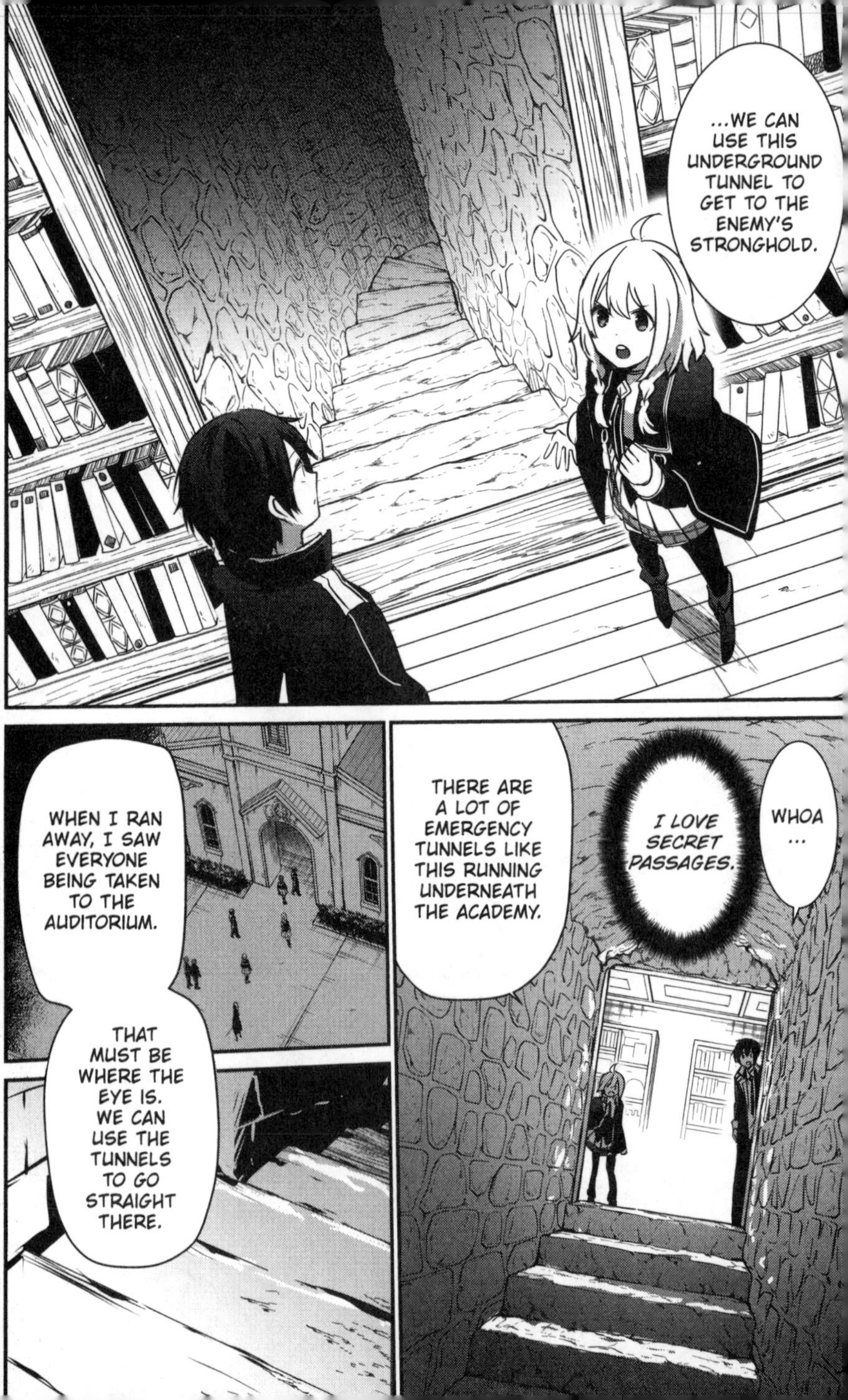
...WE CAN USE THIS UNDERGROUND TUNNEL TO GET TO THE ENEMY'S STRONGHOLD.
WHOA ...
I LOVE SECRET PASSAGES.
THERE ARE A LOT OF EMERGENCY TUNNELS LIKE THIS RUNNING UNDERNEATH THE ACADEMY.
WHEN I RAN AWAY, I SAW EVERYONE BEING TAKEN TO THE AUDITORIUM.
THAT MUST BE WHERE THE EYE IS. WE CAN USE THE TUNNELS TO GO STRAIGHT THERE.

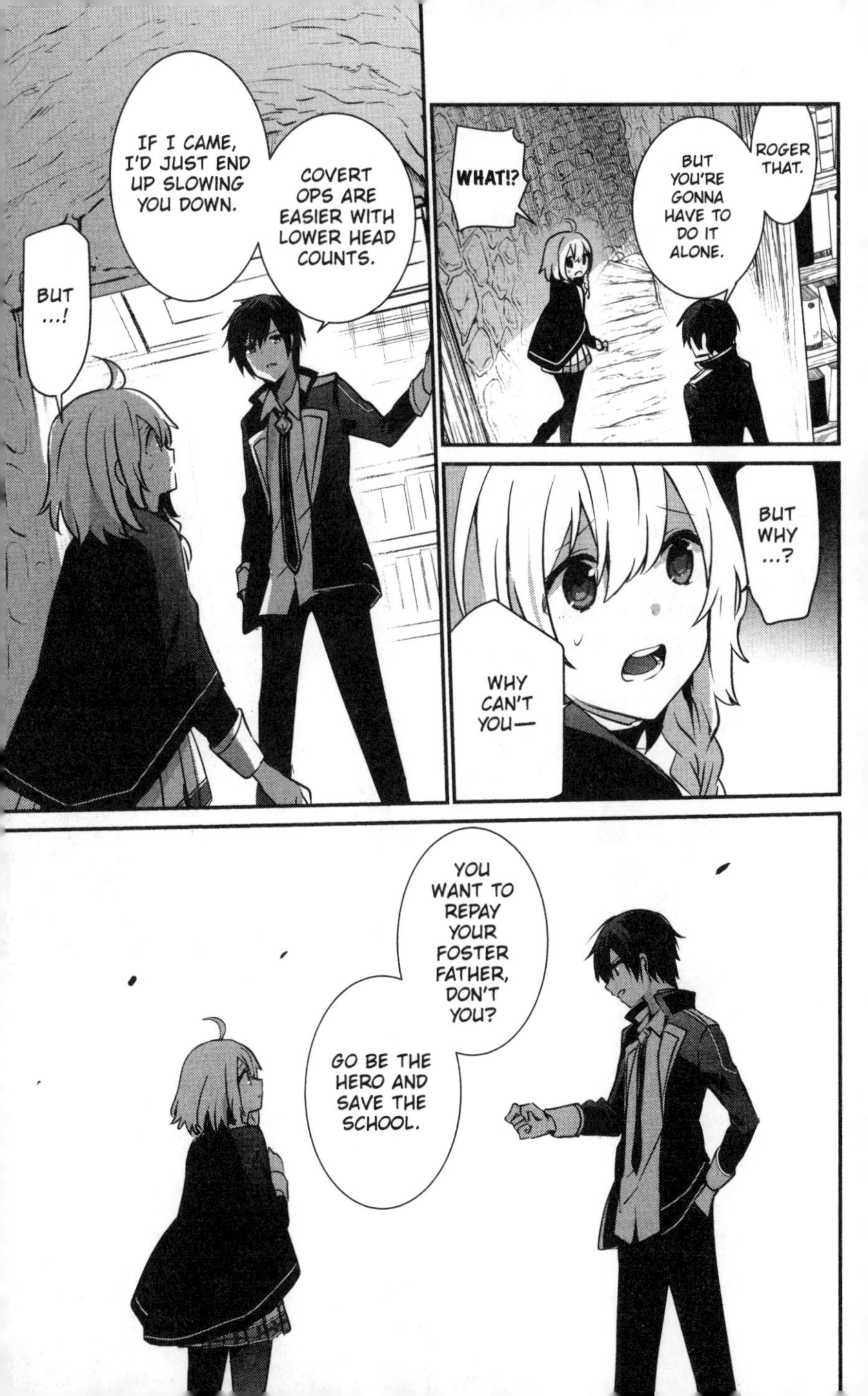
ROGER THAT.
BUT YOU'RE GONNA HAVE TO DO IT ALONE.
WHAT!?
BUT WHY ...?
WHY CAN'T YOU—
COVERT OPS ARE EASIER WITH LOWER HEAD COUNTS.
IF I CAME, I'D JUST END UP SLOWING YOU DOWN.
BUT ...!
YOU WANT TO REPAY YOUR FOSTER FATHER, DON'T YOU?
GO BE THE HERO AND SAVE THE SCHOOL.

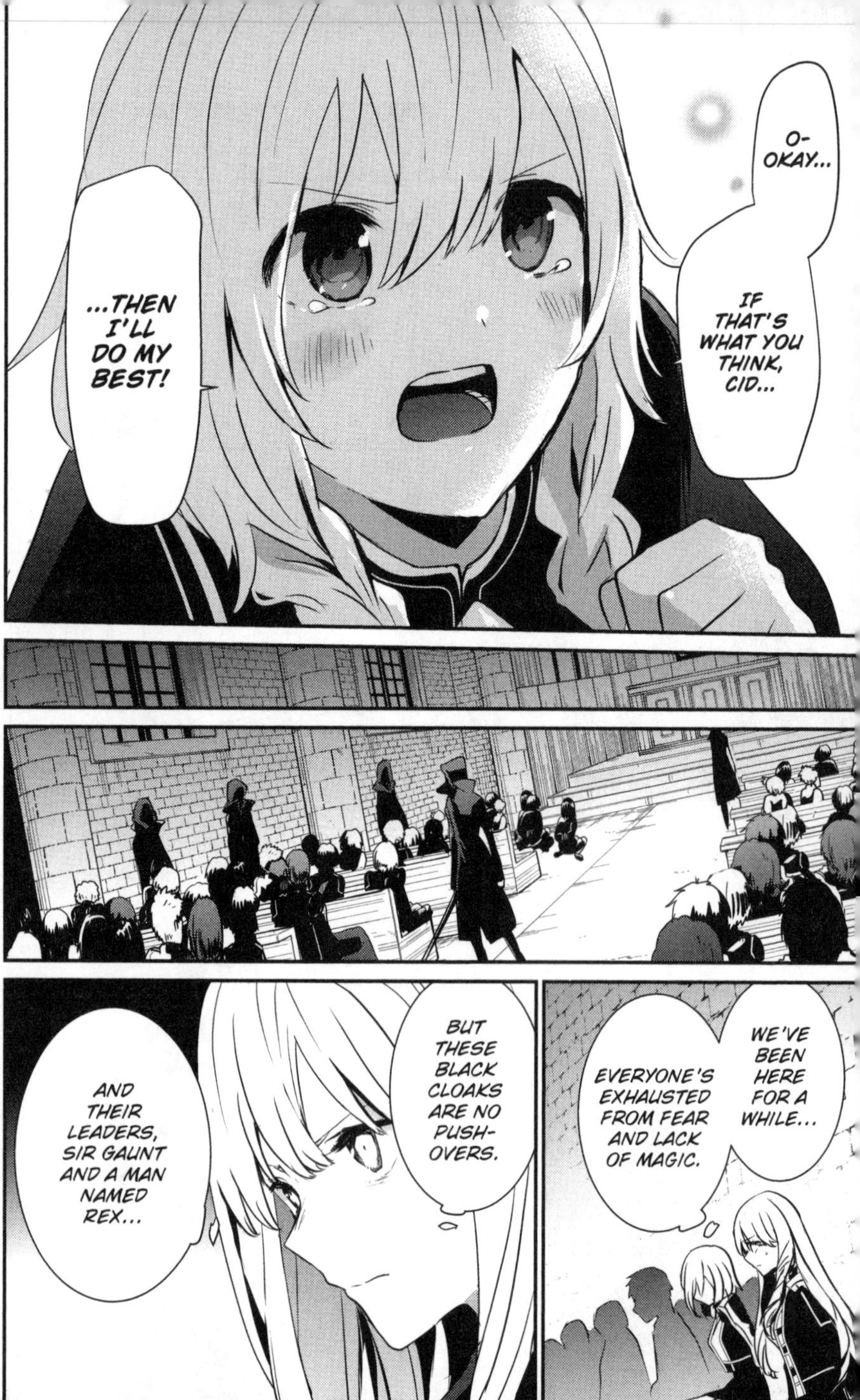
O- OKAY...
IF THAT'S WHAT YOU THINK, CID...
...THEN I'LL DO MY BEST!
WE'VE BEEN HERE FOR A WHILE...
EVERYONE'S EXHAUSTED FROM FEAR AND LACK OF MAGIC.
BUT THESE BLACK CLOAKS ARE NO PUSH-OVERS.
AND THEIR LEADERS, SIR GAUNT AND A MAN NAMED REX...

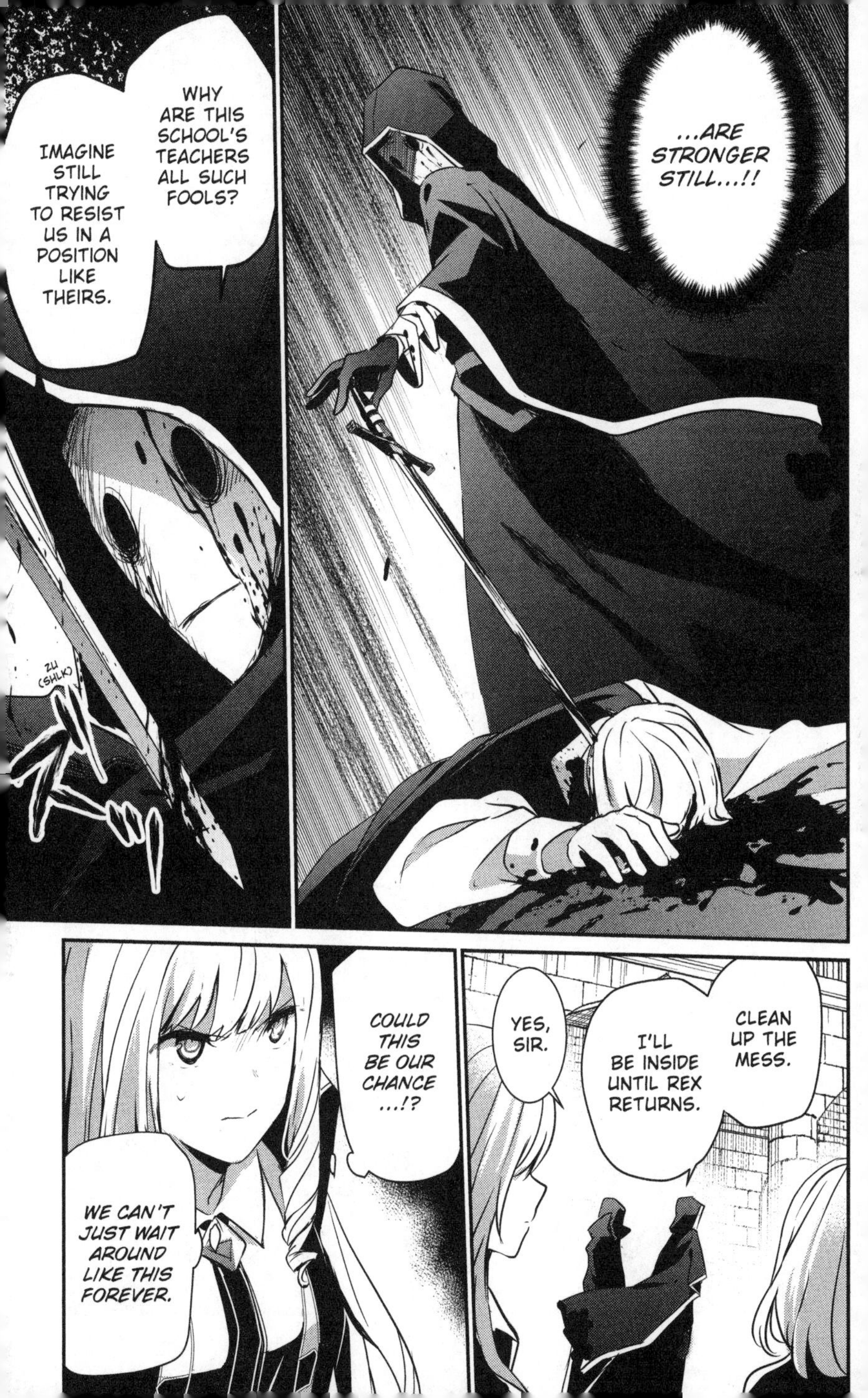
...ARE STRONGER STILL...!!
WHY ARE THIS SCHOOL'S TEACHERS ALL SUCH FOOLS?
IMAGINE STILL TRYING TO RESIST US IN A POSITION LIKE THEIRS.
ZU (SHLK)
CLEAN UP THE MESS.
I'LL BE INSIDE UNTIL REX RETURNS.
YES, SIR.
COULD THIS BE OUR CHANCE...!?
WE CAN'T JUST WAIT AROUND LIKE THIS FOREVER.

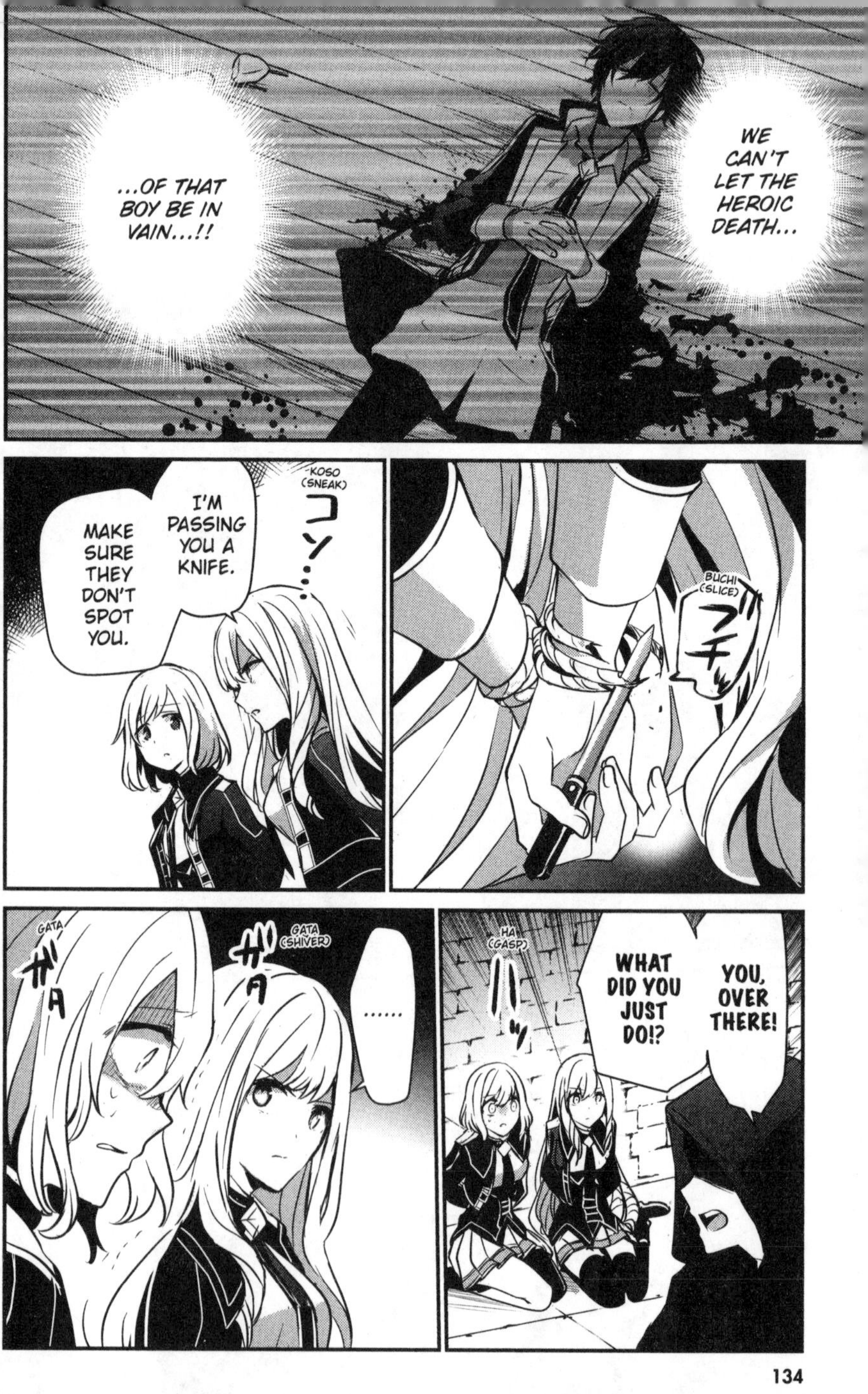
WE CAN'T LET THE HEROIC DEATH...
...OF THAT BOY BE IN VAIN...!!
BUCHI (SLICE)
KOSO (SNEAK)
I'M PASSING YOU A KNIFE.
MAKE SURE THEY DON'T SPOT YOU.
YOU, OVER THERE!
WHAT DID YOU JUST DO!?
HA (GASP)
......
GATA (SHIVER)
GATA

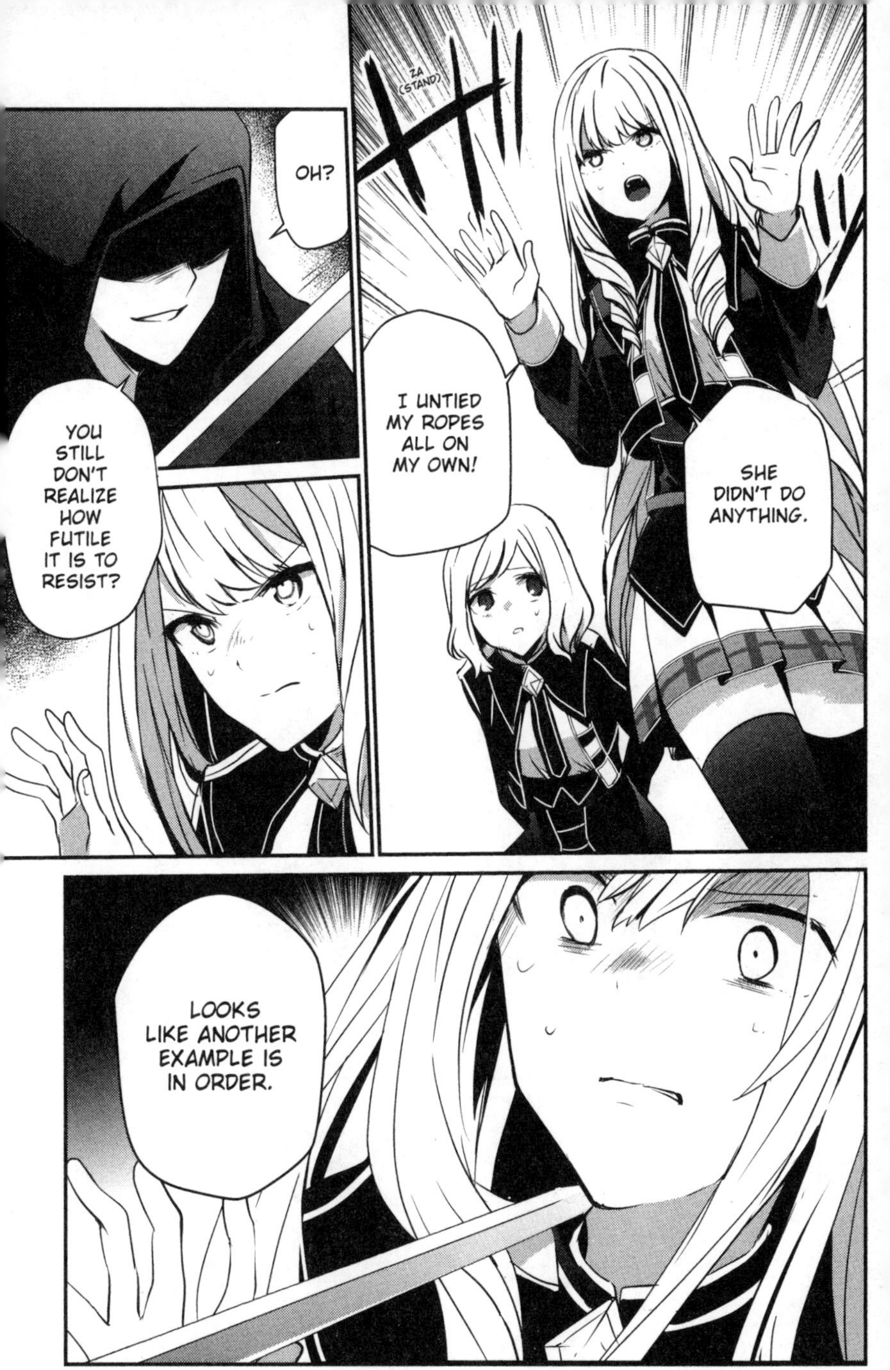
ZA (STAND)
SHE DIDN'T DO ANYTHING.
I UNTIED MY ROPES ALL ON MY OWN!
OH?
YOU STILL DON'T REALIZE HOW FUTILE IT IS TO RESIST?
LOOKS LIKE ANOTHER EXAMPLE IS IN ORDER.

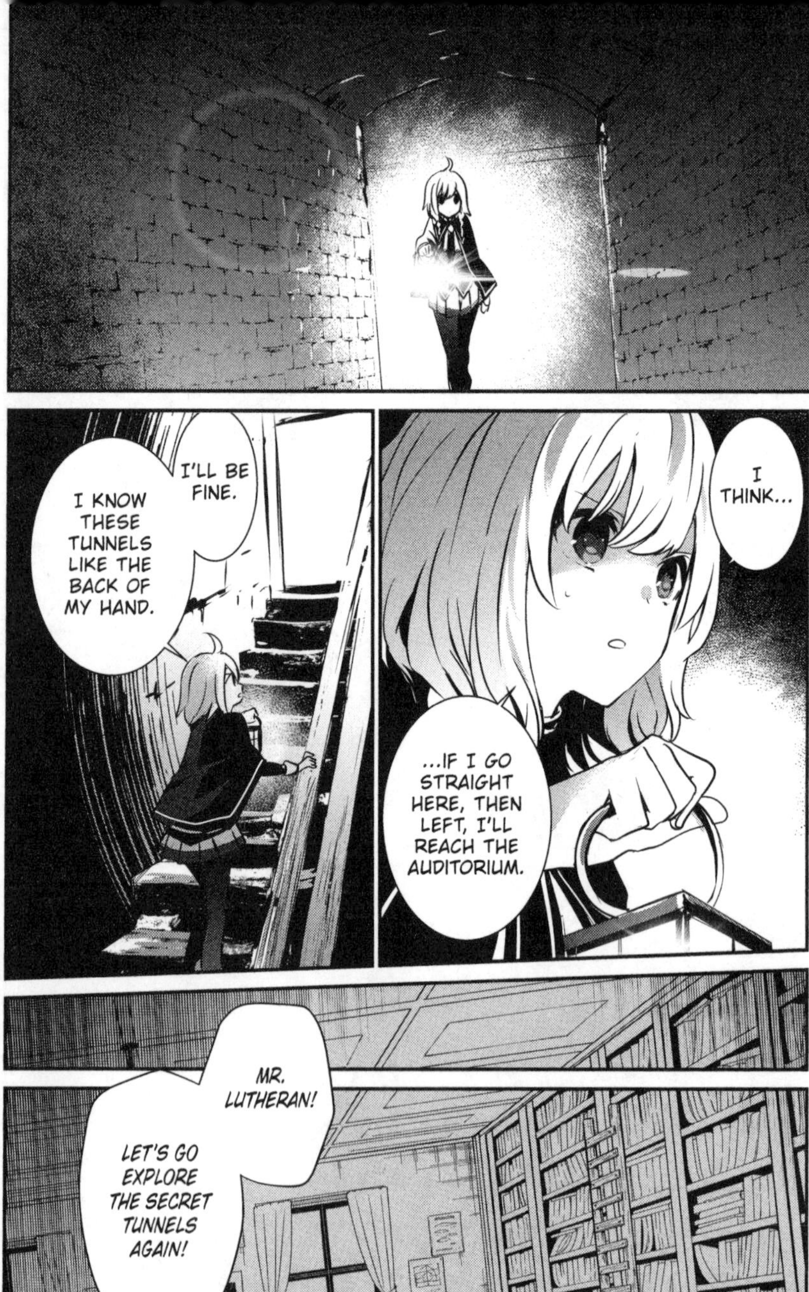
I THINK...
...IF I GO STRAIGHT HERE, THEN LEFT, I'LL REACH THE AUDITORIUM.
I'LL BE FINE.
I KNOW THESE TUNNELS LIKE THE BACK OF MY HAND.
MR. LUTHERAN!
LET'S GO EXPLORE THE SECRET TUNNELS AGAIN!

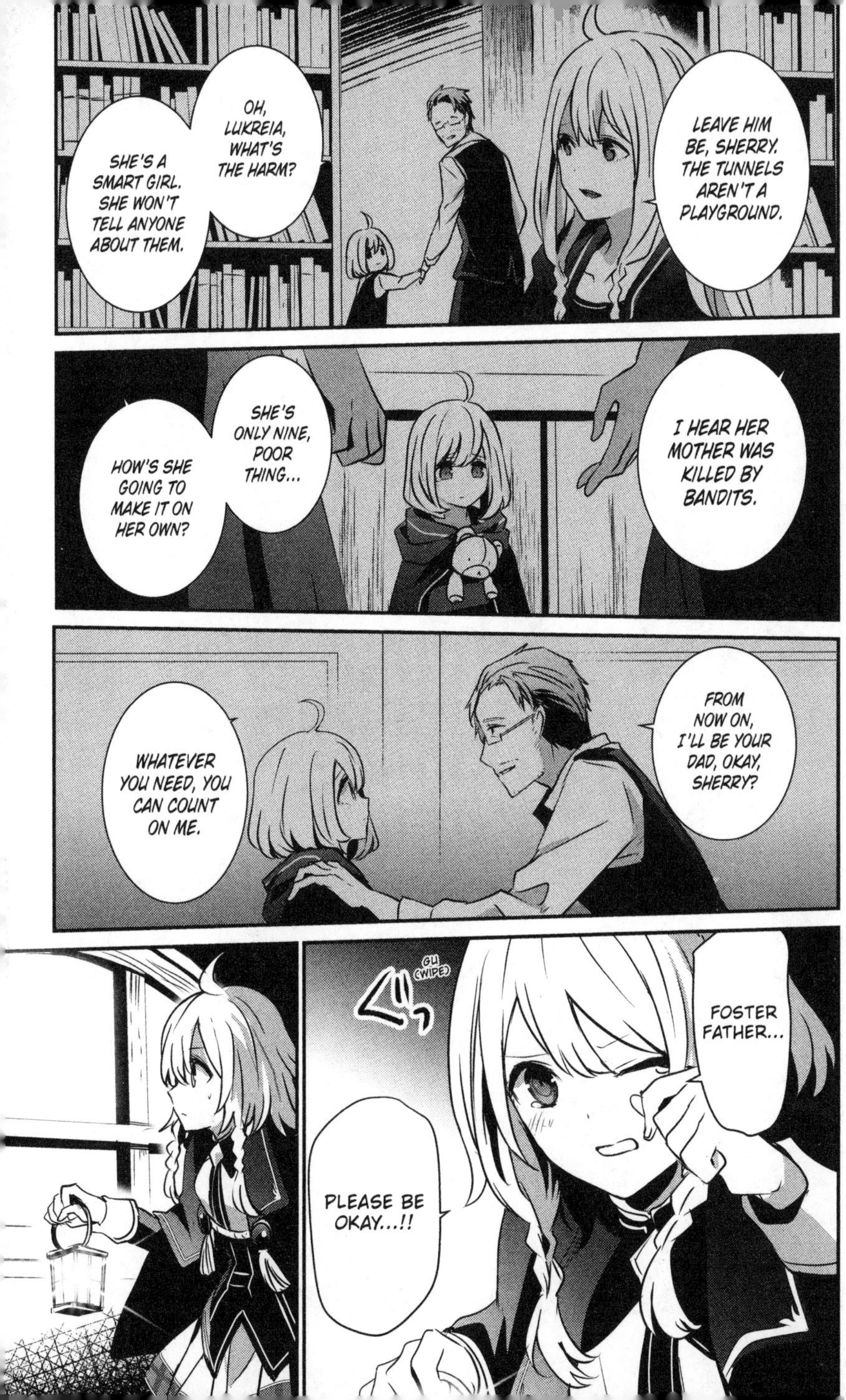
LEAVE HIM BE, SHERRY. THE TUNNELS AREN'T A PLAYGROUND.
OH, LUKREIA, WHAT'S THE HARM?
SHE'S A SMART GIRL. SHE WON'T TELL ANYONE ABOUT THEM.
I HEAR HER MOTHER WAS KILLED BY BANDITS.
SHE'S ONLY NINE, POOR THING...
HOW'S SHE GOING TO MAKE IT ON HER OWN?
FROM NOW ON, I'LL BE YOUR DAD, OKAY, SHERRY?
WHATEVER YOU NEED, YOU CAN COUNT ON ME.
FOSTER FATHER...
GU (WIPE)
PLEASE BE OKAY...!!

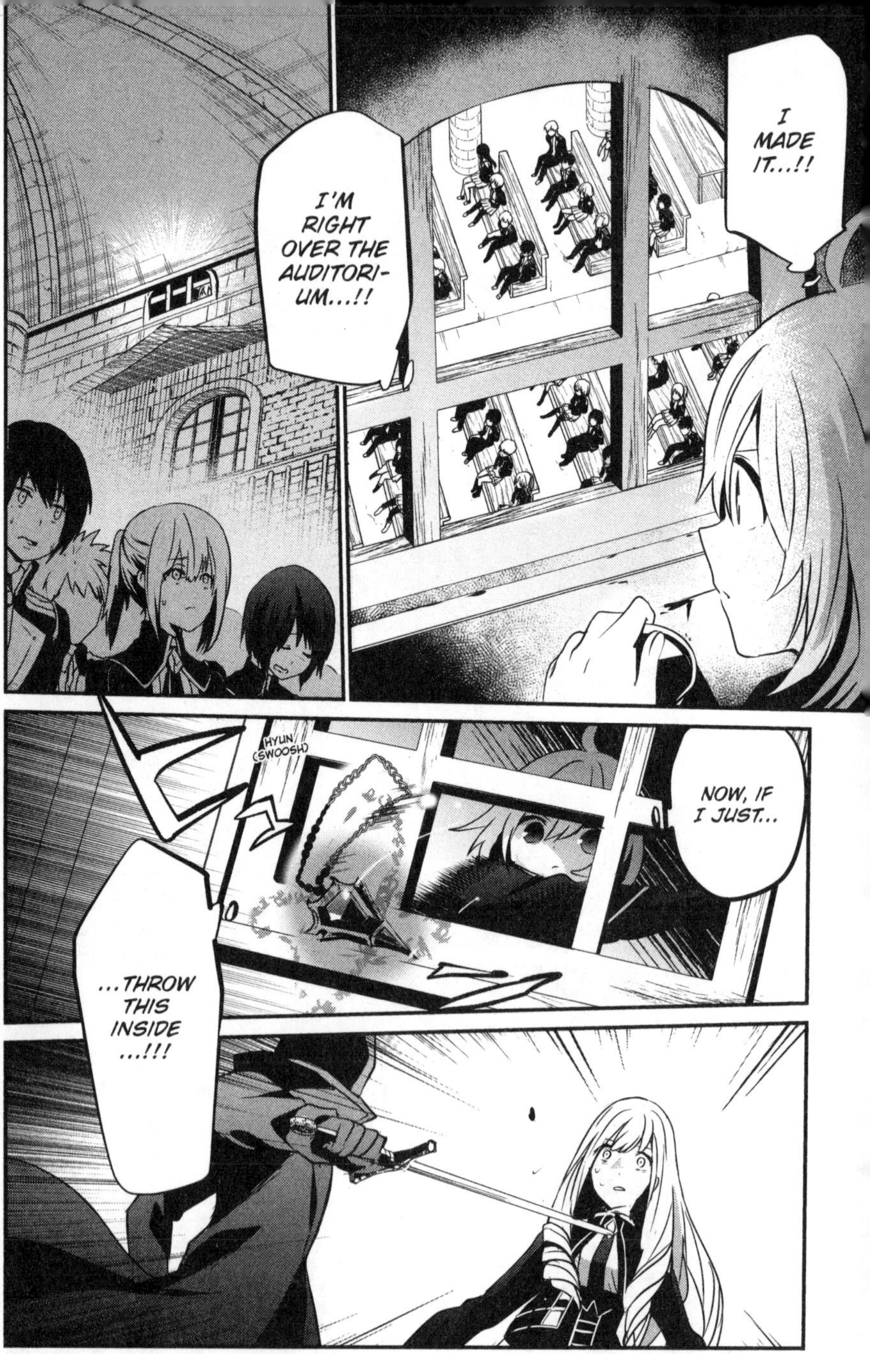
I MADE IT...!!
I'M RIGHT OVER THE AUDITORIUM...!!
NOW, IF I JUST...
HYUN (SWOOSH)
...THROW THIS INSIDE...!!!

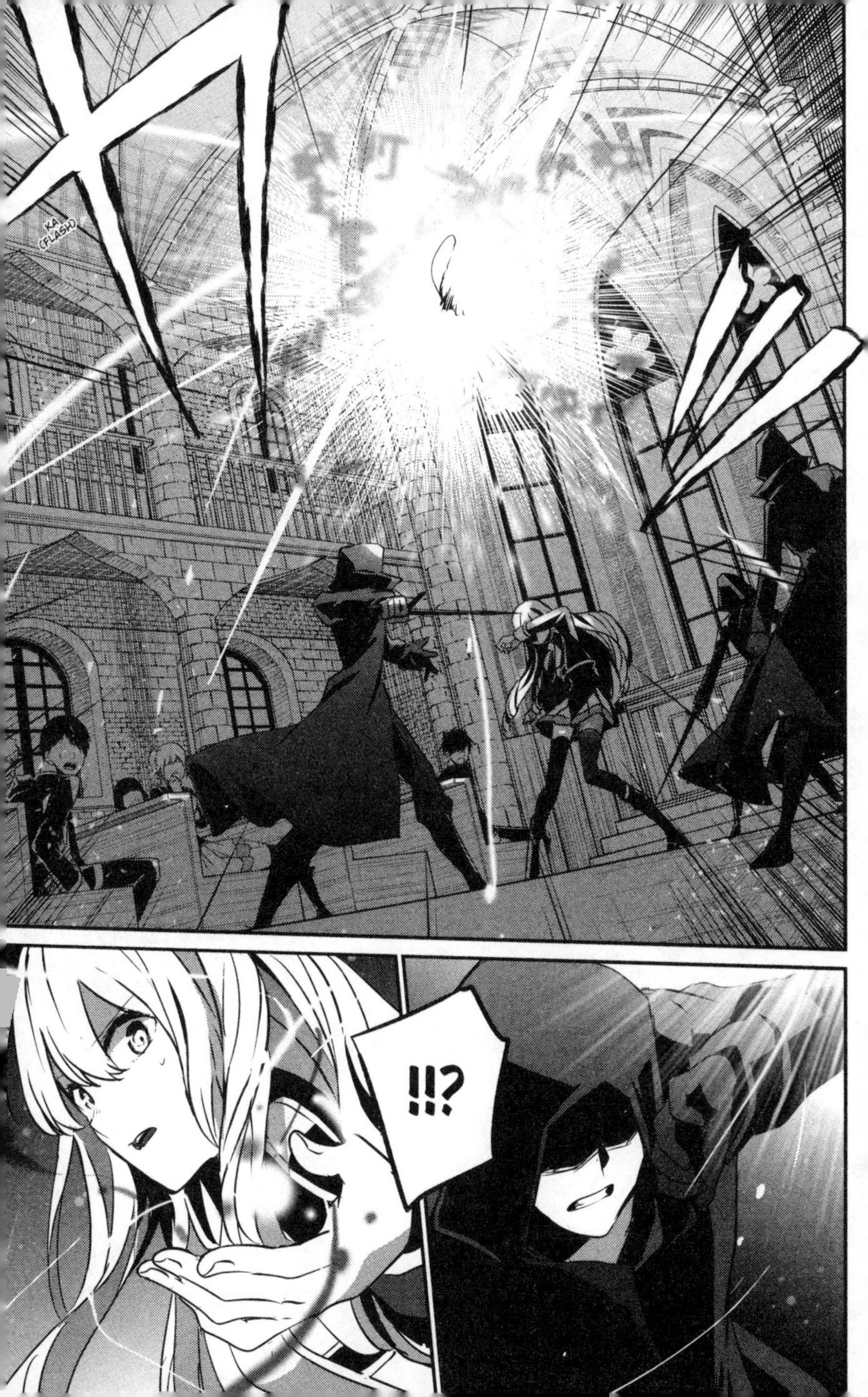
KA (FLASH)
!!?

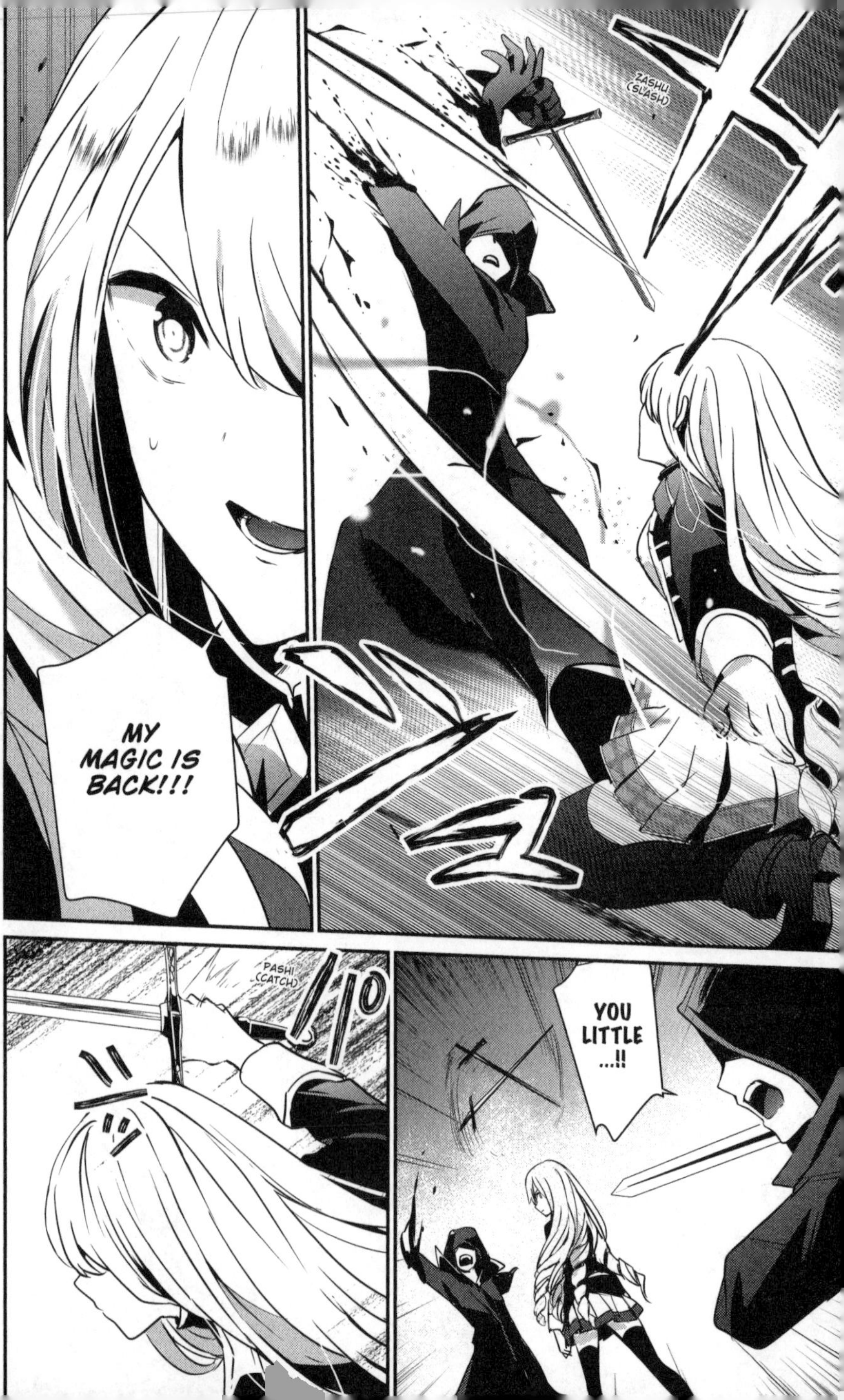
ZASHU (SLASH)
MY MAGIC IS BACK!!!
YOU LITTLE ...!!
PASHI (CATCH)

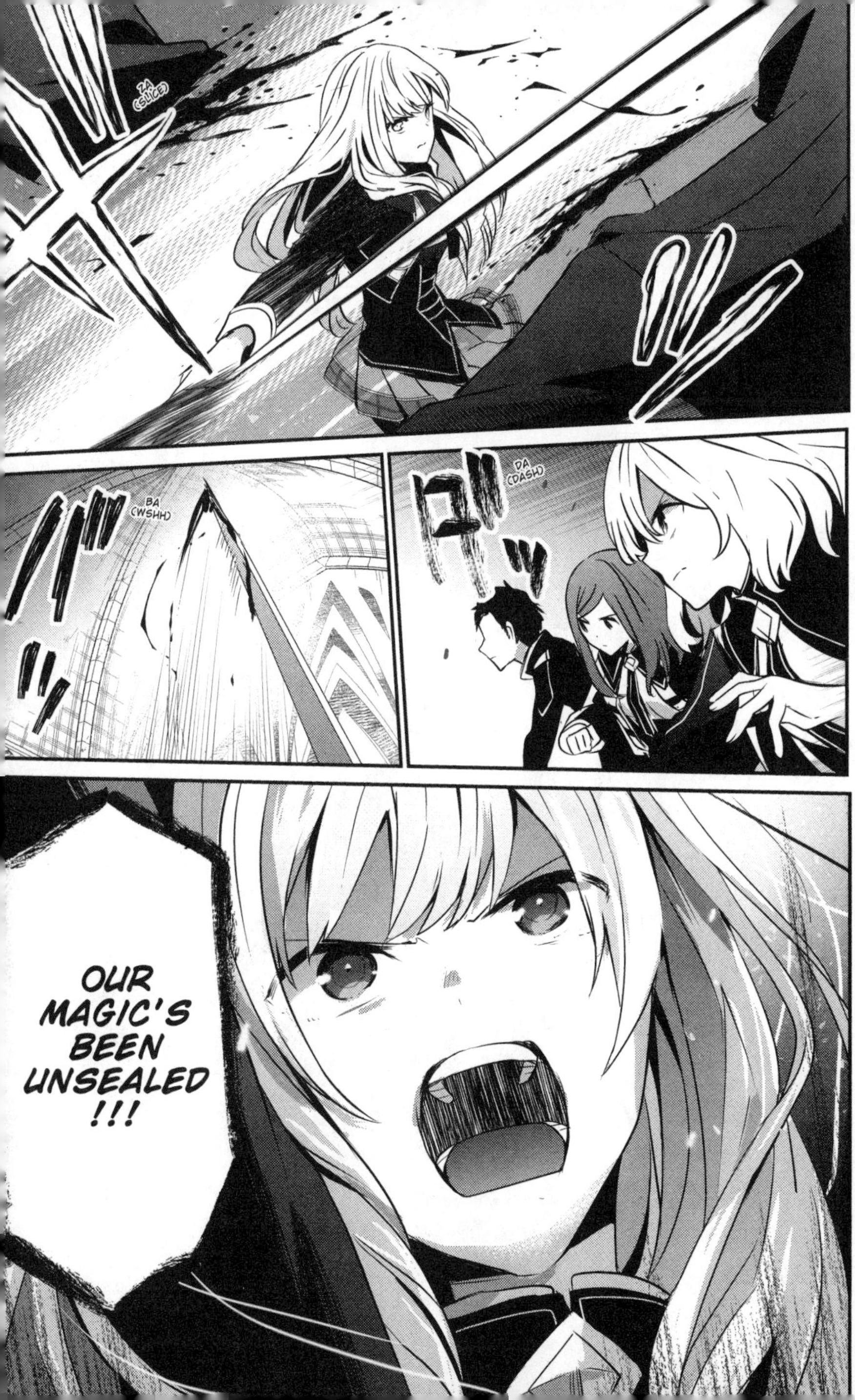
ZA (SLICE)
DA (DASH)
BA (WSHH)
OUR MAGIC'S BEEN UNSEALED!!!

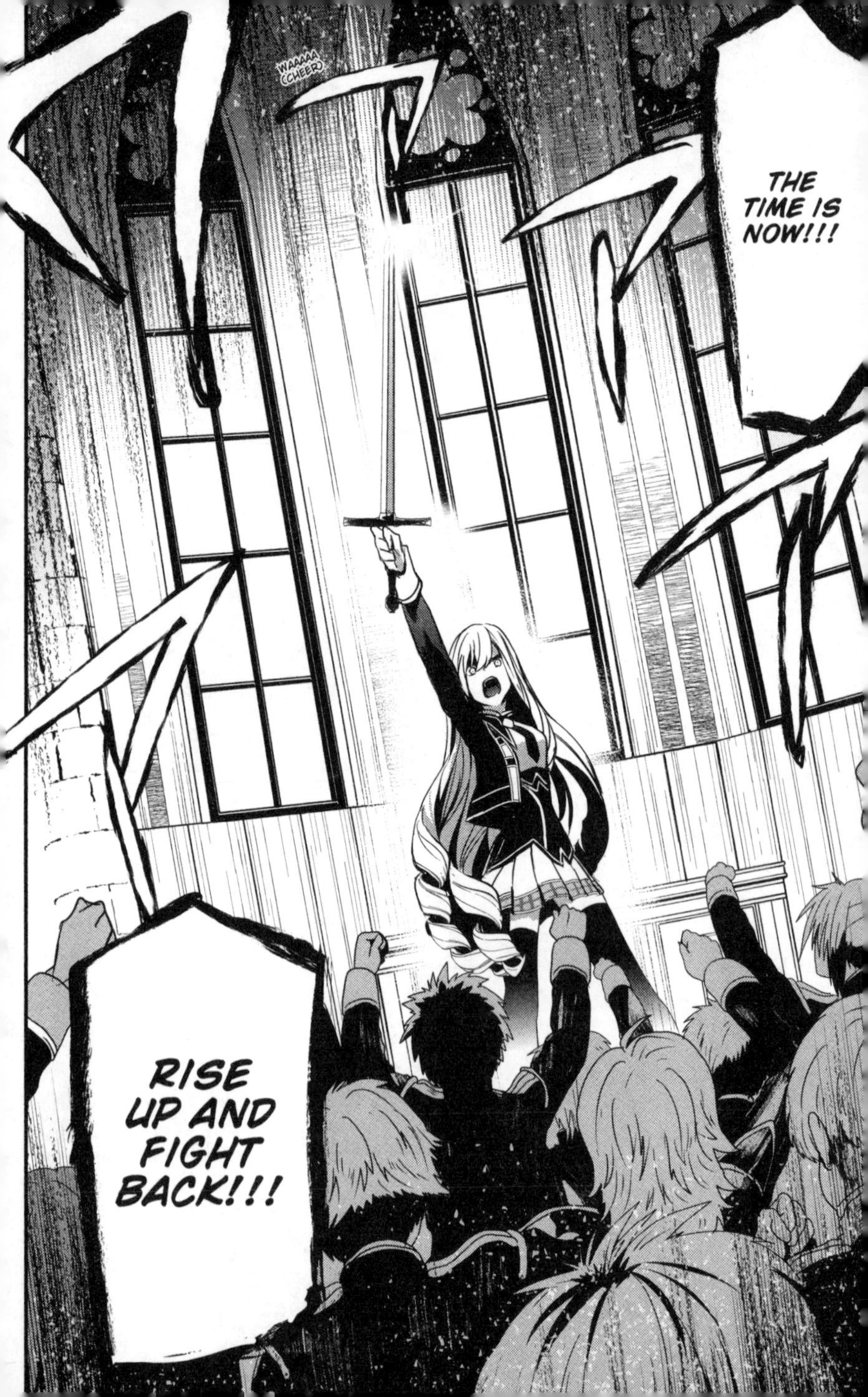
THE TIME IS NOW!!!
WAAAAA (CHEER)
RISE UP AND FIGHT BACK!!!

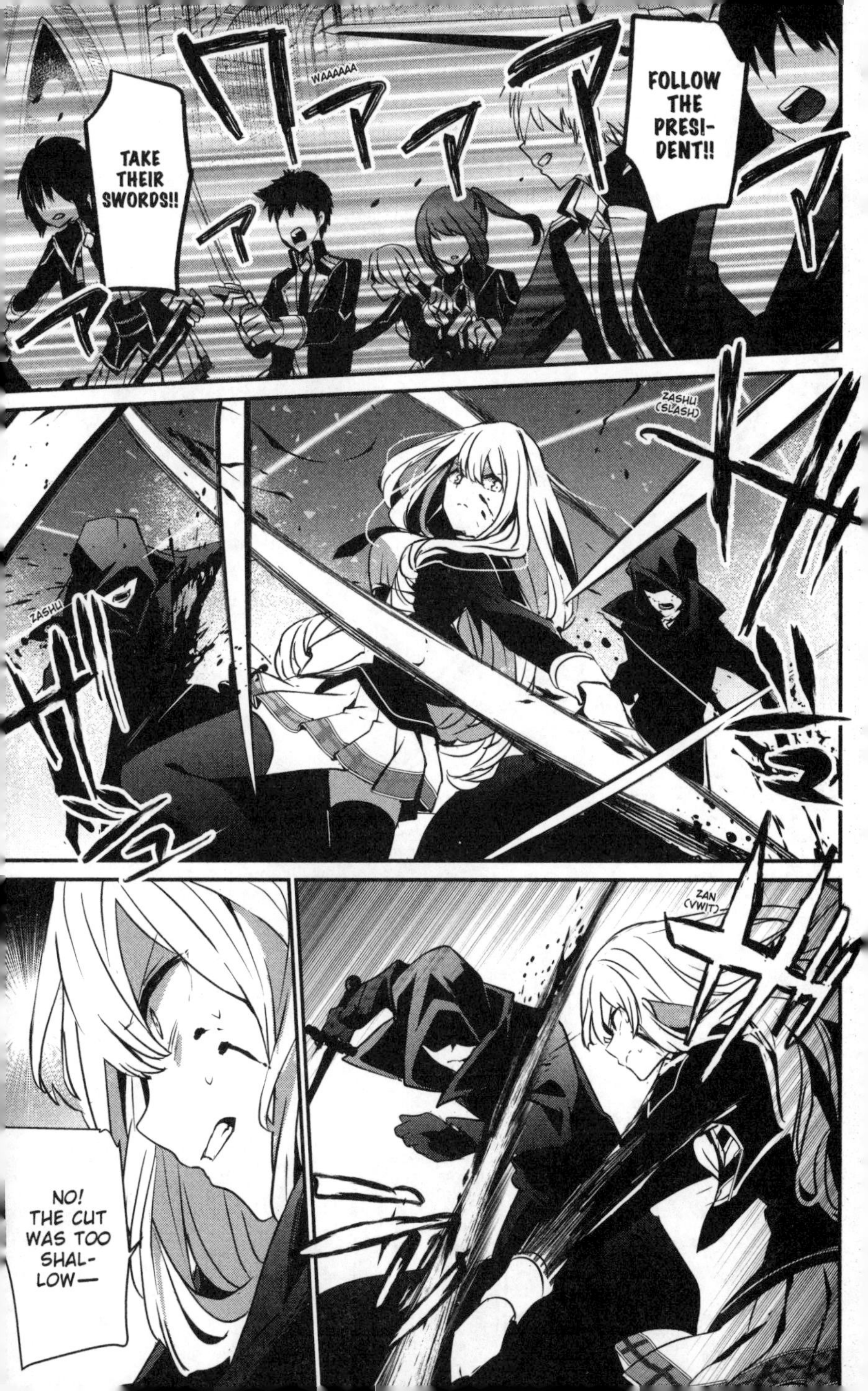
FOLLOW THE PRESI-DENT!!
WAAAAAA
TAKE THEIR SWORDS!!
ZASHU (SLASH)
ZASHU
ZAN (VWIT)
NO! THE CUT WAS TOO SHAL-LOW—

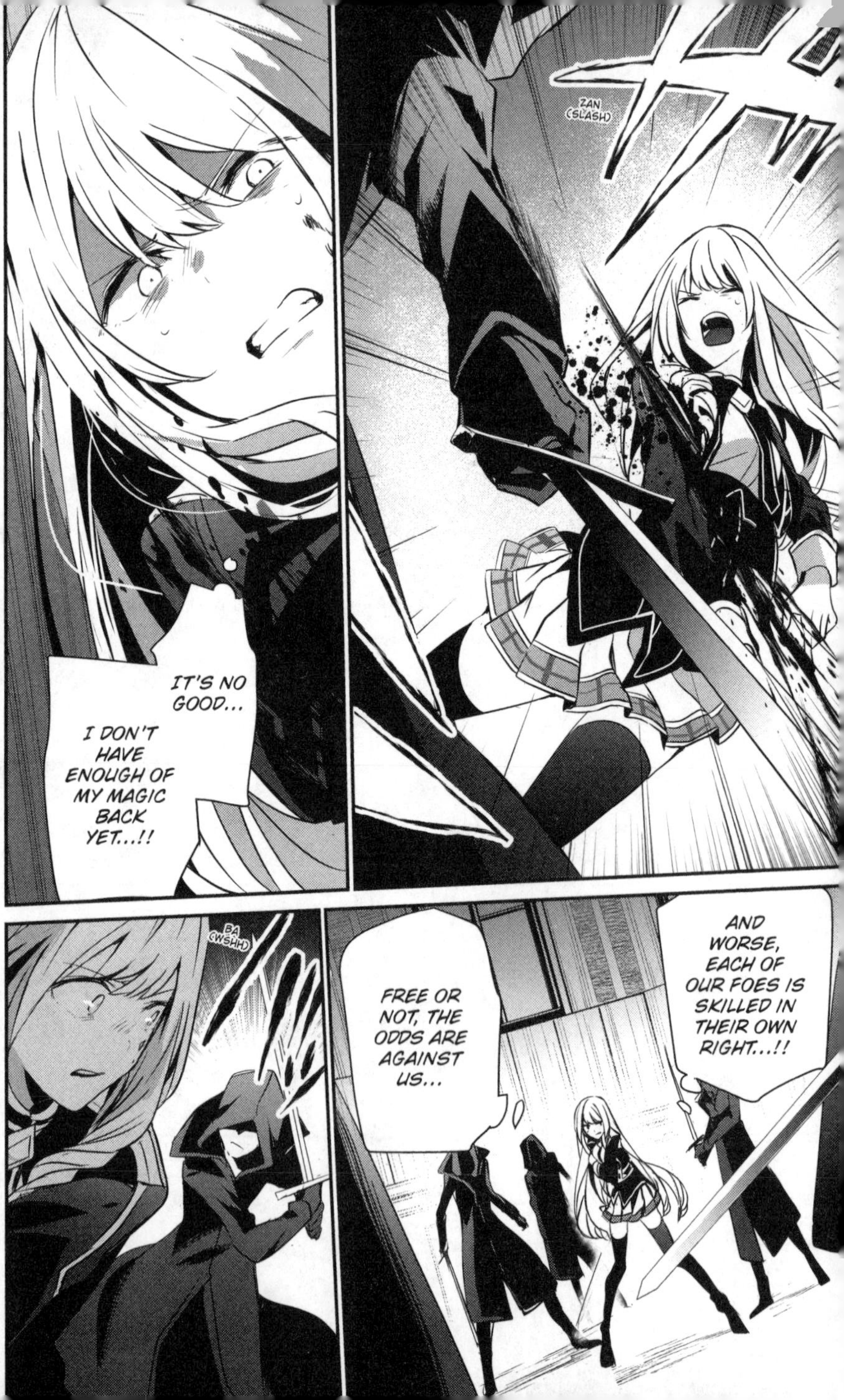
ZAN (SLASH)
IT'S NO GOOD...
I DON'T HAVE ENOUGH OF MY MAGIC BACK YET...!!
FREE OR NOT, THE ODDS ARE AGAINST US...
AND WORSE, EACH OF OUR FOES IS SKILLED IN THEIR OWN RIGHT...!!
BA (WSHH)

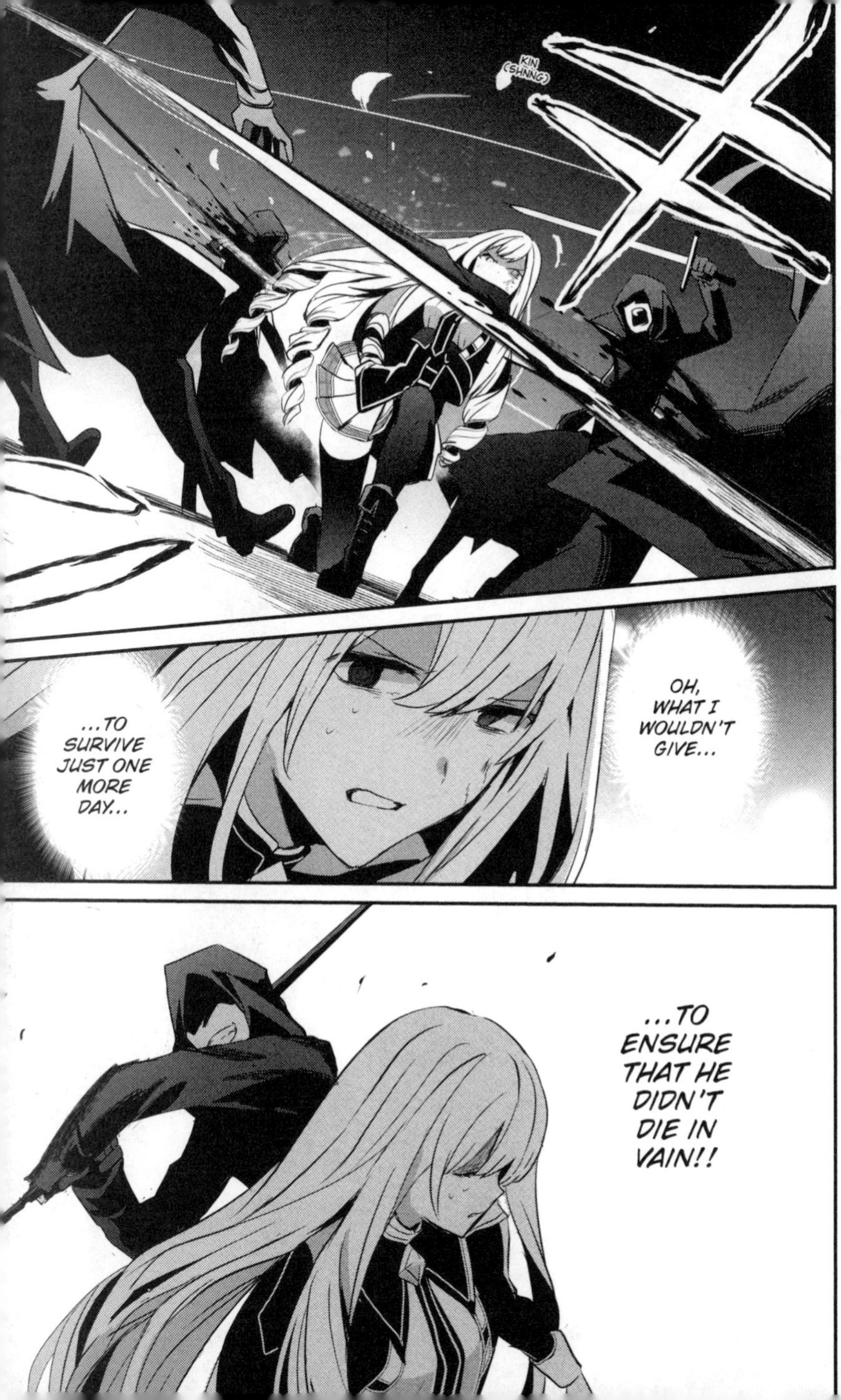
KIN (SHNNG)
OH, WHAT I WOULDN'T GIVE...
...TO SURVIVE JUST ONE MORE DAY...
...TO ENSURE THAT HE DIDN'T DIE IN VAIN!!

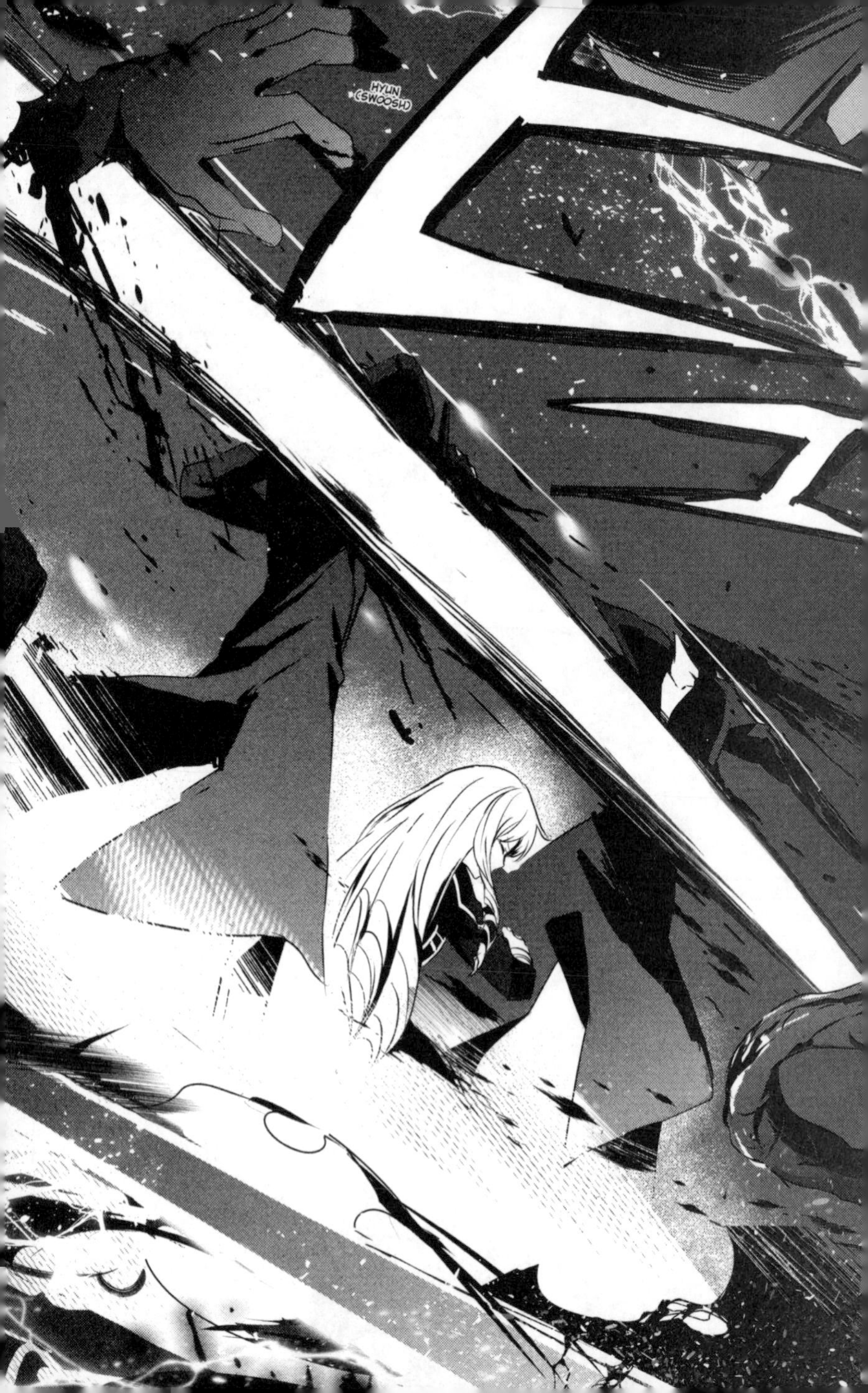
HYUN (SWOOSH)

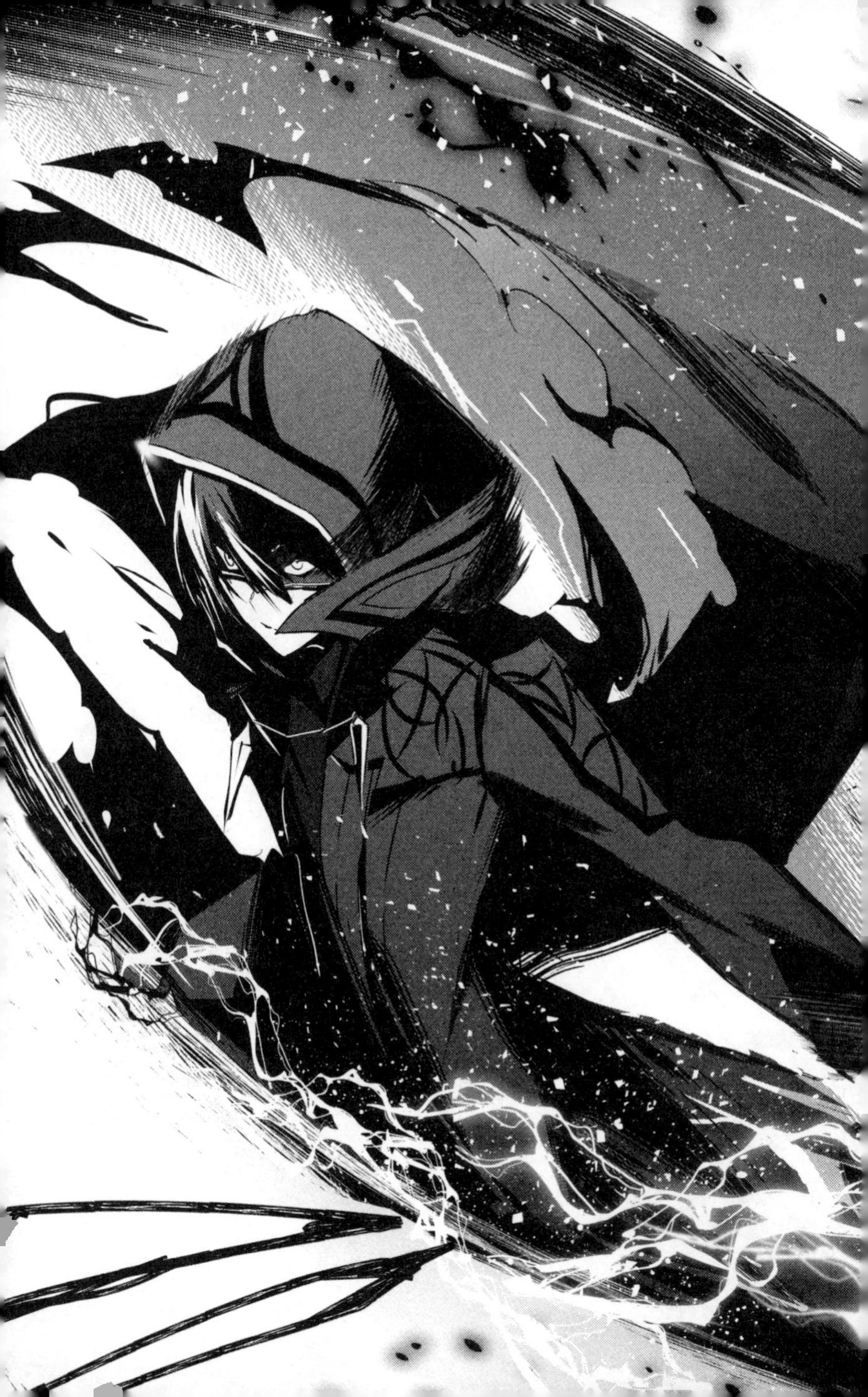

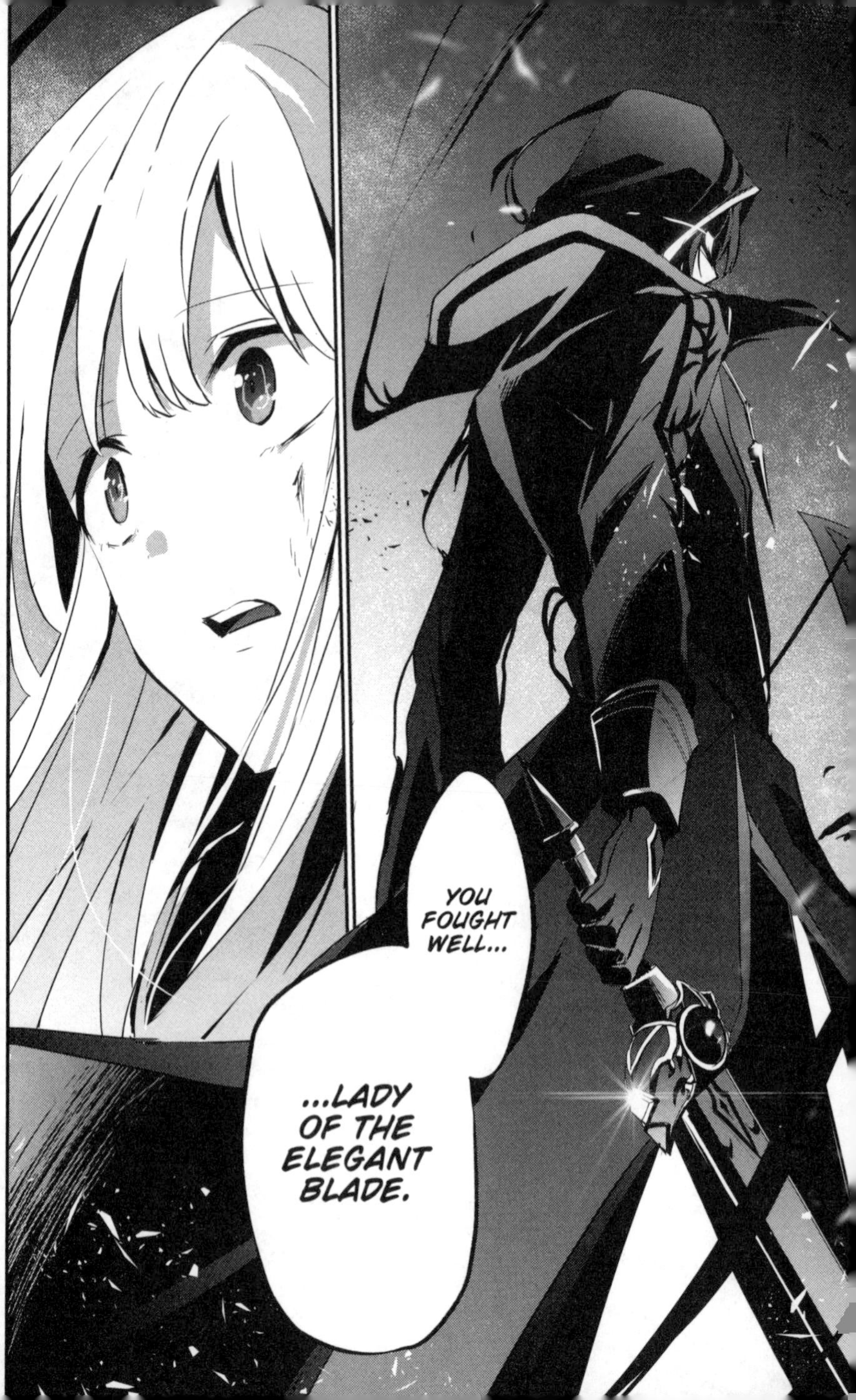
YOU FOUGHT WELL...
...LADY OF THE ELEGANT BLADE.

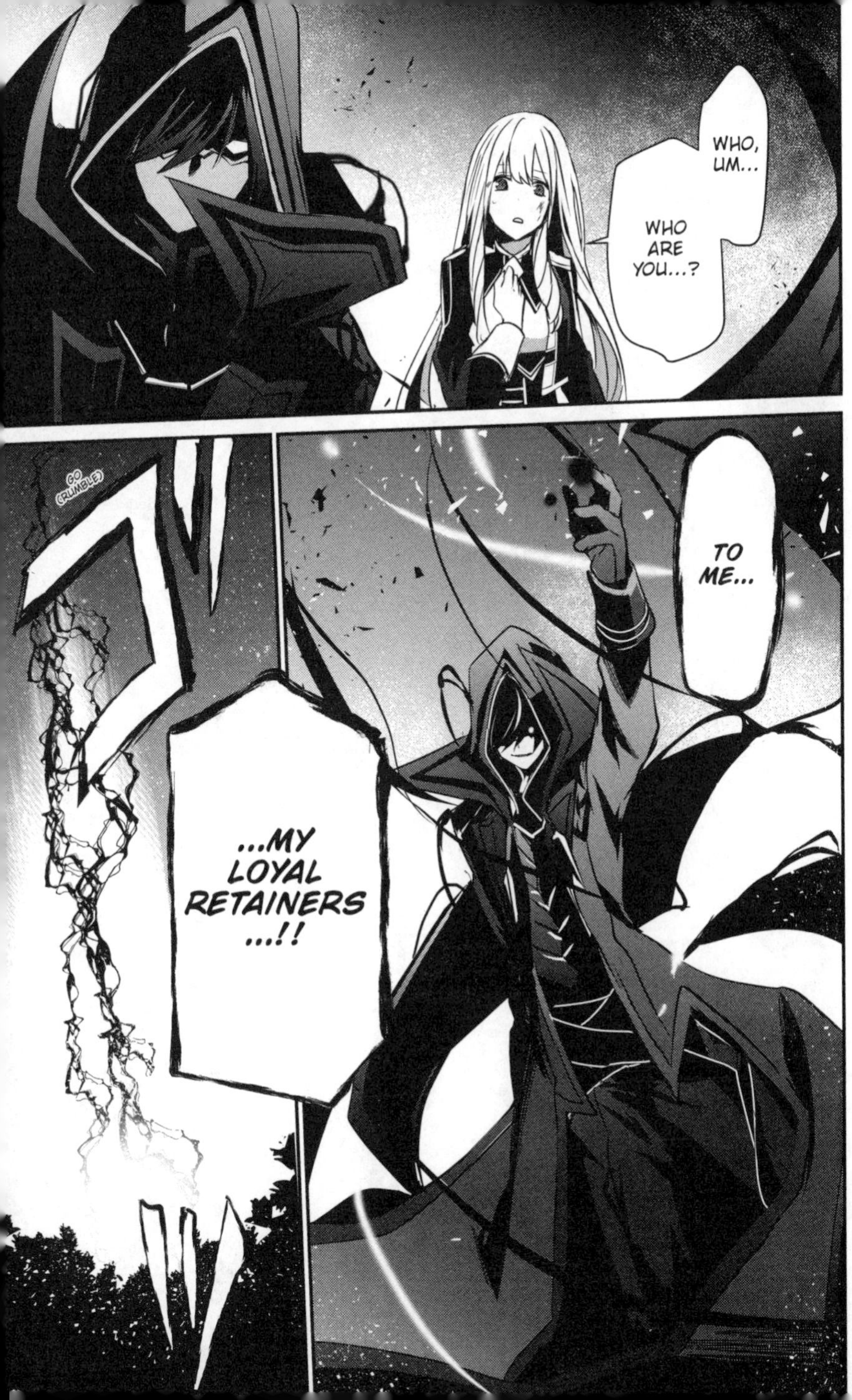
WHO, UM...
WHO ARE YOU...?
TO ME...
GO (RUMBLE)
...MY LOYAL RETAINERS ...!!

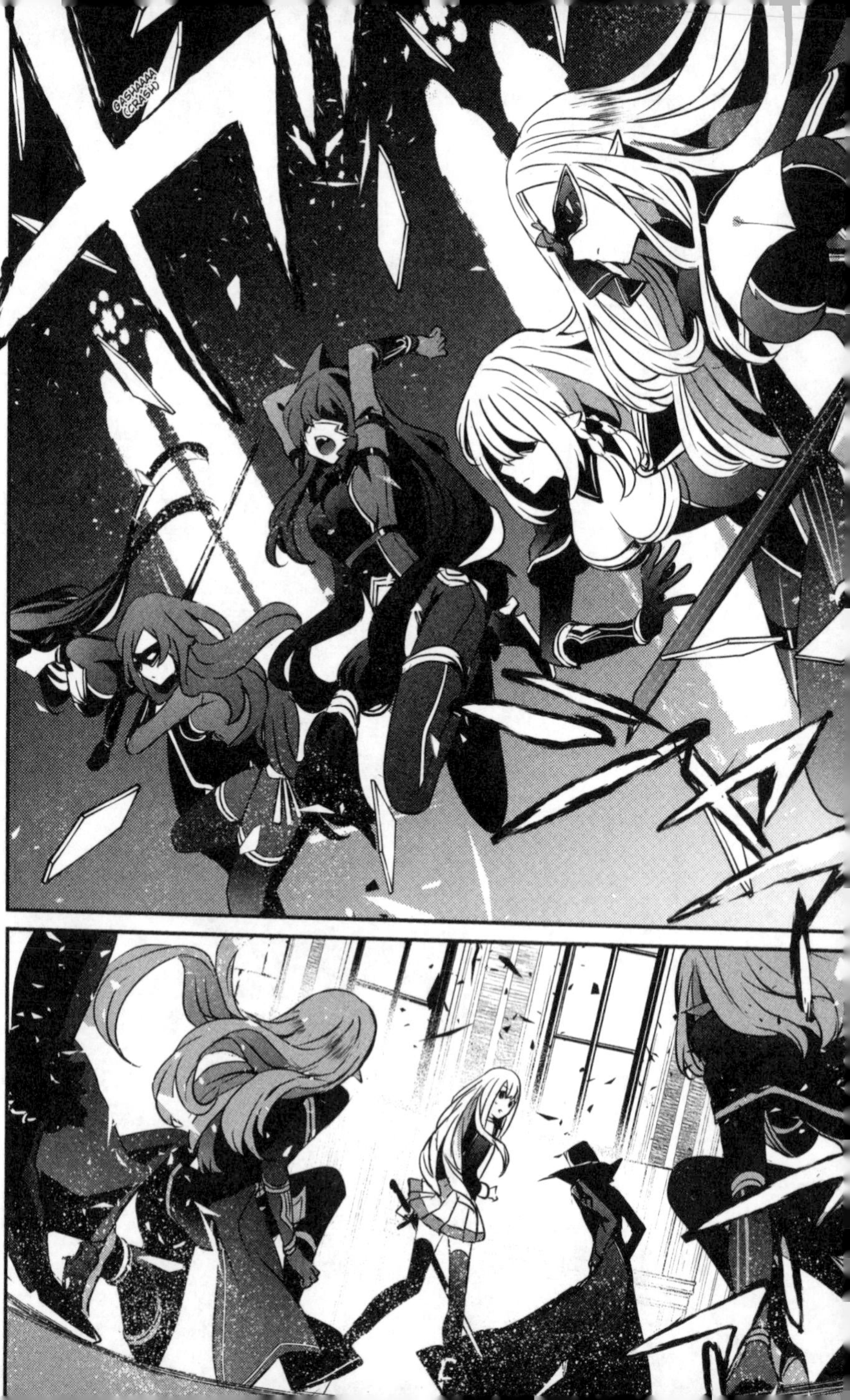
GASHAAAA
(CRASH)

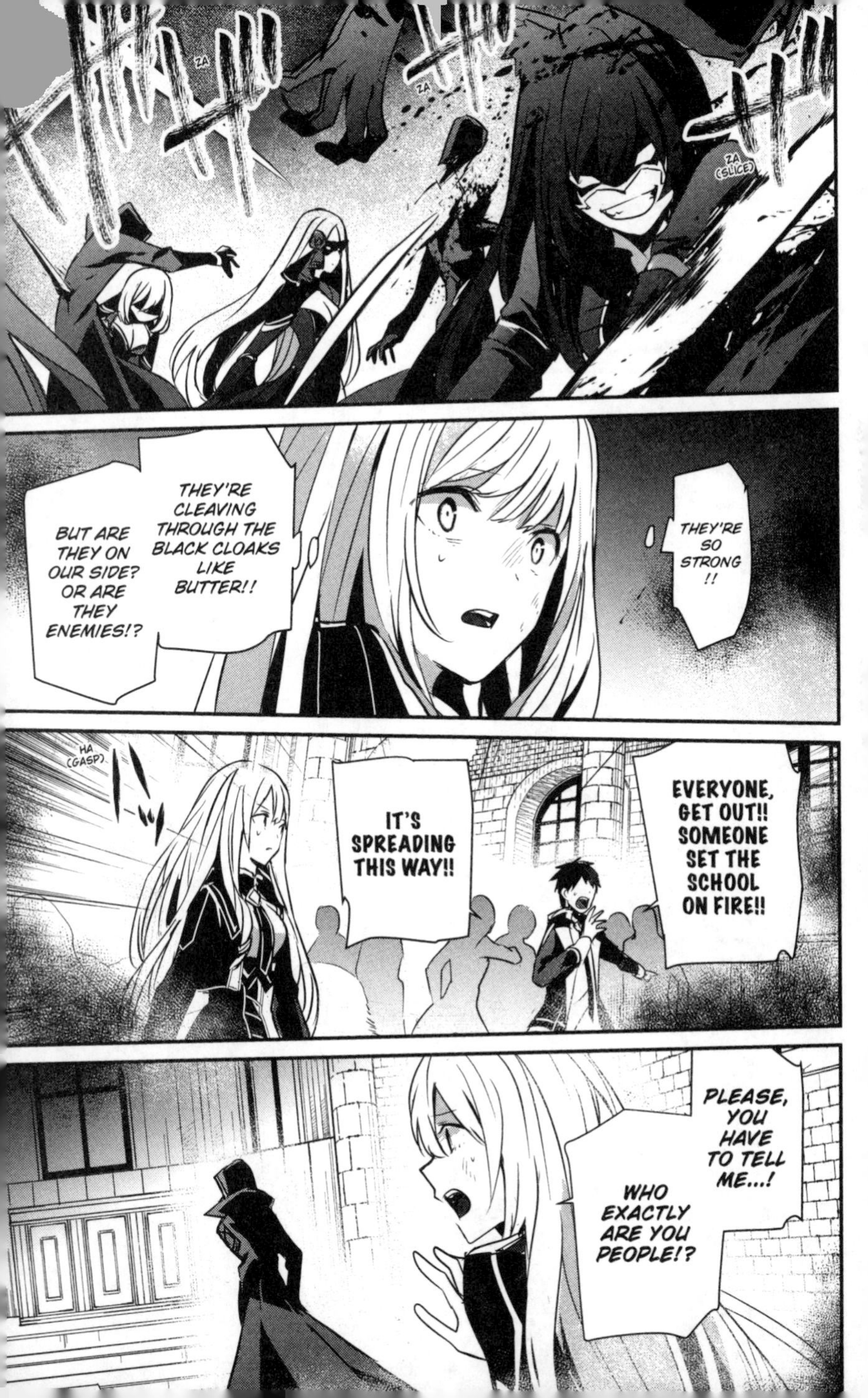
ZA (SLICE)
ZA
ZA
THEY'RE SO STRONG!!
THEY'RE CLEAVING THROUGH THE BLACK CLOAKS LIKE BUTTER!!
BUT ARE THEY ON OUR SIDE? OR ARE THEY ENEMIES!?
EVERYONE, GET OUT!! SOMEONE SET THE SCHOOL ON FIRE!!
IT'S SPREADING THIS WAY!!
HA (GASP)
PLEASE, YOU HAVE TO TELL ME...!
WHO EXACTLY ARE YOU PEOPLE!?

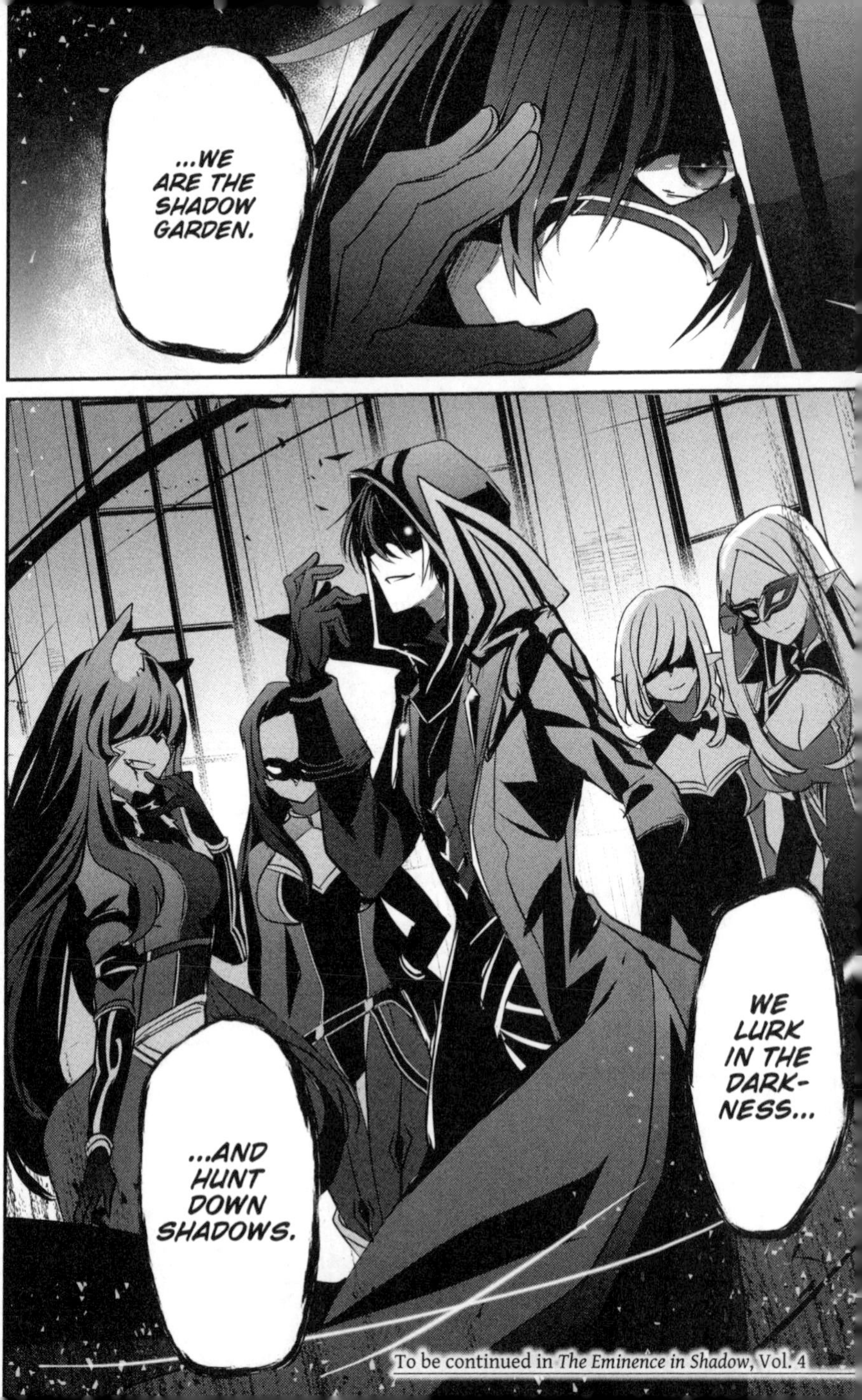
...WE ARE THE SHADOW GARDEN.
WE LURK IN THE DARK-NESS...
...AND HUNT DOWN SHADOWS.

To be continued in *The Eminence in Shadow*, Vol. 4

The Eminence in Shadow

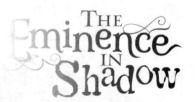

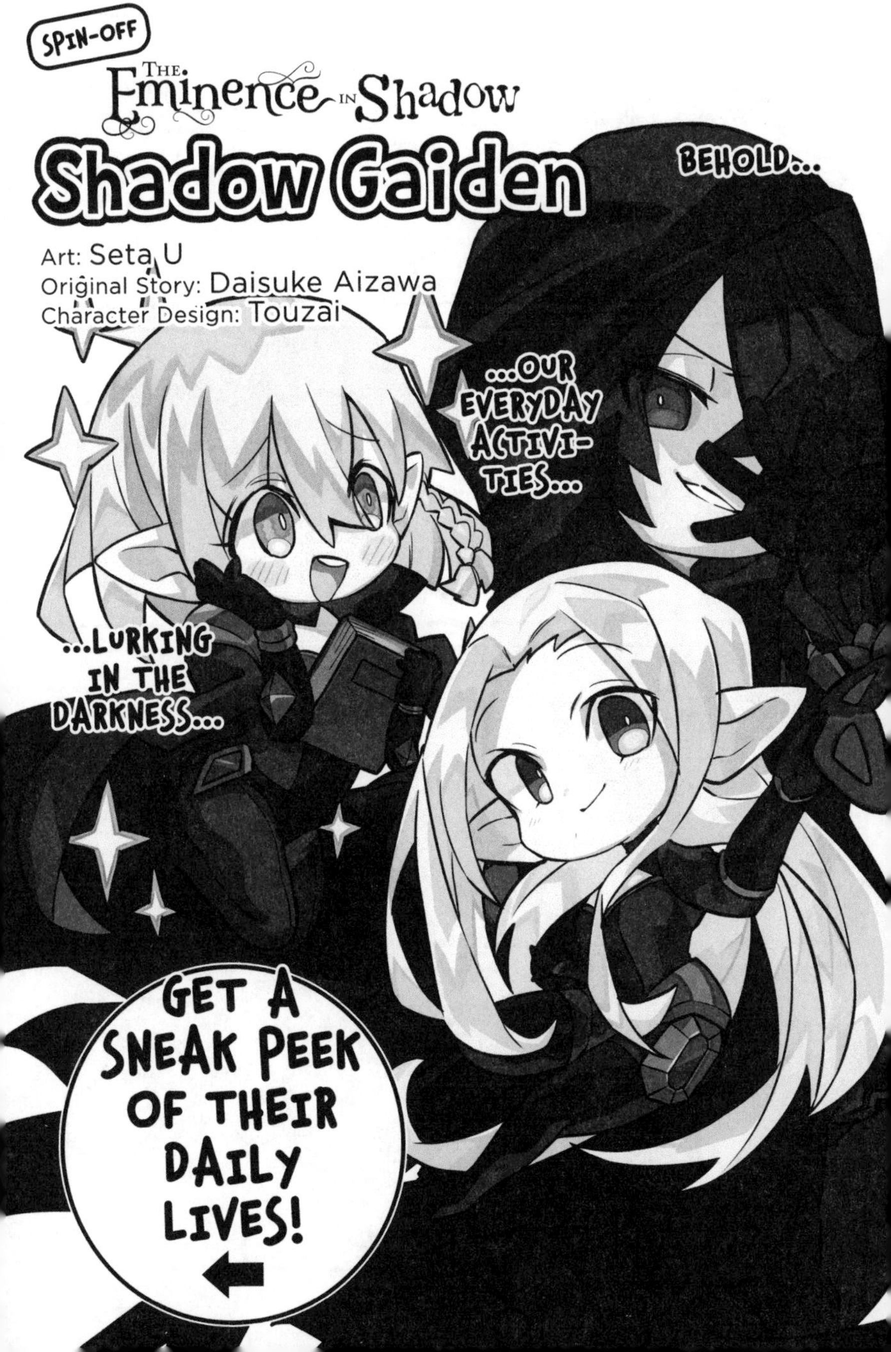

SPIN-OFF
THE Eminence IN Shadow
Shadow Gaiden
Art: Seta U
Original Story: Daisuke Aizawa
Character Design: Touzai
BEHOLD...
...OUR EVERYDAY ACTIVI-TIES...
...LURKING IN THE DARKNESS...
GET A SNEAK PEEK OF THEIR DAILY LIVES!

LOOKING AFTER LOST DOGS...

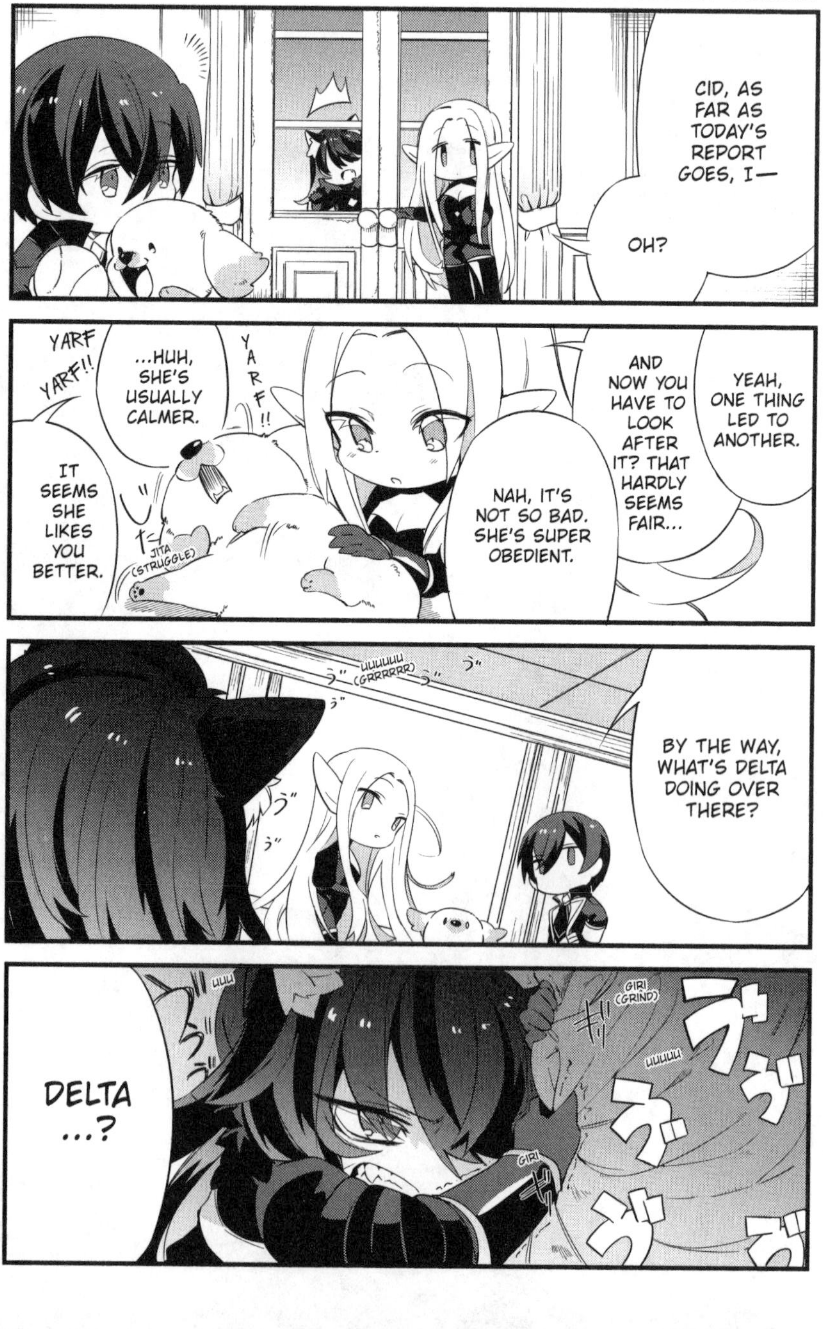
CID, AS FAR AS TODAY'S REPORT GOES, I—
OH?
YEAH, ONE THING LED TO ANOTHER.
AND NOW YOU HAVE TO LOOK AFTER IT? THAT HARDLY SEEMS FAIR...
NAH, IT'S NOT SO BAD. SHE'S SUPER OBEDIENT.
YARF!!
...HUH, SHE'S USUALLY CALMER.
JITA (STRUGGLE)
YARF YARF!!
IT SEEMS SHE LIKES YOU BETTER.
BY THE WAY, WHAT'S DELTA DOING OVER THERE?
UUUUUU (GRRRRRR)
GIRI (GRIND)
UUUUU
UUU
GIRI
DELTA ...?

SEARCHING FOR RARE HERBS...

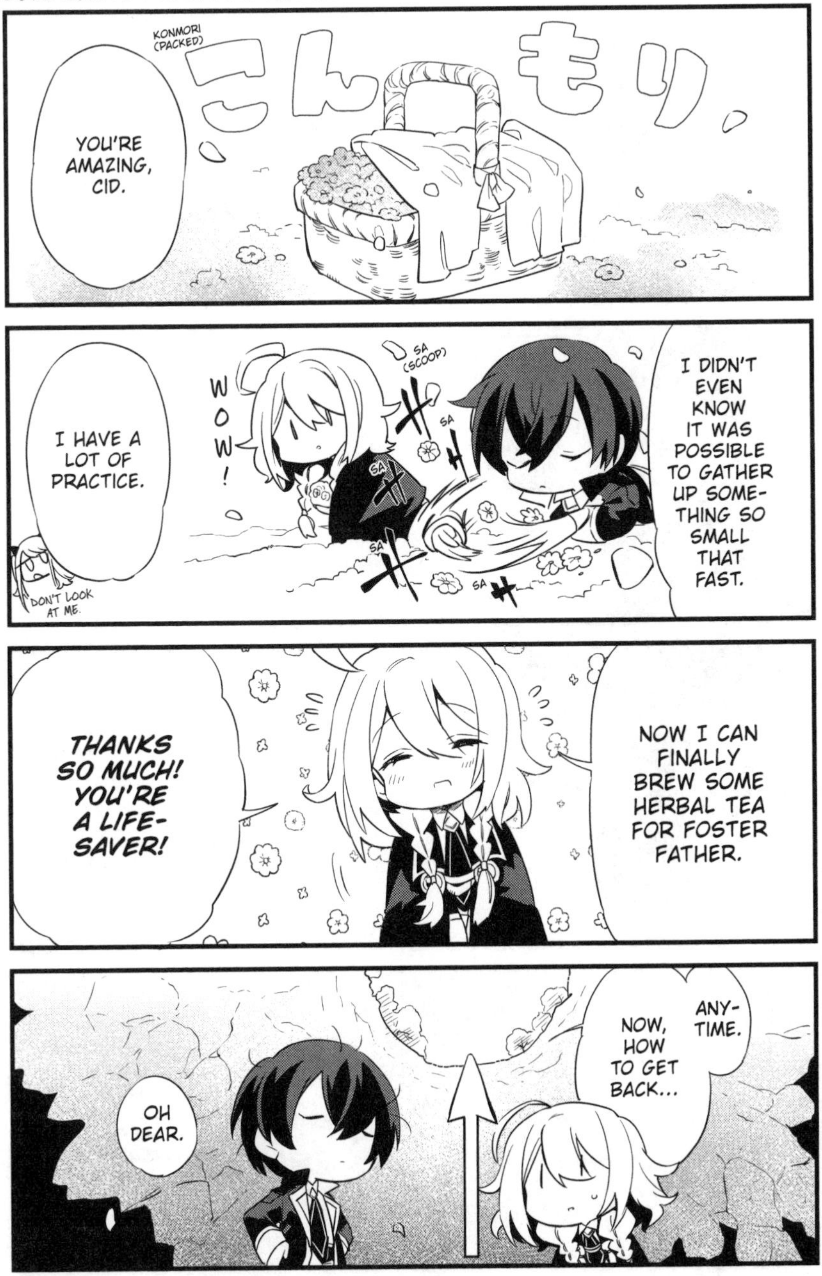

こんもり
KONMORI (PACKED)
YOU'RE AMAZING, CID.
I DIDN'T EVEN KNOW IT WAS POSSIBLE TO GATHER UP SOMETHING SO SMALL THAT FAST.
SA (SCOOP)
SA
SA
SA
SA
WOW!
I HAVE A LOT OF PRACTICE.
DON'T LOOK AT ME.
NOW I CAN FINALLY BREW SOME HERBAL TEA FOR FOSTER FATHER.
THANKS SO MUCH! YOU'RE A LIFE-SAVER!
ANY-TIME.
NOW, HOW TO GET BACK...
OH DEAR.

AND OF COURSE, MASTERING THE WAYS OF THE NPC.

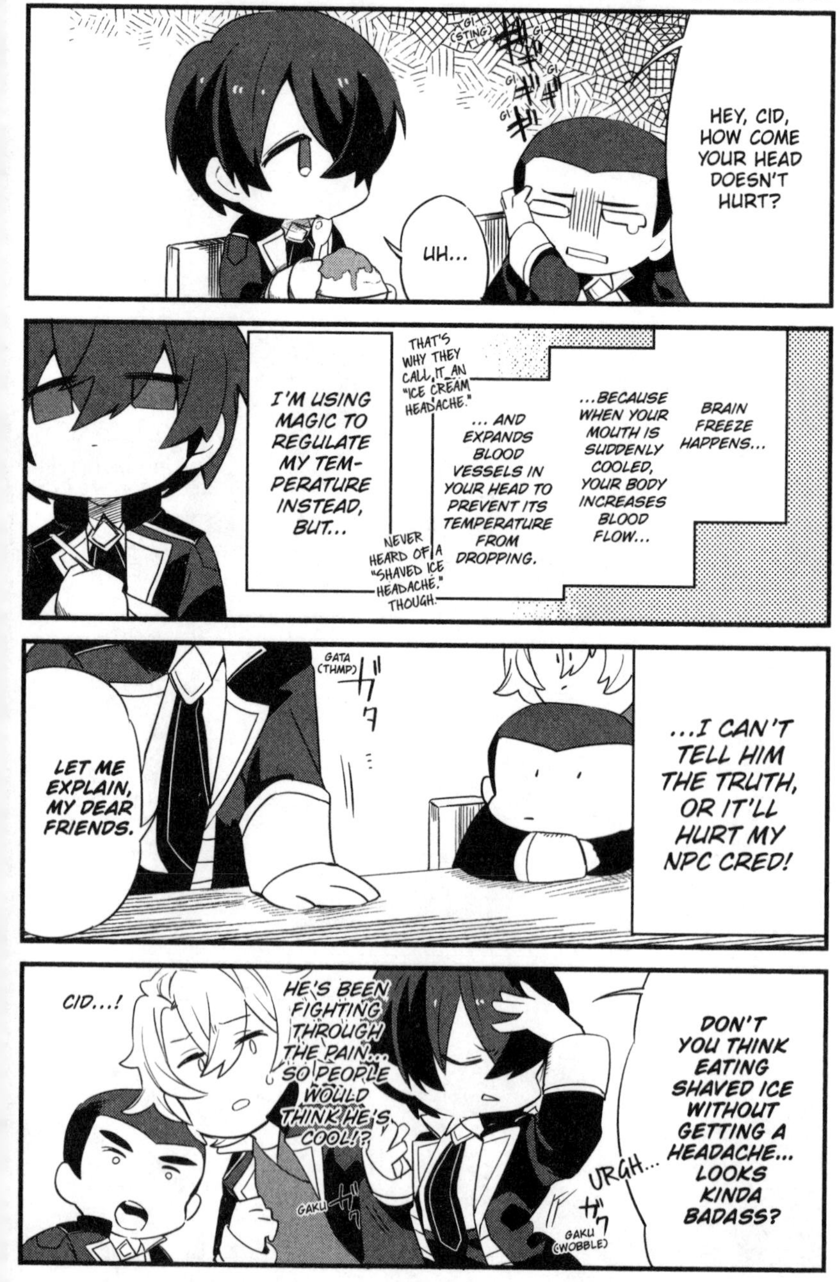
HEY, CID, HOW COME YOUR HEAD DOESN'T HURT?
GI (STING)
GI
GI
GI
GI
UH...
BRAIN FREEZE HAPPENS...
...BECAUSE WHEN YOUR MOUTH IS SUDDENLY COOLED, YOUR BODY INCREASES BLOOD FLOW...
... AND EXPANDS BLOOD VESSELS IN YOUR HEAD TO PREVENT ITS TEMPERATURE FROM DROPPING.
THAT'S WHY THEY CALL IT AN "ICE CREAM HEADACHE."
NEVER HEARD OF A "SHAVED ICE HEADACHE," THOUGH.
I'M USING MAGIC TO REGULATE MY TEMPERATURE INSTEAD, BUT...
...I CAN'T TELL HIM THE TRUTH, OR IT'LL HURT MY NPC CRED!
GATA (THMP)
LET ME EXPLAIN, MY DEAR FRIENDS.
DON'T YOU THINK EATING SHAVED ICE WITHOUT GETTING A HEADACHE... LOOKS KINDA BADASS?
URGH...
GAKU (WOBBLE)
HE'S BEEN FIGHTING THROUGH THE PAIN... SO PEOPLE WOULD THINK HE'S COOL!?
GAKU
CID...!

Art
Anri Sakano
Original Story
Daisuke Aizawa
Character Design
Touzai

The Eminence in Shadow 3

LETTERING: Phil Christie

TRANSLATION: Nathaniel Hiroshi Thrasher

KAGE NO JITSURYOKUSHA
NI NARITAKUTE! Volume 3
©Anri Sakano 2020
©Daisuke Aizawa 2020
©Touzai 2020
First published in Japan in 2020 by
KADOKAWA CORPORATION, Tokyo.
English translation rights arranged
with KADOKAWA CORPORATION, Tokyo
through Tuttle-Mori Agency, Inc., Tokyo.

English translation © 2022 by
Yen Press, LLC

Yen Press
150 West 30th Street
19th Floor
New York, NY 10001

Visit us at yenpress.com
facebook.com/yenpress
twitter.com/yenpress
yenpress.tumblr.com
instagram.com/yenpress

First Yen Press Edition: March 2022

Yen Press is an imprint of
Yen Press, LLC.
The Yen Press name and logo are
trademarks of Yen Press, LLC.

Library of Congress Control Number:
2021935892

ISBNs: 978-1-9753-2522-0 (paperback)
978-1-9753-2523-7 (ebook)

10 9 8 7 6 5 4 3 2 1

LSC-C

Printed in the United States of America